THE Hapless TEACHER'S Handbook

To Pete, whom I recall saying long ago –
'Don't do it!'

PHIL BALL

THE Hapless TEACHER'S Handbook

EBURY
PRESS

1 3 5 7 9 10 8 6 4 2

This edition published in 2007
First published in 2006 by Ebury Press, an imprint of Ebury Publishing

Ebury Publishing is a division of the Random House Group

Copyright © 2006 Phil Ball

Phil Ball has asserted his right to be identified as the author of this Work in
accordance with the Copyright, Designs and Patents Act 1988

The Random House Group Limited Reg. No. 954009

Addresses for companies within the Random House Group
can be found at www.randomhouse.co.uk

A CIP catalogue record for this book is available from the British Library

The Random House Group Limited makes every effort to ensure that
the papers used in our books are made from trees that have been legally
sourced from well-managed and credibly certified forests. Our paper
procurement policy can be found on www.randomhouse.co.uk

Interior designed by seagulls.net

Printed and bound in Great Britain by Cox & Wyman, Reading, Berkshire

ISBN 9780091908973

This book is a fictional account based very strongly on my own life,
experiences and recollections. The names of people, places, dates,
sequences and the detail of events have been changed here and there.
Otherwise, except in minor respects not affecting the overall
accuracy of the book, the contents are largely true.

Mixed Sources
Product group from well-managed
forests and other controlled sources
www.fsc.org Cert no. TT-COC-2139
© 1996 Forest Stewardship Council
FSC

CONTENTS

ACKNOWLEDGEMENTS

A special thanks to Andrew Goodfellow for shaping, encouraging, chivvying and chasing, but above all for no-nonsense honesty. Thanks to Alex Hazle, Ed Griffiths and all at Ebury. Thanks also to Rupert Lindsay, Diana Lindsay, Steve Hanford, Ekua Green, Barbara Levy, Sue Summers and Philip Norman.

PROLOGUE

There are proactive people and reactive people, and that's basically it. It took me a long time to realise that I belonged to the latter group, but once I'd admitted it to myself there was no real problem, no real trauma. Reactive people do plan their lives, but only in the most basic of ways. When their bowels rumble, they visit the toilet. When they get a job, they do that job to the best of their abilities. But there is no over-all plan. What will be will be. It's probably a more interesting way of living than the take-charge method, mainly because it is less predictable – and also because it means that you get to see a bit more of life's little collage. Years down the line, you may harbour a secret wish to have been a more assertive, more executive type, but you console yourself with the thought that along the more winding way you have bumped into a wider range of people, and that they are still hanging around inside you somewhere – a part of you, nestled down inside the soul, to have and to hold.

I was born in Vancouver, Canada, and even that turned out to be an accident. I don't mean that my parents missed out on the family-planning advice but rather that their ending up in Canada belonged more to serendipity than to design.

Six years after the war ended and England was still on ration books, the news that the governments of Canada, South Africa and Australia were offering the chance of a cheap passage to a new life was tempting indeed. My father, back from the war in Burma to a wife he hardly knew, sensed that a move might be a good idea. Decent job prospects in Bradford were few and far between. My mother, informed by her doctor that she would probably never have children, clung to the word 'probably' with desperate conviction and recited to herself the working-class mantra passed down to her by a generation of overworked women – that if you couldn't conceive, go abroad. A change of scene usually worked, according to the legend. And so in 1952 they applied to these countries, and on being accepted by all three of them, wrote out the names on pieces of paper and put them in a hat. My father allowed my mother to execute the prize draw, and Canada was the country that came out between her thumb and her forefinger.

They left by boat in August 1952 with not the slightest idea of what they were going to do once they got to Canada. They must have done something, however, because by June 1953 my brother was born, and I followed on four years later. The old-wives' tale turned up trumps in my mother's case, but the severe dose of post-natal depression she suffered on first setting eyes on me prompted her to pack her bags and sail back to England, leaving my protesting father behind in Toronto, where they'd moved soon after I made my appearance. Standing on the docks at Liverpool with two young children, a large suitcase and nowhere to go, she headed for her sister's at an east-coast resort called Cleethorpes – a national joke but somewhere that promised a temporary haven. Dad came home eventually, so pissed off that he never really forgave her, and fate settled them there, by the sluggish tides of the River Humber.

That's where I was brought up, and it comforts me to think that the whole episode was based on those three pieces of paper. Other people's parents would have planned it all with precision, weighing up the pros and cons and plumping for the best option, as they saw fit. My folks went for the lottery method. It should come as no surprise, therefore, that they have passed on this tendency to their children with unerring efficiency.

It was always improbable that I would become an officer of men, a merchant banker or even a politician. These things require confidence, planning and conviction. The total absence of any of these qualities leads me to Trumpington Street in the early summer sunshine of 1978. Destiny dances in the mild Cambridge air. The final undergraduate exams at Lancaster University are a week away and I'm feeling quite pleased with myself. Besides, just getting down here for an interview to the famous farty-sounding street has meant a major railway expedition, akin to the Trans-Siberian. But trains are good spaces for thinking, and I've had plenty of time to do that today. Not only that, I've also had the chance to read some of the book entitled *The Logic of Education* that I was supposed to have gone through on the final year's 'minor' course of my choice, but whose charms, up to now, I have managed to resist. The authors' names are Hirst and Peters, but I still cannot understand what the hell they are blathering on about. With the book tucked away in my rucksack, I pass Pembroke College to my right and look for the address on the famous street that houses the university's Department of Education.

As I knock on the door of an elegant eighteenth-century grey-brick house I can't believe my luck. About six weeks before, when I'd finally bothered to glance at the leaflets given to me by the Careers' Officer at Lancaster, I'd noticed that among the universities offering PGCE courses (Post Graduate Certificate of Education) Cambridge was the one that stood out. I hadn't expected it to figure. It seemed too good to be true. Back when I was a sixth-former, you'd had to sweat blood, flutter your eyelashes at the teachers and try to unlearn your Cleethorpes accent before you could ever dream of being considered for the Oxbridge Entrance Exam. Only the really serious guys and gals had managed to scale those heights, and that was just the exam. Then they'd had to negotiate their provincial ways through an interview which by all accounts had been as intimidating as it had been terrifying. Only two from my sixth-form group had made it to the gleaming spires, an achievement that the rest of us considered almost godly. And here I am, three years down the tracks, about to enter via the back door. Well, the front door of the Education Department, but it all seems too easy. For the last few weeks since I was called to interview, I've been dreaming of future conversations with friends, even employers. 'Oh yah – I studied at Cambridge in the late 1970s. Good times, good people.' What a wheeze. All I have to do is get through this interview, but I figure that it can't be so tough. I figure that no one else apart from me will have noticed that Cambridge are offering a PGCE. I'm practically in already.

The matronly secretary frowns slightly at my rucksack, and offers to look after it for me for the duration of the interview. I thank her and follow her instructions through the stately corridors of the old building. I know that the course that I've been following with half an ear in Educational Philosophy will also stand me in good stead. There can't be many applicants from the world of English Literature that have also been studying some educational stuff. I haven't understood any of it, but never mind. I take a seat opposite the designated room. The dark wooden door looks sturdy and portentous. Suddenly, as the secretary kindly brings me a cup of tea – 'Just another five minutes now' – I begin to feel the first stirrings of unease. Maybe this won't be so easy after all. It all seems a bit posh, a bit too sophisticated for my liking. I've grown accustomed to Lancaster's tackier, brick-dust academia, but this is something else. I smell tradition, and serious minds. Even the tea tastes intelligent. And worse still, I know that whoever interviews me is going to ask me about the twin strikers, Hirst and Peters. I've had a go at understanding it again on the train journey, but the main thing that the lecturers have been going on about on this course – Hirst's 'Forms of Knowledge' – has simply left me baffled. I don't even know what his buddy Peters is supposed to have said, but Hirst is the big cheese. That much is clear. I'm going to have to improvise something, or just hope for the best. The plan can't fail now.

When I get the big 'Come in' it's as bad as I feared. There are two elderly-looking academics in the room, one sitting behind an enormous oak desk and the other relaxing with a cuppa by the fireplace. They are both tweedy and white-haired, and despite the friendly greeting there's a grim, weighty air about the two of them, like a pair of owls at either end of a bookcase. Not good. The owl behind the desk ushers me forward.

'Ah! I see our resolute secretary has provided you with some tea! Would you like a refill?' I totter forward, terrified that the china cup might fall. The delicate little set in my hands is sliding and slurping.

'Yes, please,' I croak. 'It's been a long journey.'

He leans across the huge table and whips the cup and saucer from my hands, passing them back to his colleague who guards a pot of tea by the empty black hearth.

'So,' he begins, donning his glasses and looking down at my application form, 'you're at Lancaster. Some good eggs up there in Education. But they don't offer a PGCE. Well – one day perhaps. So you'd like to come down here for a year? Damn good idea.' So far so good. The fresh cup of tea comes back across the table. 'So you'd like to be a teacher?' he asks – a question I'm prepared for. Trying to look confident I tell him that I would like to work with children, and that it would be fulfilling to have the chance to help them to enjoy literature, just as I had done. My nose grows a couple of inches, but he doesn't seem to notice. Then the gloves come off. 'Educational Philosophy, then,' he begins, removing his glasses and looking at me with slightly more interest. 'Not many candidates that we get have studied that subject. Have you enjoyed it?' I answer in the affirmative. He sits back in his high-backed leather chair. 'But you'll no doubt have noticed that some of the issues are rather tricky, of course.' Again, I agree. It's nice to agree. Nevertheless, the inevitable arrives. 'What do you think of the main debate? I mean about those damned *forms of knowledge*.' As he throws this poison dart, he turns back to his colleague and appears to wink, although I could be mistaken. The teapot guardian smirks, as if sharing some private joke. I try to steel myself. I know that I have to say something vaguely intelligent now about a crucial topic that I don't understand. What I want to say is 'Sorry, but I don't have a fucking clue', but instead of a bit of good old-fashioned honesty one of the most insane things I will ever say begins to form on my lips. I can't stop it, and it blurts out into the still air of the room.

'I think that what Hirst has written is a little bit reactionary.'

The sentence is not mine. It belongs to one of the lecturers at Lancaster, and he had said it during a seminar in response to the only student who had actually bothered to read *The Logic of Education* and who was engaging him in a lively debate. Whatever, the effect of these words, exported down south and mouthed into the sophistication of

Trumpington Street, is quite startling. It's as if I've hit the old guy with a cricket bat. He splutters slightly, then turns to the fireplace, presumably to confirm what he's just heard. The teapot nods back, his eyebrows raised in interest.

'*Reactionary?*' the main man pronounces, turning back to me and fixing me with a much more interested gaze. 'Now there's a word. I've yet to encounter that particular one in relation to the debate surrounding the forms of knowledge. I'm intrigued. Very intrigued.' He waves his glasses at me. 'Please, go on' – which is what I was afraid he might say. I pause, I stutter, I mutter and I murmur, but there is no safety net wide enough to prevent me from drowning in the pool of shit that I have just launched myself into. After receiving five minutes of complete gibberish, the kindly academic puts me out of my misery and asks me a further pointed question, something like, 'And do you know the town of Cambridge at all? It's really quite pleasant.' As the interview comes to its humiliating end, and as my dumb little scheme expires in the limp handshake the interviewer offers me, I smile wanly at his final parting shot – 'We'll be in touch.' Yeah right. I push down the heavy handle of the door, and walk outside. Interested for one more fleeting moment as to the identity of my interrogator, I turn to look at the name on the door. Stunned, I cannot understand why I had failed to notice it before. 'Professor PH Hirst' stares down at me in large white lettering.

As a famous anthropologist once observed, the male of the human species is capable of picking out a wild boar on the plains at two miles distance, pursuing it with stealth and killing it cleanly with a throw of a spear from thirty yards. As a female columnist more recently observed in *Cosmopolitan* when talking about men, they cannot see a pair of underpants staring at them from a distance of two feet in the drawer. We were made to chase wild boars. Drawers in drawers and names on doors are far more complicated matters.

1

STUMBLING

I'm pinned to the floor, the youth's face so close to mine I can feel the smutty caress of his bum-fluff. His knee lies heavily across my arms, preventing me from moving. 'Gizza kiss!' he yells, pursing his lips and nodding up and down, like a woodpecker hammering at a tree. I squirm away from his cigarette breath, but there is no way I can escape from his strength. Behind my frozen head, a wet draught blows in from the January playground and mixes with the sickly smell of school dinners. Echoing voices chuckle at my plight. Behind my assailant's skull the harsh glare of the corridor's strip-lighting is too bright for my eyes. Closing them, I decide to relax and pretend that nothing is really happening, and that if I cease to resist I will just wake up from this nightmare. The boy's lips finally connect with the cheek that I have turned over for his delectation, and he springs up, apparently sated. As I pick myself up slowly from the wet linoleum, the huddle of youths runs out into the playground, cackling with glee. Welcome to the teaching profession.

Their leader is a boy named Alan Plant, but I don't know

that yet. Neither does the boy know that I am about to become his English teacher for the next two months. This is the beginning of the fabled 'TP' or teaching practice, an emotional assault course for the singular breed of people who decide to try their luck on the other side of the school desk. It can only get better from this point. That's what I'm hoping. The morning walk from my temporary lodging (my parents' house) to the school chosen for me by the course tutor at Hull University has been a significant one, measuring in its all-too-brief distance the gap between boy and man, student and professional, slob and schoolmaster. It's the big wake-up call, the one that comes too early in the dawn for comfort. And for those who have chosen, for whatever reason, to stagger out into the half-lit morning of the teaching profession, the prospect of an easy baptism is an unlikely one. You know this with every passing step. I am about to come face-to-face with large groups of young people – and large groups of young people are unpredictable things.

My young assailant has confronted me after a mere two hours in the school building, when under instructions to find some administrative forms from the secretary's office I have foolishly attempted to cross a barbed-wired strip of land close to the bomb-pocked territory known as the playground. Like an innocent soldier on his first day in the trenches, the earlier warnings from the hardened troops have failed to register. I am already missing in action.

Turn back the clock to 8.15am and everything seems to be moderately tailored to expectations. A polite and helpful sixth-former has shown me to the staffroom where I am to meet my new colleagues and mentors. Walking slowly through the open door into a warm cloud of instant coffee and pipe smoke, things are as I had anticipated. There is an adult world here of pattern and enterprise, none of which I share or understand. People stand around in a swirl of jackets, ties, briefcases and mugs of hot liquid. Their sense of routine closes me out from their Monday morning. Nobody notices me as I stand by the door. After several minutes in which I shift the weight from foot to foot, stare up inanely at some unfathomable messages on the noticeboard and generally attempt to look like a lost lambkin, I spy – with my little eye – something beginning with 'c'. It represents contact, and it is coming in the shape of a small hand, its arm raised in the far corner. The hand is beckoning to me, quickly and impatiently, but there is so much dense human undergrowth between us that I cannot see clearly to whom it belongs. Stepping cautiously and edging my way past the soft hum of impenetrable chat, I find the arm. It belongs to a small wizened man, with greying blond hair, a sailor's fair beard and large blinking eyes. He has a pipe clasped between his teeth and he looks like a garden gnome. He is sitting in a large rocking chair, one of a corral that seat his obvious accomplices. He holds out a tiny hand – 'Welcome to the Dirty Corner!' He says it with relish, as if he wants the rest of the staffroom to hear. He has a Scots-porridge accent, and his handshake is firm. It leads me across to his right, where the last chair remains vacant.

'So you're the new boy, eh?' he begins, blinking madly. 'The name's Mr Hamish – Hamish to you. Head of English,' he chuckles, pulling the pipe from his mouth and collapsing in a wheeze of tobacco-stained coughing. On recovering, he introduces me to his companions in the Dirty Corner. 'To my left, Jim Drewery, specialist in Wordsworth, Blake and the names of the best-looking sixth-form girrrrls.' Jim extends an arm, grinning. He looks as young as me, has a face scarred with acne, but appears encouragingly friendly. 'To your right, Tony McCall, MA in history and wife-swapping.' Tony nods, proud of the title. 'And last but not least, Bill Brown – one of the worst teachers ever to inhabit the western hemisphere.' Bill also confines himself to a nod, but seems less amused by Hamish's introduction. Hamish then turns back to me, scrabbling with a scrap of paper. 'I have your name somewhere now … um, let me look here. Ah yes. Philip Bull. Bull-of-the-walk, eh? Ha! We'll find you a nickname soon enough.'

Apologising, I correct his mistake. 'Sorry – it's Ball. Philip Ball. As in football.' Hamish takes this in his stride.

'Well, that's a pity. I like Bull better, but if you prefer the spherical version, I suppose we'll have to go for it. Now then, if you want to belong to the Dirty Corner, and benefit from all the various things that it has on offer, you only have to answer the following question.' At this point, a bell sounds and Bill Brown, the worst teacher in the west, appears to challenge my new head of department's authority.

'Oh, put a sock in it, Hamish. Leave the poor kid alone.

He's only been here for five minutes,' and he makes as if to leave. Hamish bites on his pipe and grins. He's not for turning.

'The question is this. Can you, or can you not, control a class of thirty children?' As the massed ranks of teachers with their briefcases and their registers begin to disperse, the Dirty Corner awaits my response. I decide that they might be looking for honesty. They've been nice enough to speak to me, at least.

'Erm, no. I've never really taught a class of thirty children.' I shrug. 'So I suppose not. I guess it must be quite difficult.' Hamish wheezes and stands up, squeezing me affectionately on the shoulder as he goes.

'You stay here, sonny, and read the papers. I'll be back in twenty minutes, and we'll discuss your teaching practice, or whatever it's called nowadays.' Evidently I'm in. The new member elect of the Dirty Corner.

With the school suddenly snapped silent by the exodus to the classrooms for morning registration, I survey the wreckage of the Lynton Comprehensive staffroom, Cleethorpes. It looks tousled and infested. Random scraps of paper, 'Wish-you-were-here' postcards and cheesy flash photos of Christmas piss-ups adorn the peeling walls. The lime-green carpet that partially covers the concrete floor is dotted with black cigarette stubbings, its fraying edges rising upwards as if praying to the gods for release. The heating is oppressive, steaming up the windows as in every school in the country, cutting off the inmates from the outside world and its more comforting realities.

'The thing about this place, Philip, is that there are a lot of bullshitters.' Hamish is back, and he tells me this in little gulps as he holds a match to the end of his pipe and sucks. Jim the Wordsworth expert nods vigorously. The staffroom is empty save us three. 'Whatever, I've given you two classes, one from the third year and one from the fourth. That should be enough. And one *dramma* class, twice a week. It says here that you're doing some *drrramma*.' He pronounces the word with peat-bog intensity. 'That's the good news. Now back to the bullshitters. There are some teachers here that have been around for years, like me for instance. Long in the old tooth. And if ye were to ask them what I asked you, sonny, not half an hour ago, they would have said that they were fine, that they could control a class of thirty lunatics. That's because they're mucked up in the head, wee laddie. They're lying. Everyone has problems. I'll tell you that for nothing. Isn't that the case, Jim?'

Jim, clearly Robin to Hamish's Batman, is happy to be asked to contribute.

'That's the way, man!' he shouts out, in a Geordie accent as choppy as the Tyne. 'Hamish has given ya ma fooking loonies from the fourth, year man. Ah hope you don't mind, now!'

It begins to dawn on me what they're driving at. I'm to be given one soft option and one tougher one, just in case I get the wrong idea about teaching, at this delicate stage. Hamish smooths the edges a little.

'Och man, the third-year class is fine. It's got more top-of-the-range swots per square metre than I've seen for many a season. They'll nay give you problems. But there's no point you just having them. Besides – it's the way the timetable worked out,' he adds, shooting a quick glance at Jim. He then hands me my timetable, almost apologetically.

'Well, thanks,' I reply, uselessly. 'I suppose I have to take the rough with the smooth. I'm looking forward to it.' At this, Jim lets out a friendly guffaw.

'There's one thing we have to tell you about, mate.' He grins, showing a jagged set of amber teeth. 'We're not supposed to – you know – the code's unspoken, like. We're not supposed to give you any prejudices towards the kids. You're supposed to form your own opinions of the little bastards. But now you're a member of the Dirty Corner we feel a certain compulsion … to warn you about Plant.' I ask him if Plant is a pupil from his fourth-year class, an assumption that is quickly confirmed. 'Sure fooking is. I won't tell you any more, Phil ol' son. But I'll just say this. If a machine gun worked on the big twat, you'd take one in there, spray him full o' lead and get on with the lesson. But the bullets'd bounce off him man, I swear. He's like a cockroach – indestructible. If he gives you shit, tell us and we'll haul him out. But anyway, you've always got the Dirty Corner. It's like a confessional – if ya see what I mean.' And with that candid assessment of what I am likely to encounter on my first teaching practice, with the fourth-year slot flashing red on the nine o'clock square for Tuesday on my new timetable, my two new colleagues leave me to prepare myself for Judgement Day.

Of course, it would have been a teeny-weeny bit easier for me if I had not been forced to lie beneath Alan Plant before he even knew that I was to be his teacher for the next couple of months, but such is fate. *As flies to wanton boys are we to the gods.* I had almost reached my destination when the incident occurred, and had I possessed the presence of mind to simply answer 'I happen to be the new English teacher, so if you'll just stand aside, please' then all might have been fine. But I was still unused to responding to such confrontation, and as Plant challenged me in the doorway which opened out onto the playground – where I had obviously stumbled upon him having a quick fag with his mates – I made the major mistake of showing fear, or hesitancy, or both. 'Who are you then?' enquired this large youth, beaming a crocodile smile my way. He signalled for his troops to block the doorway. Before I could answer, he began a rapid interrogation, as if my silence had been an affront to his authority. 'Are you a sixth-former?' I shook my head. 'You're not a bloody inspector?' I shook my head and tried to move past him. Mistake. 'You're a student! We've got a student!' he whooped, and grabbed one of my arms, shoving me with his free hand and then skilfully tripping me off-balance as I toppled backwards. The kiss was soon to follow.

As for what I intended to do with Plant's class, Geordie Jim had given me a fairly free hand – on the sole condition that I should use the class reader from time to time with them, and set them the occasional writing task. Beyond that, there was a decent-looking book of short texts with related questions that Jim used from time to time, and a dog-eared old resource book called *Topics for Discussion* which had caught my eye in the afternoon, as a possible source of inspiration. The first drama class wasn't until the Wednesday, and the third-year class would, according to Jim, fail to bat an eyelid if you told them you were about to give them a crash course in colloquial Japanese. Anyway, they were deep into a class reader about the Romans in Britain, and were apparently very happy with it. So it was Jim's class that I really had to work on, and Jim's class was first on the Tuesday menu.

How does one prepare for Armageddon? That night, back at my mum's place, I sat for hours at the desk in my old bedroom working on how I was going to conduct the class. Every minute of the fifty-five ticks of the clock had to be planned. I needed a script. The idea of running out of things to say or do was too terrible to contemplate. No one on the PGCE at Hull University – where my Trumpington Street gaffe had landed me – had thought of teaching a course in the first term entitled 'How to plan a lesson' or anything as useful as that, and so I was forced to make it up as I saw fit. The trouble was that every time I thought of something, the vision of Alan Plant loomed into view. Of course, I'd told neither Jim nor Hamish of the impromptu snogging session, but had casually asked Jim in the afternoon if Plant answered to the description I gave, pretending that I'd seen him with a group smoking in the playground. To my dismay, on hearing Jim's sketch of the youth's distinguishing features, I knew that I had already met my nemesis.

In my desperation, it seemed to me that some sort of disguise might come in useful. All actors improve with their real faces hidden. I felt too young to impart any wisdom, too clean-shaven to look as though I had left the pupils' world and joined the more serious communion of adults. I'd have preferred Jim just to have told me what to do, of where to build the doors and the walls, instead of offering me the open-plan approach. It felt like induction week at university all over again, back to eighteen and the self-discovery method of life. Couldn't someone just give me some instructions?

By midnight I'd decided to work from *Topics for Discussion*. Each chapter of the book worked its way around a theme, but with the reassuring presence of a text at the beginning. This meant that I could ask them to read and write for at least half the class, without me having to talk too much. Then they themselves would have to talk, in theory at least. Staring at the white spirals in the furry yellow wallpaper silence of my childhood bedroom that night, I felt that the topic of 'School Uniform' might get me through the first fifty-five minutes. Beyond that, the future seemed a trifle unclear. What did these teachers get up to for ten months of the year? How on earth did they keep things going? As my head hit the pillow with a version of the next day's events dancing in my head, I resolved to be like the teacher I had observed before Christmas – a person with enough self-confidence simply to trust the kids to get on with things. That was surely the safest way. I wouldn't talk too much, and I wouldn't give too much away. I was going to be fine.

The next morning was suitably cold and drizzly, as I set off on foot to my destiny. My mother waved me from the door with a timid 'Good luck', but the tension in her voice made it sound as though she herself were about to face a classroom of student-eaters. Every turn around a street corner, every other house passed was a silent push along the path to my doom. Like Charles I on the morning of his execution, I wore a thick vest under my shirt to prevent me from shivering on the scaffold – lest the people should think of me as frightened. To compound my misery, all the kids that morning were running, or swishing past through the drizzle on their bikes. I'd not really taken notice of this human traffic since leaving school myself, but now it became all too significant. They all seemed worryingly keen, as if they couldn't wait to get to school to torture some poor bloody apprentice. It suddenly looked like some massive conspiracy – a morning full of Midwich Cuckoos.

I felt slightly better after a coffee in the Dirty Corner, during which Geordie Jim's casual confidence in my abilities boosted my own a little, up from rock-bottom to faintly visible, but I was grateful for small mercies. Even though he'd failed to ask me what I was thinking of doing with his class – probably because he preferred not to know – I told him anyway. He just slapped me on the arm and concluded, 'Fooking great, man! They'll luv that. Sock it to 'em!', and he was gone, off to the new free period that my presence afforded him, to do some 'research'. The bell clanged out the end of morning curfew, and I rose to my fate. Perhaps it wouldn't be so bad after all. Never send to know for whom the bell tolls, it tolls for thee.

I walk briskly down the series of echoing corridors, holding myself upright like I had seen an authoritative teacher do, many years before. Try to look vaguely irritated by everyone, and keep your poise. Urchins scurry past, doors swing open, doors slam shut. 'Can you be *quiet*!' someone bawls to my left, as I spy the porthole of the classroom door, down at the end of the final corridor. A lookout scout is peering through it, down the alleyway towards me. The face disappears like a shot and I hear his warning shout just as I extend my arm to push open the tangerine-coloured door. 'He's here. Keep it quiet!' I stride in and there is a deathly hush. The door swings on its hinges and squeaks back into its frame. The air smells wet and farty. Thirty youths, anonymous for now in their blackish-blue uniforms, look expectantly towards me. There are girls, boys, and other creatures of indeterminate sex. Some of them have turned fifteen, and some of them look surprisingly large. Go for it. Try out the first words of the script and see what effect it might have on this gathering. But the bell cuts me short. A girl's voice pipes up: 'That's the bell, sir. It means the lesson's started.' The sound of 'sir' floats on the air, somewhere slightly distant. I feel no connection to such a word.

'Yes – thanks,' I reply to the voice, thrown temporarily by the change in the script. Two words. I have pronounced two words to a class. My feet carry me to the large teacher's desk at the front, beneath the blackboard. I take a piece of chalk and turn my back to the audience, hiding in the temporary shelter of the empty black expanse. 'My name is Mr Ball,' I announce to the board, 'and I'm here to teach you for the next couple of months.' I squeak my name on to the blackboard, with the shiny new piece of chalk. The silence continues. Encouraged by this apparent obedience, I turn to face the uniforms again: 'I know that Mr Drewery has been doing certain things with you, and although I intend to carry on with some of those things, I'll also be doing other things differently.' Something I have said has caused a slight stirring in the ranks. Someone wants to burst the silence. As I open my mouth to continue to the next part of the rehearsed speech, someone says: 'What things, sir?' quickly followed by a girl's comment to my right which helpfully adds, 'It's cos Drewery's a pervert, sir.' The phrase is couched in the classic Cleethorpes-Grimsby accent, suggesting suicide and boredom in equal measure. The word 'sir' extends tiredly to '*seer*' and 'pervert' comes over as '*pear-vert*', a deviant who does unspeakable things with fruit.

Time to steady the ship. 'I'd like to look at the topic of school uniforms today, and so could you take out your books *Topics for Discussion*?' There is a rumble and a groan, followed by a horrible fidgeting. The old desks have the traditional opening lids, into which the pupils' heads suddenly disappear in a collective kerfuffle for the book. A boy to my right makes a vomiting sound, and opens his mouth wide into the depths of his open desk. Others snigger or begin to speak quietly to each other. Someone flicks an ear in front with a ruler, someone else belches. I look for Plant in the quiet meltdown, since I still haven't located him. Maybe he's out in the playground having a fag. I sincerely hope so. Nevertheless, I sense that maybe I should have taken issue with the girl who has just accused my colleague of being a pervert, but I am reluctant to face any further justification of the description on her part.

'Could you turn to page eighteen, please? Unit four.' The desk lids close, some more noisily than others. Pages flicker and then a lid slams, too loud for me to ignore. It's Plant. He's sitting at the back, of course, and he's grinning up at me. As the class surprisingly does as I have asked them, Plant does nothing of the sort. He has no book, his red school tie is now wrapped around his head like a bandanna, and he is clearly looking for me to comment on his interpretation of the school uniform into which his expanding body is squeezed. He has yet to make any mention of the fact that we are already acquainted, but that clearly depends on the way that I decide to play it with him. His whole grin says as much. I'm new to teaching, but not to subliminal messages from a future killer. This time I decide to act.

'Could you not slam the desk like that again, and could you take that tie off your head, please?' I manage. Pleased momentarily with my bravado, I suddenly sense a change of temperature in the classroom. To my consternation, some of the rougher-looking pupils dotted about the room have taken their eyes from the book and begun to stare at me, as if I were insane. Worse, some of them are beginning to look back at Plant, not egging him on, but in some kind of fear. Five minutes into my first class, and I've obviously done something very wrong.

At first, nothing happens. The only thing to do is to carry on with the trusty *Topics for Discussion*. Defaulting back to the most boring methods I can think of from my old schooldays, I have already decided to ask someone to read out aloud. The unit has the heading 'School Uniforms? A blessing or a curse?' and the opening lines of the text begin with a verse from an old song I vaguely remembered:

> *And the people in the houses all went to the university,*
> *Where they were put in boxes and they came out all*
> *the same,*
> *And there's doctors and there's lawyers, and business*
> *executives,*
> *And they're all made out of ticky tacky and they all*
> *look just the same*

I pick out a boy at random from the middle row of the serried ranks that line the classroom. He points to his chest, his eyebrows raised in alarm. 'Yes – you. Thanks,' I confirm. 'Can you read up to the end of the first paragraph?' Some more sniggers. The boy heaves his frame straight, then sags again. He takes a deep breath and begins to read, but in a staccato rhythm, toneless and awkward.

'Sing it for us!' shouts the '*pear-vert*' girl, but the boy drones miserably on. When he gets to the third line, his mouth collapses around the word 'lawyers', and the class begins to fray at the edges. 'Lawyers,' I prompt, apologetically, but then he blunders over 'business executives', mashing the two words into something unrecognisable. By the time he gets to 'ticky tacky' at least two-thirds of the class are roaring with laughter. I shout above the sudden din.

'So what is ticky tacky? Can anyone tell me what it is?' It's a question I'd rehearsed in my bedroom. I'd thought it would be a good one to ask, but no one raises their hand. Instead, there is a cacophony of colourful suggestions, ranging from the lewd to the indescribable.

'Spunk!' shouts a voice.

'Tampons!' shrieks another.

'Ticky-tacky wicky-wacky,' shouts Plant, and thumps the desk lid down again.

I focus on the serial snogger and walk a little way down the aisle towards him, ignoring the rest.

'Don't do that again – OK!' I snap, shouting above the din. Plant stands up, suddenly indignant.

'Don't do what? I never said nothing. What about the rest of them then? I was answering your question, *mate*,' he sneers. The act of getting to his feet has hushed the class, and the truth hits home. Plant is a lone wolf. Whoever his bodyguards were the day before, they're not here now, in this class. But I have no idea of how to cope with him. In life beyond the classroom I always shy away from aggressors. I even prefer, pathetically, to get on their side. Here, the only solution that occurs to me is to use the rest of the class's obvious dislike of him as the weapon, but the problem is that he has an ace card up his unwashed sleeve. He has yesterday as evidence to use against me. All these things occur in a flash. There is no time to think them through.

I back off and ask a girl on the front row to continue the reading. The fact that she's at the front suggests a conformist – one of the few things we have actually talked about on the course. This time I get it right, and the girl begins to read acceptably, punctuated every few seconds by Plant. He has sat down, but has begun to make curious noises every time the girl reaches the end of a sentence. First a howl, then a dog's bark. When he does an impressive horse-like whinny, the girl who is trying to read suddenly turns around and shouts, 'Why don't you piss off you twat!', which confirms my suspicion as to his popularity. Plant responds, of course.

'Hey Mr Balls! Don't let her get away with that. She's swearing. She told me to ... ooh, I can't use that kind of language. Wouldn't hear me using them words!'

No mask can hide my obvious inability to cope with this. I want to morph into a series of people whom I know could easily handle this, but my cover's already blown. All I can do is crank up the confrontation.

'Look – just shut up, OK?' I appeal, almost tearfully. 'I'm here for a couple of months, and we don't want to be doing this every day, do we now?' I say this to the whole class, taking the exclusive focus away from Plant, but it backfires.

'We 'aven't done anything, sir!' says a bossy little girl, over by the window. A murmur of agreement accompanies her little pout. I shrug, conceding the point.

'Mr Plant,' I begin, in a final attempt, but before I can

read out the ultimatum that Jim has implied I use, he shouts out, 'How do you know my name then?', standing up again. It's a very good question, laced as it is with the paranoid implication that the other teachers have warned me about him. I'm beginning to wonder if he remembers me struggling beneath him. Maybe the cigarette smoke clouded his vision. Maybe he assaults teachers every day. Fortunately one of the girls comes to my rescue.

'Oh come on, Plant!' snarls a peroxide-blonde from the window side. She looks older than the rest, and is chewing gum furiously. 'You really think he doesn't know your name? Crawl back inside your kennel,' she spits, with the necessary touch of steel that I so obviously lack. Plant points across the room to my saviour and mumbles a threat, but he sits down nevertheless, barking one last time at her suggestion of the kennel, so as to appear undefeated. I make a mental note of the girl. I'll need her name for future classes, as she is clearly the one to cultivate. I feel suitably low, already stooping to such tactics, but the show must go on – even though I'm painfully aware that it hasn't even started.

The class stutters along in this stop-start fashion for what seems like several decades, until the bell finally releases me from the torture. Never have fifty-five minutes seemed so long, and as the pupils effect their departure in a frenzy of pushing, shoving and mutual insults, the only positive thing I take from my educational debut is that I have done what I said I would do. We have read the text, written out some answers to the discussion points in rough – and I have told them that for the next lesson they must write them up in their exercise books and prepare to discuss the points in a kind of open debate. I'm not sure of how I intend to manage this debate, but the next lesson seems a far-off event. I've got over the first hurdle, which is all that matters in the here-and-now. Plant has given me trouble, but after the blonde's little put-down he retired into a kind of fidgety silence, broken by the occasional howl at the moon. But he's obviously not stupid. He's keeping back the humiliating fact of the kiss for a more serious occasion, or perhaps retaining it as a bargaining tool for not doing his homework. We shall see. Others in the class have not been easy to control either, but in a perverse sort of way the presence of Plant has eclipsed them all. Any other misdemeanours have looked small beer in comparison.

I'm not sure as to whether I have succeeded or failed, or even if such considerations are important at this stage of the game. All I feel is a tremendous sense of fatigue, mixed with a curious sensation of relief. For the entire duration of the class, I never seemed to manage more than a five-minute stretch without some challenge to my authority, without some woodworm of an incident nibbling away at the chair legs of my fragile throne. That's what has been so difficult – the constant feeling that at any moment it might all fall apart, landing me on my backside. Standing for a moment in the middle of a sea of desks and blue uniforms, for one blissful moment in which the entire class appeared to be doing what I had asked them to do, the strangeness of the entire edifice of education had suddenly welled up inside of me. What compelled thirty adolescents to sit in their desks for six hours a day and obey a series of apparently random orders from the likes of useless people like me? And despite their better selves, they did exactly that – not without some protest, of course, but the whole creaking construction seemed to be holding up for now at least. Or maybe they'd just given me the benefit of the doubt, and would rip me to shreds next lesson? Meanwhile, there was the Dirty Corner in which to confess, and the other two classes to face. I'd only just begun.

2

OBSERVING

Perhaps what kept me going was that I already knew it could be better. There did appear to be another way. Two months before, in the early November, all trainees had been sent out from Hull to various destinations for a three-week 'observation period'. This seemed like a decent enough idea. Besides, all we had to do was watch and take notes. We didn't have to teach, unless we had some massive desire to do so. We were each assigned to a different junior school in the region, since the policy back then on teacher-training courses was to observe younger children, and to learn some of the basics. The idea seemed slightly odd, but nobody at the university had bothered to explain it to us. I thought that if I was going to teach older, more unruly youths, then it would be better to observe some of them being unruly – but no such logic prevailed.

Nevertheless, I was looking forward to this observation business. I felt that it might tell me something – that it would confirm or disclaim my choice of profession. Whether I was prepared to take any notice was another matter, but I went along to St Peter's Primary School in Cleethorpes that first

Monday with a reasonable spring in my step. I put on a tie, dusted down the jacket that I'd bought for the graduation ceremony and generally made a bit of an effort, which was not like me at all. When I arrived at reception it was the first time I'd actually been inside the school – despite being brought up in the town. I had gone to the other 'harder' primary school, from whose crumbling walls we had considered St Peter's to be a somewhat snobbish place. This was nonsense, of course, since there are no snobs in Cleethorpes. If you were a snob, you would immediately move out of the town in order to confirm your status. Cleethorpes doesn't do posh. I think it was the name 'St Peter's' that confused us, as if by aligning itself with a saint the school was somehow giving itself airs. Whatever, we used to throw half-bricks over its fences on the way home from my school, and I recall peeing through its gate one afternoon in response to a dare from one of my mates, but I decided not to share this information with the teacher to whom I was assigned that Monday, the wonderfully named Bonnie Howden.

Mrs Howden, as I thought it fit to address her, was like something from one of those Fifties or Sixties' girls' comics – *Bunty* or *Judy* – in whose pages life consisted of boarding schools, jolly hockey sticks, and lashings of ginger pop. On walking into the small staffroom that morning, accompanied by the school secretary, my leader sprang up from a sofa as if she were a jack-in-the-box and greeted me like some long-lost nephew.

'How absolutely lovely of you to choose to come here!'

she enthused, spraying spittle hither and thither. 'It's really lovely. No one's been here to see us for so long!' she screeched, almost hugging me. She was unable to form her 'r' consonants, so that they morphed into a 'w' sound – 'wea- lly lovely!' It made her sound even kinder somehow. She must have been in her mid-fifties, wiry and smart, with her grey hair tied back in a bun. The only nod to unorthodoxy was the shocking-pink trouser suit that she had chosen for the Monday, presumably to wake up the children. Dynamic wasn't the word. She grabbed my arm and marched me out of the staffroom 'to meet the children'.

We flew into the classroom hand in hand, Peter Pan and Tinkerbell. The tiny children, a group of seven-year-olds, were sitting quietly at their desks. Mrs Howden had already prepared them for me, it seemed. Without a further word she plonked me down on a chair to the side of her desk and suddenly raised her arms, like the conductor of an orchestra. The children, blinking like startled rabbits in the aura of her trouser suit, began to sing the welcome they had clearly been rehearsing the week before.

We welcome you, oh Mr Ball, we welcome you into our class
We welcome you like a sunny day,
We welcome you as you sit on your ass

Or something along those lines. But it was very touching. I hadn't been expecting to make such an impact on their lives. I smiled awkwardly as Mrs Howden wound up to full amphetamine mode. Leaping across the classroom to the piano, she launched into a couple of hymns, pounding on the keys like a deranged concert pianist working up to the climax. The children, on the other hand, already seemed to be exhausted, singing the song like little automata, their mouths opening and closing like stoical goldfish in a tank. But there was no stopping Bonnie. Music was her muse. At the end of the second hymn she turned to the class, flushed and trembling with the emotion of it all. Obviously determined to include me in some way, rather than just let me dip into the pool little by little, she shot to her feet and addressed the class with the following dreaded questions: 'Perhaps Mr Ball plays the piano? Perhaps Mr Ball can sing?' I looked at the floor. 'James!' she bellowed, pointing at some poor child in the front row of desks. 'Ask our new visitor if he can play the piano,' upon which the tiny child rose obediently and walked slowly to where I was sitting, the two of us hopelessly exposed in the bright lights of the Mrs Howden show. He stopped just in front of me, and with an almost reverential bow squeaked into the silence, 'Please, Mr Ball. Can you play the piano?'

Yes I could play the piano, albeit poorly. Mrs Howden, despite the thrashing she'd just given the poor instrument, was clearly a competent pianist. She belonged to that lost generation for whom piano lessons had been second nature. As such, I was unsure as to whether I should lie or just go for it. The little boy still stood there, looking vaguely expectant. In the lingering silence, I decided to admit it.

'Yes,' I replied, smiling at the boy. 'But I'm not very

good.' On hearing this, Mrs Howden began to clap, hopping up and down with the sheer excitement of it all.

'Mr Ball can play! I just knew he would. We just know – don't we, children – that he will play beautifully for us? Now what do we say?' As I stood up from my chair and began the slow walk to the gallows, the children began to recite mechanically another of their teacher's mantras:

You must never be shy
You must always try
Always break the crust
Of life's steaming pie

Or something along those lines. I sat at the stool and wondered, in the sudden silence, how I might break the crust. Self-taught on this instrument, in the usual messy way – plonking out chords in the freezing front room of my idle youth, I had none of the wonderful trained fluency that Mrs Howden had just displayed. Scrabbling through the mental files of my limited repertoire, I decided to try out one of the few hymns I could half play – *Now Thank We All Our God*. I began to plink plonk the unrecognisable chords, then began to sing, out of desperation. Mrs Howden, rushing to the rescue, suddenly began to accompany me from the opposite side of the class, in a voice trembling with emotion.

'*Who from our mother's arms, hath blessed us on our way...*'

After what seemed like an hour, as we hit the final verse I was beginning to feel some strange sort of love for this woman. Our voices had begun to gel, hiding the appalling piano-playing. Within ten minutes of my arriving at the school, I was engaged in a duet with a complete stranger, in front of twenty-five open-mouthed little urchins.

'*For thus it was, is now, and shall be evermore!*'

The final line bounced from the poster-coloured walls of the little room and tripped across the silent heads of our startled audience. My leader was taking some time to recover from the ecstasy of it all.

'That was quite splendid!' she announced, on finally opening her eyes. 'A *wound* of applause for Mr Ball!'

And thus began my teaching career, on a cold November morning – with the windows steamed up and the world outside doing whatever it was doing. It felt as though I'd never really been away, that I'd not taken long enough, perhaps, to see what else there might be in the affairs of man, beyond the walls of life's classroom. But it felt right, in a comforting sort of way, as the children settled back that morning into something resembling their daily routine. It felt right that I had at least chosen to work with human beings, as opposed to pushing a pen or even making money, however one did that. Mrs Howden was the type of person from whom I would normally have hidden – and from whom I might have run screaming had I not been obliged that morning to have shared a classroom with her. I would never have guessed at her range of skills, at how a simple enthusiasm for things – anything really – could have such far-reaching effects. As I watched her that first morning I found it impossible to write anything at all on my official observation sheet. There were various criteria provided for us

– Habitual position in the classroom? Range of voice and intonation? Use of blackboard? Discipline – Firm? Authoritative? Authoritarian? Lax? Permissive? I had no idea. The things that I was being asked to consider seemed to me to be of little consequence. There was no checklist, for example, to measure sanity – Mad as a hatter? Utterly barking? Mildly insane? Besides, I was far more interested in the pink trouser suit. It seemed to me to be of much greater significance. A question on the sheet such as 'What colours has the teacher chosen to wear?' would have focused me much more clearly on why Mrs Howden was a successful teacher. The pink trouser suit said 'I love you all!' in a clumsy but endearing way. She could easily have chosen black, which would have made her look elegant, or a more businesslike blue. But the pink communicated happiness, and Bonnie would probably have been bouncing around in the same manner even if she'd just come home from her mother's funeral. And sure enough, as their Monday morning weariness began to wear off, the children began to respond in kind. Who knows what fears and dreads kids bring to school with them? Few of them would tell you. The only escape is to go to school and hope to find something brighter, which is why Mrs Howden's shocking-pink enthusiasm did just fine.

By the end of the first week, I was smitten. I had not been asked to repeat the musical performance, but Bonnie had encouraged me to wander around the classroom, to lend a hand where I thought I could, and to just talk to the children. One thing I did notice for the observation sheet, however, was that she didn't really *teach* very much. I'd not considered this point before. It also surprised me, given the hyperactive kick-off that she'd treated us to. She would set them tasks, put them into little groups and let them get on with it – which they invariably did. The observation sheet seemed to only ask me questions about her performance, not about what the kids actually got up to themselves. I resolved to raise this point when I got back to my tutors, but it seemed to me that Bonnie was effective precisely because she trusted them to get on with it, and they trusted her, of course.

The only thing that seemed to bore the kids was some of the music lessons, oddly enough. But they weren't Bonnie's fault. To my amazement, the radio programme *Time and Tune* was still on the air, and every afternoon at three o'clock sharp Mrs Howden would tune in, presumably under orders since she could have done the music much better herself. The children wearily sang the same stuff as I had sung fifteen years before: *Home, Home on the Range*, *Little Brown Jug* and the promiscuous *Grand Old Duke of York*, who had ten thousand men. Given Bonnie's obvious enthusiasm for all things musi-cal, this particular part of the day was maybe just designed to give her a rest – although she never seemed to be the kind of person who needed one.

Walking home on Friday afternoon at the end of my first week, a bitter east-coast wind was dancing the first sparse snowflakes around in the gathering gloom. I hunched up against the cold and decided that I should have done more that week, despite the orders that we were only to observe. Bonnie's wonderful acceptance of just about anything – she would probably have applauded if I'd walked into the classroom naked – had made me think that maybe I should try to write a song for the kids, and play it on the last day, in a fortnight's time. It was the least I could do to return her kindness. Problem was, I'd never written a kids' song, and the only grown-up ones I had attempted to write had been wrist-cutting bedsit anthems, songs best kept from the public domain. Turning a corner into the howling wind, I suddenly got it. I saw a small, snowman-type creature, alone on the North Pole, lonely but friendly, waiting for visits that hardly ever came. As the cars whooshed by in the gathering sleet, the name Jomble-Wimp formed itself in my head. I had no idea where it had come from – maybe from the North Pole. In this kind of weather, Cleethorpes didn't feel that far away from it, in truth. As my mum cooked the bangers and beans that evening, I tried to extend the idea of this chap, sitting there lonely but expectant. I thought the kids might like that.

I hardly ventured out that weekend, partly because of the weather but mainly because the issue of the Jomble-Wimp had assumed vital importance. At times the whole thing seemed vaguely preposterous, and I thought it would be far healthier to go and get drunk in my local, added to which I feared that the kids might not even like it – assuming I ever summoned up the courage to play it to them unsolicited. Nevertheless, by the Sunday evening I'd got it, tune and all.

Deep in the north, where the white wind blows
Where there's snowbergs and icebergs

And no one ever goes
I went to see the Jomble-Wimp
A friendly chap you'll see
I always went there once a year
When he asked me round for tea:
Chorus
The Jomble-Wimp the Jomble-Wimp
Was always kind to me
The Jomble-Wimp the Jomble-Wimp
Ate buttered snow for tea

There were two more verses, in which I made my annual visit to the Jomble-Wimp, and in which he cooked for me generous helpings of icicle pie, frost cakes and frozen flimble, finished off with hailstone sandwiches – but still I wasn't sure. The only thing that made me feel good was that I'd carried it through. Mrs Howden was having some influence. At the end of that second Monday, I casually mentioned to her after the class that I'd written a song for the children, on guitar. I was hoping that the piano plonking might now be a distant memory and in truth I couldn't wait until the final day to try out the song. Predictably, she hopped up and down with glee.

'You've written a song? Oh how wonderful! You must play it to the children. Yes I insist. Tomorrow morning, just before playtime!' Of course, her trust was implicit, as ever. It was a great gift that she possessed. Anyone else in their right minds might have gently enquired as to the subject of the song, or even as to the genre. I could just as easily have written one entitled 'You're all going to die one day', or 'School sucks', but Bonnie just assumed it would be kosher. She could see no bad in anyone.

So I took my guitar to school, and tried to make some contribution. Still too raw to stand there and teach them anything, and unsure as to what kind of wisdom I could impart to them anyway, I opted for the performance method. The guitar made me feel safer, stuck there as it was between me and the unfortunate recipients. Bonnie, to my consternation, had asked the children to clear the desks at the front, leaving a floor space where they could sit down in a circle and gaze up at me. It all seemed a bit *Watch with Mother* for my liking, but I was in no position to protest. I sang the song. The children listened, attentive as ever, the lights of the classroom glistening on their snotty little noses. When I finished, life was never the same again. There was a pre- and a post-Jomble-Wimp period. It took a couple of anonymous snowflakes on a Friday evening to change my life, but from the moment I stopped singing that ditty there was no turning back. The children applauded, of course – but I was expecting that. Bonnie would make them applaud if you picked your nose. What I hadn't been expecting was the following interrogation. Almost all the children had their hands up, straining to ask their questions. Mrs Howden nodded at me to take over. I pointed to a tiny little girl by my feet.

'Please Mr Ball. Does the Jomble-Wimp have a mummy?'

'Yes he does,' I replied, hoping to reassure her. 'But

Jomble-Wimps don't stay very long with their parents. They're expected to be able to live on their own.'

Another question: 'Can we go to see him?'

I turned to Mrs Howden, pretending to ask her permission for a trip. 'Possibly. But it's a long way to the North Pole, and it's very cold. Maybe you could just write him a letter' – a suggestion that Bonnie immediately took up with the effortless skill of an experienced teacher.

By lunchtime we were still working on the Jomble-Wimp. Some tables had tried to write rudimentary letters, in their scrawny unformed handwriting, whilst others had opted for pictures. Some had drawn the dishes mentioned in the song, which Bonnie had helpfully written out on the blackboard. Another table was busy on a task deciding what things they should take to the North Pole, in order to keep themselves alive and to make the Jomble-Wimp happy. Their concern for his loneliness was utterly genuine, and each table kept me occupied with a constant volley of questions: 'Does he like peanut butter?' 'Shall I send him my duffel coat?' 'Does he watch telly?'

Thus did Jomble-Wimp fever grip the small school of St Peter's that chilly November. Like that magical moment when you score the only goal of the match and you feel the sudden pleasure that comes from having an influence on things, so did the furry white creature from the North Pole show me the value of trying to break the crust of life's steaming pie. So flattered was I to have invaded the primary syllabus that second week, so astonished was I to have set such a fuss in motion, that it sent me into a creative frenzy. Children's songs spewed forth from me and multiplied in frightening quantities. Bonnie invited me to her house one evening so that I could sing them all to her and so that she could score them on her piano. She had three daughters, ranged in age from sixteen to twenty-one, and she introduced each one to me by opening a separate door, like giving me a peep into the rooms of a large doll's house. Each daughter was apparently engaged on some musical activity, cello between knees, violin on shoulder, clarinet in mouth. Each one smiled, and went back to her duties. I had never asked her about her husband, but she sensed the question. 'Ron died ten years ago!' she laughed. 'But hey what – you have to get on with things. No point in hanging about.' I suspected that he'd died of chronic fatigue, but decided not to ask.

I kept those song-sheets, and I never forgot Mrs Howden. She had magically transformed my nonsense into real notation, like a musical alchemist. I was awestruck. One of the songs, *The Camel with a Purple Hump*, had a daft chorus that went:

> *Nibble Nobble Neeble*
> *Wibble Wobble Wump*
> *Have you ever seen a camel with a purple hump?*

On the word 'neeble' there was a sharp note that the children found rather difficult to sing, but the sight of Mrs Howden, sitting upright at her piano and insisting on them doing it correctly, was surreal, in the nicest of ways. 'No, children!' she scolded, as kindly as possible. 'It is nibble nobble *neeble!*'

Exactly. You have to get the neeble factor right in life. Nothing less will do. And so I went back to Hull with nothing much written on those observation notes, and a strangely heavy heart. I had gone to Cleethorpes for a bit of home cooking and some live football, prepared to put up with the minor inconvenience of attending school for three potentially tedious weeks – at the end of which I had felt unexpectedly transformed. I'd imagined all sorts of Dickensian scenes, but instead had come across some kind of fairy godmother and a happy school. All that faced me now was the emptiness of the course, a big unfriendly city and the faintly queasy feeling that the real teaching practice after Christmas could not possibly turn out to be as easy and rewarding as this little episode had proved to be.

The undergraduate years had been anxious, shapeless ones, and as a result I'd dropped my expectations down the well of life. I could never have guessed that I would be dragged back into the light by a hyperactive widow from the pages of Enid Blyton. Mrs Howden was a genius, a revelation. She came from a generation that saw teaching as a public service and vocation. But it's one thing to see your job in that wholly respectable light, and quite another to do it well. I arrived at St Peter's with the casual air of the graduate who thinks he's seen it all, after three years away from the nest. I left the school three weeks later with the conviction that I knew absolutely nothing. I knew that it would take years to get anywhere near Mrs Howden's level of expertise, and even then I wasn't sure that it was something you could really learn. All I wanted to write in my observation notes was that this woman had treated every single one of the children as if they were intelligent beings, whatever they had done or said. It made a lasting impression on me. Watching her turn the dumbest remark into something clever, watching her encouraging the slowest-witted kid to believe he could do it next time, watching her carry out her innocent conviction that everyone was as well intentioned as herself, you couldn't help but feel that somewhere in the rotten old world there was a corner that was forever Bonnie, keeping things going, chivvying us all on and teaching us to be kind.

3
CONFESSING

Morning three of my teaching practice. Bill Brown, the teacher described by Hamish as the worst in the western hemisphere, is over by the kettle in the staffroom shrugging and confessing to another elderly colleague. Having come in early I can hear him easily over the half-empty room.

'I said to Joan this morning over breakfast – why the hell do I *do* this every day? Why do I allow myself to turn up for work every morning in the full knowledge that I am to be ritually abused and slaughtered by various groups of disgusting adolescents? Since I manifestly don't want to teach, and they have no desire whatsoever to learn, what is the bloody *point*? What am I *doing* here?' he groans. The colleague to whom he is discharging his spleen is actually the deputy head, a sympathetic woman by the name of Geraldine who has asked me a couple of times already if I am settling in, and whose kindly appearance has given me a feeling of potential comfort, should I ever wish to seek some crumbs of it outside the confines of the Dirty Corner. But Brown's little speech has struck me as depressing, as something that I wished I'd not heard. The worst thing about him is that he looks the part. Smartly turned out with a shiny leather briefcase in hand, he appears confidently academic, an efficient transmitter of knowledge. He doesn't look for a moment like the kind of man you would mess about, and yet evidently he is. Or perhaps it makes no difference in the jungle of the classroom. They are the predators and we are their prey, and since it's just a question of staying alive maybe it's not so disheartening after all.

Tony McCall comes over and settles into the armchair to my side. Each teacher has his or her own place, and it's clear that although I'm admitted to the circle, I will have to continue to drag over one of the less charismatic wooden chairs from the outer regions of the staffroom for the duration of my stay. McCall is large and from Liverpool, with a boxer's flat nose and that air of wise and funny composure that seems to come with the package.

'So how'd it go then?' he asks, speaking entirely through his nose.

'Fine – just fine,' I respond, raising an eyebrow to indicate that I don't quite mean what I've said. He takes the hint.

'How'd you get on with Plant? Didn't give you too much bother, did he?'

'He was a bit difficult,' I say, unsure of how clean to come, 'but he seemed to shut up in the end. I struggled a bit, but I did what I set out to do. I suppose that's all I can hope for at the moment.' McCall laughs briefly, but he's listening carefully, fixing his eyes on mine.

'Plant's pretty fucked up, of course,' he begins. 'His

47

mother topped herself about three years ago, and the old man's a disaster. He's remarried, but as you can imagine, the stepmother doesn't have a doctorate in human judgement. So young Alan's a bit of a tearaway, as they say. He gets shit at home, and he gets the same when he comes here. So naturally, he'll fling some of it back in your direction.' I ask if the other kids get on with him. 'Nah. He's a bully too. Classic profile, of course. He's got a little band of disciples, but he's not Mr Popular. We had a shrink in last year to talk to him, but it hasn't made much difference. If anything he's worse. Did Kelly shut him up or did you?' Assuming Kelly to be the blonde, I admit that it was indeed her in the end, although I try to make out that I also confronted him.

'Yeah, Kelly's all right,' confirms McCall. 'She's smarter than any shrink. If Plant goes too far, she wades in. He won't cross her, for some reason. When she leaves here, I'm first in the queue to marry her. So don't get any ideas, young apprentice.'

With that, McCall sits back and begins to read a series of essays that he's pulled out from a folder, ending the confessional. The only concrete advice that I have been given is not to propose to Kelly, but the chat has calmed me considerably. It isn't going to make the next class any easier, but it's nevertheless evident that no more dung has been flung at me than is normally the case. Things are making a little bit more sense, but the main problem is still how to fill the two months that stretch ahead of me, like some interminable marathon. Not only that, but during this period of purgatory

I am to be visited twice by my new tutor from Hull University, an elderly but amiable lecturer, washed up on the tide from some other age. Alice Roberts is a curious woman, like a harmless little granny mouse from a Beatrix Potter tale. She took us for only a couple of sessions before we left for teaching practice, but it was difficult during those classes to decide whether she was a subtle, all-knowing practitioner who would cut her knife through our bluff, or an entirely harmless creature who didn't know her fanny from her fundament. I'm hoping for the latter, of course, particularly as I simply can't imagine how she might react to Alan Plant. But her first visit is scheduled for about the third week, so there's still time to work out a strategy, the most obvious one being to ask her to visit when I am teaching the two easier classes, if indeed they turn out to be as such.

For now, there is day three to get through, but it might turn out to be easier than I'm expecting. As the staffroom fills up there's an unusual sense of excitement and anticipation in the smoky air. It's already snowed on the way to school, and now the skies look leaden. Crossing the playground earlier, I'd noticed that strangely muffled atmosphere that prevails before a snowfall. It's bitingly cold, and as red-faced teachers walk in shivering and blowing out their cheeks, the snow begins to fall again. With the ground already semi-frozen, the big thick flakes presage a possible late-morning abandonment of classes, which is the reason for the celebration. Some kids from further out of town have not come in at all, and year tutors are checking on which of the younger ones they know they can't send home. Bill Brown clenches his fist and shakes it at the window. 'Snow! For God's sake, snow! Anything to avoid double maths with the fifth year. Please God!' As Hamish puffs on his pipe, Jim scratches at his spots and joins in the chorus, treating the staffroom to the Newcastle version of the meteorological phenomenon 'Snoo!', whilst McCall walks contemplatively across to the window.

'If it carries on like this,' he announces, 'we can anticipate philosophical dialogue in a certain hostelry come lunchtime. Hamish?' The garden gnome, temporarily obscured by a bank of pipe mist, sits up and assumes his role as expedition leader.

'Well, it'll be The Dolphin then,' he instructs. 'Assuming continuation of current conditions, 12.30 sharp in the snug. Philip – you'll be there, of course. Compulsory attendance for all new members.' I know where The Dolphin is, and nod.

The first class of the day is with my third years, and I'm not expecting any trouble. I don't get any either. Although they're chatting when I walk into the classroom, continuing to do so as I step up to the desk and take out the class reader and my script for the morning, there is no malice in the soft murmur. Inexperienced as I am, I can detect something positive in the air. There is a delicacy in the atmosphere that reminds me of the scent of fabric softener. They're also happy, of course, at the potential closure of the school this morning, but I can imagine the scene in Plant's class. He'll be jumping up and down on his desk, whooping the snow down, with the rest of them probably joining in with the chorus. I clear my throat.

'Good morning. My name's Mr Ball and I'm here to take you for the next couple of months.' As soon as I speak, the burble dies away and those pupils who have been sitting chatting with their backs to me immediately about-face and sit up. 'I hear you've been reading a book about the Romans in Britain. *The Eagle of the Ninth*.' There is a faint nodding, a polite ripple of confirmation. 'I thought it might be nice this morning to read some of it in class, partly because I don't want to break the flow of what you've been doing, but also because I don't know the book very well,' I disclose, hoping that they'll detect some valid strategy in this. To my astonishment, the entire gathering begins to shuffle around purposefully, taking out the book from their satchels or from the desks. No one makes vomiting noises, no one protests. In a perverse sort of way it's almost annoying, since I haven't actually told them to take out their readers, but I'm not complaining. Within a matter of seconds the shuffling has stopped, the books are open at the page they have previously reached with Hamish, and thirty faces are looking up at me, awaiting instructions.

'Erm right,' I begin, temporarily fazed by the lack of confrontation. 'Of course I've looked through the book, but perhaps someone might give me a summary of the plot so far?' Thirty hands shoot into the air. I pick out a smart dark-haired girl at random from the first row, close to where I am standing. Despite the apparent docility of the gathering, I'm still a little wary of the back row. But the girl is already off. Straightening her back and staring into space as if I were just another object in the class, she begins.

'The story is about a young Roman named Marcus and his friend Esca as they travel through northern England, sir. The purpose of their journey is to recover the lost eagle of Marcus's father's legion – the Ninth Legion that marched into the mists of the north and never returned. There has been a rumour that the eagle banner has been located amongst the wild tribesmen of the north, and so Marcus is determined to find it. We're on page fifty-two now.' The girl returns her eyes to the book and awaits the beginning of the next instalment, but I'm feeling a bit neglected.

'So do you like the book so far?' I try. Some human contact might be nice. Silence reigns. Scanning the tops of thirty heads, I alight on a boy's face which has made the mistake of looking up for a moment. He looks strangely old and wise for a fourteen-year-old.

'Peter. Peter James,' he announces stiffly, which presumably means they've all been trained to give me their names on first acquaintance. Interesting how the rule seems to have lapsed in the other class. 'Well now,' he begins, pausing like a critic about to give his judgement on a late-night literary review, 'it's quite good. I would say it's quite gripping now, although there was a slight lack of tension in the early chapters.'

'Thanks for that. Now we have some good words there,' I bluster. 'Peter has used the words *gripping* and *tension,*' I manage, walking backwards towards the board. Fumbling around for the chalk, I spider the two words on to the dark abyss. 'Can anyone give me some other words to extend these two that Peter has already used?' Again, instead of yesterday's chorus of spunk and tampons, the hands shoot up to offer me all sorts of wonderful words. I get *absorbing, intriguing, captivating* ... the list goes on, to which my only reply is the vague and useless 'Good! Good!' There are no words in my head any better than these.

'OK. That's fine then. Shall we read for a while, and perhaps I'll be able to see for myself what is absorbing and captivating – or *gripping*, to use Peter's word.' On the course, a tip we have been fed is to remember people's names as quickly as possible, because this encourages them and boosts their self-esteem. Boosts their self-esteem? Bloody hell. The air is thick with self-esteem. It's bursting out of satchels, pustules, mouths and postures. But it's quite relaxing. As the snow settles on the gym rooftop outside, I am transported to some other place of comforts and desires. Peter's voice is a soft indeterminate hum.

After a while, in order to look a little more involved, I walk slowly down the central aisle as Peter continues with his excellent rendition of the soldiers' march northwards. Forcing myself to concentrate, I listen as the author describes the fear of a couple of Brit children, running off as they see a column of soldiers marching towards them.

'That's interesting,' I suggest. 'You can see there how the Roman presence in ancient Britain was not always a good thing for the natives. Maybe they would have preferred to have been left alone. It's an example of the problems of what we call imperialism.' Pleased with myself at this little intervention, I look around the class for a new reader to relieve Peter of the burden. A slight shuffling has started, and hands have started to go up, which I take to be volunteers for the reading slot. Another serious-looking pupil up at the front has turned around, but he seems to have something important to say.

'Lloyd Wright, sir. I don't think that's exactly true, sir!' he scolds. 'The Britons were happy for the Romans to stay, in the main.' The boy remains in his twisted posture, as if awaiting my response. Several others have murmured in agreement, making it clear that I've missed the whole point of the book by several galaxies. It might have helped if I'd actually read it.

'Well, yes – that's a fair point, Lloyd. The Romans made some good roads, for instance. But they made them for their own purposes. It wasn't out of kindness for us.' Hands are straining, but no one shouts out of turn. Inviting the next broadside, I point to a blonde girl.

'Claire Johnson,' she announces primly. 'Before the Romans came, sir, Britain consisted of various kingdoms, each one at war with the other. The Romans made things much better, sir. They made things more stable.' More nods from the gallery. At any point, I expect to receive the thumbs-down and be fed to the lions.

'Anything else they contributed?' I ask miserably. The hands strain higher to the ceiling.

'They showed us how to build forts!' says one.

'They showed us how to cook,' says another. What did the Romans ever do for us? Quite a bit, it would seem.

'OK, OK. These are all fair points,' I concede. 'But what I'm trying to say is that whatever you manage to do for the country you occupy, people will never really accept you. The author is trying to make that point, by showing the children's fear of the marching soldiers. In the end, the Roman Empire began to fall apart, and they left Britain because it was no longer of any use to them. When did they leave?' I ask, without a clue as to the answer. Hands shoot into the air. Lloyd Wright looks the keenest again.

'Four hundred AD, sir!' he barks, in a puppy voice still trying to break.

'Very good.' I nod. But hands are still straining upwards. I release one child from his pent-up silence and he bursts forth into the air with the fact that it was actually 406 AD. Lloyd gives the new information a cold but sombre stare. Like an academic born and bred, he nods quietly, accepts the correction, and turns back towards the front. Since the hands have gone down, even I can see that the second date is the correct one, not that I care particularly.

In the empty classroom twenty minutes later, the last pupil quietly gone, I feel that I am unprepared for this kind of life. I'd worked hard on the lesson with Jim's class because I knew that it was going to be difficult, and it was. Now, with the snow covering the roof of the school's new swimming pool outside, I know I've belly-flopped on my second dive – and as the flakes plummet down, it's the random nature of my actions that disturb me the most. Student or professional? Teacher or trickster? The latest recruit to a profession of losers? I'm not entirely sure, but it seems to me that Hamish's kids have actually deserved a bit better. Besides, what am I going to tell the Dirty Corner?

I'm spared the confessional because on approaching the staffroom it's obvious that something's afoot. Certain unlucky teachers have been assigned the duty of looking after those who cannot go home, but no one from the Dirty Corner has drawn the short straw. The bells begin to ring and tutors appear with registration books tucked under their arms. It would seem that for the rest of the day, my only further duty is to make my way through the blizzard to the snug room at The Dolphin, on Cleethorpes's bleak winter promenade. As I gather up my books and notes for the next day – assuming there is one – Bill Brown suddenly appears in the staffroom, slaps down the register in a gesture of contentment, and prepares to head off to the pub. He waves to me as he goes, a happier version of Captain Oates. 'I may be gone for some time.' He smirks, waggling his hand in a pint-downing simulation.

'See you later,' I say, smiling, and wave back.

In normal circumstances, Cleethorpes looks as though a bomb has hit it, but trudging through the deep snow that Wednesday morning a strange silence has descended on the town, like the morning after the apocalypse. After half an hour's footslog, a weak yellow light shining through the still-falling snow indicates that I have reached base camp. Inside, all is warmth and animated chatter. The members of the Dirty Corner are all there, huddled in a temporary corner by the window that looks out on to the promenade. Sea and sky meet in a greyish-white mass, visible though the hole in the steam that Hamish is wiping.

'Sit down, apprentice!' he says, upon which bums shuffle along the bench to accommodate me. 'So. You've had the swots now. What did you make of them?' Hamish asks, leaning across to me as if my answer will not necessarily be for general consumption. The rest of the gathering is chattering away about other matters, perked up by the excitement of an unexpected day off.

'Oh, not so bad.' I shrug. Hamish puffs on his pipe.

'Ah, indeed! Not so bad. There are some clever little buggers in there, I'll grant ye. Sometimes I wonder if it wouldn't be better to mix them all up, like they've done in some other more *prrrrogressive* places.' He blinks through his pipe smoke at me, waiting to see if I can take up the idea. He wields a strange power over the other members of the DC, whilst teachers who occupy other corners of the staffroom seem to view him with a mixture of fear and resentment – at least that's how it seems to me. But Hamish the gnome is my first boss, and I want to be sure that he's happy with me. I take a sip from the pint and tiptoe into the issue.

'Well, they were pretty awesome. I suppose it might hold them back a bit – I mean, if you put Plant in there. Or maybe it would do him some good. I don't really know,' I concede.

Hamish nods, pulls his pipe from its dental home, and swills down some beer.

'Aye – it's a tricky one,' he answers finally, revealing a beer-frothed moustache. 'But I reckon if you had Plant in there he'd learn something, as ye say. Something would rub off, I'm sure of it.' To his side, Jim Drewery and Bill Brown are roaring at some anecdote or other, but Bill catches the end of Hamish's sentence.

'Ah, Hamish!' he proclaims, turning to face us. 'You're not proposing mixing them up again, are you?' He aims the next bit at me. 'Now just so you know. Hamish was a radical zookeeper in a former life. He came to the zoo when all the animals were nicely tucked up in their separate paddocks, doing their separate things and minding their own – and then he decided that it would be much more interesting to have open house, didn't you, Hamish?'

Since Hamish merely grins across at his adversary, Bill continues: 'And on the Seventh Day, He let them all out of their paddocks, and He saw that it was good. It was an open-plan zoo. The lion lay down with the lamb, because Saint Hamish thought that the lion might learn something from the lamb. Is that what he was telling you?' I nod in the zookeeper's direction. 'What he probably hasn't told you is that the lion ate the lamb and the zoo collapsed into anarchy. Don't listen to him!' Slowly but surely, the volume around the table begins to drop as the others realise that Bill and Hamish are locking horns again.

'Leave the apprentice alone,' McCall says, smirking. 'You're just an old fascist, and you owe me a pint. As long as the trains run on time, eh? Never mind about the rest of the poor sods.

Just as long as it looks good. Just as long as the streets are swept clean. That's your zoo, isn't it? Genetic management, survival of the elite. You'd have made a good Nazi.'

Bill throws his arms in the air. 'Oh, all right. Here we bloody go! Why don't you save your speeches for next month, Prime Minister?' McCall is apparently standing for Labour in the forthcoming council elections. 'Mind you, he's quite good at knocking on lonely housewives' doors and persuading them to do his bidding, aren't you, Tony? Vote for me and I'll show you a good time!' – at which Bill roars at his own joke and picks up his beer for a triumphant swig. At the mention of sex, Jim intervenes.

'Tony's going to win, man – an' the first thing he's going t' do, man, is bring in early retirement for teachers. You can get out the zoo before the paddocks come down!' Bill ignores him and steps back up to his soapbox.

'Bloody socialists. All for one and one for all, eh? You live in a dream world where every Tom, Dick and Harry are the same. Chairman McCall and his Long March. You'll have us all wearing the same uniform and marching up and down the promenade, never mind early retirement. You're the Nazis, not me. Now, for example, let's look at Mr Plant ...' and at the mention of the dreaded surname, the pub seems to tremble – or perhaps it's just a lump of snow falling from the roof.

After a few seconds of Plant-induced silence, Hamish revs up. He claims that Plant is basically acting, and that he actually wants to learn. 'Planty's the worst – for sure,' he says, 'but he wants to be like the swots. He wants to be like Lloyd Wright and the rest of them. There's no such thing as the pupil who doesn't want to learn. Haven't you ever seen him, when he's really interested?' The comment receives various guffaws.

'Interested? Interested in what, Hamish?' laughs Bill Brown. 'He's beyond saving. It doesn't matter, say I. The only pupils who matter are the ones that are *able* to learn.' At this, he gets up to go to the bar. 'I'll drink to that if no one else will. Sometimes I think I'm working in some parallel universe, where all the people think that everyone is inherently good and thirsting for knowledge. But the only thing Plant wants to do is to make my life a misery, and the bastard has succeeded with flying colours.' He hovers between the table and the bar, beginning to sway slightly. 'And besides, you can't base your whole bloody philosophy on one pupil. Without him that class would actually be manageable. Who needs mixed bloody ability?' He staggers off to the bar. Tony McCall waits a few seconds, then calls after him.

'Ah, Billy boy! The trouble is that you can't base a whole philosophy on the fact that even if Plant wasn't there, they'd be running rings round you. What you need is to rediscover sex. Then change your flag to red and be a little bit calmer and more collected, like Philip here, for example. What do you make of all this, young apprentice?'

I didn't know what to make of it. I'd never sat in a pub with a group of seasoned professionals, and so I felt that they were the real adults and that I was a kid, allowed in for crisps and shandy. If I'd understood correctly, Bill had slurred out his approval for the old grammar-school selection system, but the Dirty Corner believed in the new comprehensive dawn. As for Bill, despite my feeling sorry for him, I didn't want to end up like him. More to the point, I didn't think that I'd said anything too out of place to Hamish. And apparently Plant wanted to learn. It was all I could think of saying back to McCall.

'If Plant wants to learn, um ... I'll drink to that,' I managed, raising my glass. Hamish raised his and winked. Behind him, through the steam hole in the window, I could see that the snow had stopped. If no more fell, then there would be no postponement of the second helping of that very pupil the next morning.

4

WHISTLING

Overnight a slight thaw set in, so that by the morning all hopes of a second day of freedom were dashed – as I'd feared. I had Plant and company again before I could experience the dubious pleasures of drama, and had spent the evening worrying about how the 'open debate' that I had set up would go.

Again, the smell of hormones working overtime almost choked me on walking into the classroom. Resolving to look more busy and confident this time, I asked if they had written up the answers to the ticky-tacky text on uniforms (a question they chose to ignore) and then enquired whether they had thought about the debate (a question which they also chose to ignore). Pushing on regardless and avoiding any eye contact with Plant, whose cold blood was warming up on the rocks like an iguana in a Galapagos dawn, I divided the class in two, randomly assigning the pros and the cons. I also made the mistake of writing these two abbreviations on the blackboard. The undemocratic election of sides had immediately sparked a protest.

'But sir! I want to be a con!'

'And I want to be a pro!' shouted a girl. The class howled her down.

'She wants to be a pro! Like her mother!'

'Fuck off the lot o' yuh!' she screamed, and ran out of the room.

When I finally settled them, I asked both sides to work in groups of four, to prepare arguments for the debate. I also asked them to think of two arguments that the other side might come up with, so that they could refute them, if necessary. No such luck. First of all, the noise and chaos that ensued when I asked them to form groups of four could have been heard over the North Sea. No one wanted to work with anyone else, it seemed.

'I'm not working with *her* – Christ!' or 'Not with him. He's a *perv*!' When I finally got the class back to order, Plant was left sitting alone at the back, in splendid isolation. I had thought it might happen, but had prayed to the gods of fortune that it might just work itself out. Plant seemed perfectly happy to be there, and as the rest of the class vaguely got on with what I'd asked them, enveloped in a vile cloud of gas and noise, I approached the boy that Hamish had been talking about in the pub. He wanted to learn. He had the right to learn. But before I even reached the back, he began to point at my nether regions.

'Your fly's undone! Been having a crafty one?' he opened, slouching over the desk. Fortunately, no one heard.

'I was wondering, Alan,' I tried, pulling up my fly, 'maybe you'd like to choose which side you want to be on?'

Plant thought about this. 'I don't want to be on either side, really, mate. Can't I just sit here and go back to sleep?' Having assured him that he had to choose, he then asked me what the rest of the class was doing.

'But we were doing it last lesson, Alan. We were looking at the topic of uniforms. And you did some homework for me. Have you got your exercise book?' No he hadn't. He'd forgotten to bring it. He'd bring it tomorrow.

Neither did he have a pen, nor any books of any description. I couldn't understand why he was allowed to get away with this, but fearful of starting a further brawl if I tried to incorporate him into a group, I gave him a piece of paper and a pen and asked him to write down a couple of points, a pro and a con. When I looked up from the safe distance of the other side of the class some minutes later, I saw him staring into space, completely cut off from the tide. He wasn't even being disruptive. He just seemed to want everyone to leave him alone. I thought of his mother. Apparently she'd hanged herself, and he'd walked in on her, one afternoon after school. The rest of the class was making a half-hearted attempt to prepare the debate, but they weren't very interested. I should have gone over the questions with them, I thought, before putting them into groups, but it was too late now. At least Plant was being honest. He couldn't give a toss. He'd probably stopped giving a toss the moment he'd walked in on his dead mother. School uniforms – a matter of life and death? Probably not.

The debate was a disaster. Manfully as I struggled to inculcate the spirit of the Oxford Union into them, hard as I tried to make them use some appropriate language such as 'In my opinion' or 'With regard to what Kelly has just said' – all of which I had written up on the board as cues – the comments hurled across the central divide of the classroom had sounded more like the kind of banter heard in a pub on Grimsby docks at last orders.

'What you fucking talking about? I never said that, you cow!'

'See you outside!'

Plant had nominally joined the 'pro' side, amused as he was by the word, and had spent the duration howling like a wolf, loudest whenever a slanging match was in full swing. All I had hoped was that no other teacher would hear the chaos and the noise, and come to the class thinking that there was no teacher present. The girl accused of being a 'pro' had not come back, and was officially missing in action. I was beginning to see why teachers didn't really confess, since the only way to retain a scrap of dignity from this farce was to say absolutely nothing about it. All I learned from the experience was that debates were tricky affairs, and that it was good I had found out so early; I might otherwise have risked one when Alice came to visit. The idea of another adult witnessing this pantomime made me feel like drinking a bottle of turpentine.

I knew from my own time in purgatory as a pupil that good teaching was a state of grace not easily attained by mortals. What I hadn't predicted was the loneliness. Despite the comforts of a Dirty Corner, I wasn't in an office surrounded by people whose behaviour I could copy. I was on my own, exposed on stage in the white light. On top of this, nobody had presented me with a classroom recipe, and although I was surprised by this, I knew in my heart of hearts that it was unlikely that anyone ever would. Like snowflakes, no two classes could ever be the same, and thirty pairs of eyes will never see you in quite the way you might have planned. Besides, at the age of twenty-two, who the hell are you anyway? If adolescence is about identity crisis then I, for one, was certainly suffering the fag end of it by the time I was thrust upon Cleethorpes's youth and required to teach them. With my pale face betraying all sorts of insecurities, I was groping for a mask that would turn me into a bolder figure. I felt that I'd slipped through the net and been given responsibility under false pretences. I didn't feel much older than the kids. They had obviously noticed. I was trying my hardest to be somebody else – someone more mature. Desperately seeking charisma, the only place I could find it was in the not-too-distant past.

The man who first offered up this idea of the mask was Dr Richardson, the lecturer who taught the module 'Teachers through the ages' on the PGCE at Hull. This involved weekly seminars in which the affable part-timer kindly took the day off from his fishing to assign us readings from a wide-ranging list of authors, all of whom had had something to say about the profession. The idea was to give us an historical perspective on the schoolmaster's lot, and although they seemed of no obvious practical use at the time, I'd rather enjoyed Richardson's seminars that first term. He actually turned up one week with his fishing rod in tow, propped it up in a corner of the room and proceeded to ask us questions about the week's reading with his back to us, all the time disentangling a fish hook. But I really remember the silver-haired Richardson not for his fishing rod but for the last seminar he taught before we parted our ways for the dreaded TP. He had asked us to sit in pairs and discuss 'the teacher who had most influenced us' at school. Halfway through the session he stopped us, closed his copy of *Angling Times* and pointed a lazy finger at Karen, a talkative and witty fellow trainee.

'Now then, love. Tell me something. When you stand in front of that first class, who are you going to be?' Karen, for once, was lost for words. She shrugged, opened her eyes wide and turned her mouth downwards, in a gesture of defeat. Richardson prompted her further. 'Who was that teacher you were talking about – the one that influenced you?' Karen replied that it had been her English teacher. Richardson scoffed. 'Ah! They always are. Why is it always bloody English teachers?' he drawled, inviting the rest of us to intervene. But Karen defended her choice anyway: 'Because they usually have something to say that you can relate to. Instead of talking about photosynthesis or something.'

'So who will you be in that first class – yourself or that English teacher?'

'Me? No, no. Never! I don't want them to see me. Anybody but me!' This was exactly what Richardson wanted.

'Then you'll be that teacher you liked. You'll want to be him or her. It's a time-honoured tradition, from which only the most confident and gifted are exempt. It's a perfectly natural state of affairs. There's nothing to be ashamed of.' And then he bestowed upon us the line that he presumably recited to all his students, year after year: 'There'll be plenty of time to be yourselves.' He then gathered up his fishing magazine and left, as if there were no more to say.

He might have added that all such copycat attempts are doomed to failure, but his words were prophetic nevertheless. Once cast adrift from studenthood and washed up on the lonely shore of that first classroom – Plant and all – all I could think about was survival, about gathering together all the defences available to cope with the climate and the hostile natives. I wasn't too good at the chameleon trick, but I'd definitely tried it. The chap I'd really wanted to use as camouflage had loomed very large in my life. His name was Johnny Roe.

Roe had the gift, and was something of a legend even before I became a pupil at the local grammar school on a sunny morning back in September 1968. My older brother was sixteen and had been taught English by Roe for two years. While my brother dismissed most teachers as despots, Roe was accorded the unique privilege of a Christian name. This was no mean feat in a decade that had been tuning in and dropping out, blowing its dope-scented smoke into the face of the mortar-board values of the doomed grammar-school system. And because my brother had the longest hair in the school and had all the albums of all the hippest bands,

I guessed that there must have been something in this Johnny Roe business. But it wasn't just my brother. You could sense a collective feeling in the air that the surname or nickname treatment was somehow wrong for him, resulting in the simple 'Johnny' moniker. I would have to wait a further three years before I was actually taught by him, and when that fortunate year began I was treated to a double whammy of the man, as English teacher and class tutor.

It's difficult to avoid clichés here, because the idea of someone changing your life, influencing you or even saving you can sound mawkish or false. I don't suppose, looking back, that Johnny Roe 'saved' me at all. I was just an average pupil, short on confidence and unsure as to where the future might lie, as befits the reactive soul – but I was no disaster. I would have muddled through. But he did change my life. If he hadn't come along and brightened things up in the way that he did, then I would have grown up a different person – a better one or a worse one it's impossible to say – but without doubt a different one. Others will have similar stories to tell, but it's unlikely that many will have come across a teacher quite like this one.

He was no obvious rebel. In his late thirties, he looked conventional enough. In the main hall at morning assembly he would sit with the rest of the staff on the raised stage behind the headmaster's lectern, wearing his university gown and a pained expression – as if he were suffering from a permanent migraine. His hair was jet-black and immaculately cut, and he was handsome in a square-jawed sort of way. He sported the classic uniform of the aesthete – grey slacks and brown Hush Puppies, overhung by a green cord jacket with leather patches at the elbows – but he walked carefully and upright, with a don't-fuck-with-me strut straight from the army. Even the older, cockier pupils at the back of the hall were wary of him. During the assemblies our barking head-master, an unstable religious fanatic sitting out his retirement, would have a weekly fit – storming off stage hollering the fatwa 'Assembly is abandoned!' At the slightest sign of disorder or rebellion in the ranks below, Roe would step off the stage. Although he held no official senior rank he was always the one to descend into the pit.

My first year at the school was a good one for apoplectic headmaster walkouts. The first I witnessed was when a small boy in the front row of seats below the lectern dared to whisper something to his neighbour, right in the middle of a wailing benediction. The headmaster suddenly stopped his chant, pointed down at one of the boys and shouted: 'Who is that boy sitting next to East?' The hall twitched as one. 'West, sir' came the plaintive reply, upon which the assembled school – some 500 pupils – exploded in spontaneous combustion. Even the po-faced teachers on the stage found it hard to keep their expressions straight. 'This is a *religious ceremony*!' bellowed our leader, thumping his fist down onto the lectern and sweeping off stage, his face as purple as a plum. As matters threatened to get out of hand, Johnny Roe appeared from nowhere, floated down the aisle and stilled the waters. No one dared speak with him hovering in the vicinity. It was the look that you feared, the withering glance. Where the rest of the teachers borrowed from the system for their authority, Roe preferred to use his eyes. He had some scary aura about him that would have worked in San Quentin.

By the age of fourteen, I'd accepted that school was a sort of obstacle course to be endured. I crept unwillingly through its darkened corridors each morning with neither choice nor expectation. As long as you didn't buck the system no one took much notice of you, and nobody really seemed to care. It was the natural state of affairs, and you adapted as best you could. But then along came Johnny. The first lesson was like losing your virginity and being introduced to drugs all in one go. As they say, I remember it well. With his migraine face and killer eyes he swept into the room, slammed the door shut, strode down the central parting of the desks until he reached the back wall, then stopped dead and swivelled theatrically on his soft brown shoes to address his slack-jawed throng. I'd been waiting three years for this – hoping he wouldn't disappoint. The shoes squeaked slightly as he pirou-etted. 'I have in my hand a book,' he pronounced, in a mean, tight-lipped voice. Despite this being my fourth year, I had never heard him speak before. He held the book up for us as we craned our necks to watch him. 'It is called *English Four*. You probably remember *English Three* from last year, and *English Two* from the year before that.' He paused. 'They were all written by the same imbecile. Only an *imbecile* could have written a series of books like this.' He paused again in the silence, breaking it suddenly with a contemptuous 'Pah!'

– a sound that had become his trademark, according to my brother. 'But have no fear,' he continued, sneering at the poor publication, 'because I have no intention of foisting this nonsense upon you,' whereupon he strolled more slowly to the front of the class and dropped the book with a thud into the large metal litter bin. 'Pah!' he hissed again, looking down at the bin as if to make sure that the book was dead. We looked around uneasily at each other. It was difficult to believe that it was happening. This was revolution, and there was more to come.

After a long and acrid silence he resumed his walkabout, gliding down the central lane of the class. 'I was brought up in Rhodesia,' he began, in a more story-bookish sort of tone. 'We had a small weekend house up in the hills and when I was a boy I would take off on my own, climbing the rocks and cliffs that formed the first steps of the mountainside. I used to enjoy being alone up there, away from my parents. I thought I was invincible because I could climb those hills. You often do when you're a child. But then something happened. *Baboons.*' He pronounced the word 'baboons' with a strange inflection, to show us his more exotic African side. 'A group of them were watching me in a most curious manner. I had passed them earlier on the way up the cliffs, but when I had paused to drink some water and eat some biscuits I noticed that they must have been following me, although they kept their distance. Most odd.'

Thus passed the first five minutes of Johnny Roe. Everyone was thinking the same. Genius or serial killer? But it was entertaining – an entirely new concept. What did he want us to do? Surely there was some catch? Was he expecting us to take notes? He couldn't possibly want to tell us a story – to simply interest us. No, no – that was impossible. Teachers couldn't possibly do that kind of thing. I knew he told stories, because my brother would come home cracked up sometimes, claiming that Roe had been telling them madman tales about when he was abducted by aliens, when he had spoken to a ghost, or when he'd had to kill insurgents during his time in the Rhodesian army. Every time my brother had come home scoffing, I'd ask him the same question: 'So what did you say?' and every time he'd answered the same: 'You don't say anything. If you laugh he goes mad.' And as the baboon story became progressively more barking, the only way to avoid wetting myself was to avoid my classmates' eyes. Most were focused on the door anyway, calculating the chances of escape should things begin to get any weirder.

They did. Roe carried on, straight-faced and deadly serious. 'The baboons were clearly following, which is something that baboons never do. Worse than that, I could see that some of them had gone ahead, and were waiting for me above the rocks. I turned around and tried to shoo them away, but they only retired a certain distance. When I resumed walking, so did they. I had heard stories about baboon attacks, but they were almost all in specific circumstances, such as a mother protecting her young, or when walkers had suddenly come across a group, unexpectedly. But here there was more deliberation on their part.' As a signal that we were about to reach the *denouement*, he walked across to the large side windows of the classroom and looked out contemplatively over the small quadrangle. Suddenly, like a viper whose siesta had been rudely disturbed, he let out a deathly hiss. 'And suddenly I remembered what an old chief had told me years before about baboon attacks. He had told me that if they ever began to look threatening, the only thing to do was to whistle at them.' Having got to the crucial point, he paused again and faced his public, as if challenging them to laugh. But no one did. Satisfied, he returned his look to the window. 'And so I began to whistle. I'm not a particularly good whistler,' he snapped, as if he resented the fact. 'But it made no difference. The baboons behind me were getting closer. There must have been about two dozen of them. For one of the first times in my life, I began to experience true fear. The fear of an animal that knows that it is about to be killed. And then I remembered. I remembered that the old chief had told me that if the whistling didn't work, you had to change the pitch. Some baboons only respond to a certain key, and so I tried something around middle C.' As if the story were still not quite wacky enough, Roe actually began to whistle at this point in our direction, turning us into the watching baboons. Just when I thought I was about to burst, he supplied the final line: 'Remarkably, the baboons scattered.'

After this performance, he ordered us to write an essay about fear, about the first time that we could remember experiencing it. We were handed no prompts, no planning, just the order to hand in the piece for the next lesson in two days' time. As people began to look at each other quizzically, he wafted his arms up and down impatiently. 'Get out your composition books and start – now!' he huffed, with a withering stare. As he returned to his seat at the large desk in front of the class I felt, for the first time in ten tedious years of schooling, a surge of something like excitement. Looking around, the majority of the class seemed flummoxed by the essay demand, whereas I couldn't believe that someone had asked me to do something that I fancied I could actually do. This was a revelation.

Back in those days, schools believed in competition. Not the sort that posts up league tables in the nation's newspapers, but rather the sort that pitted you against your mates, whether you liked it or not. In the old version of dog-eat-dog, based loosely on the notion that if there were another world war it would be won on the playing fields of the grammar schools, your exam results and your class 'position' in every subject were mercilessly published on the windows of the classrooms, so that you couldn't help but be affected by the rat race. From a class of thirty, the system threw up three annual winners and twenty-seven losers. The three got the prizes on speech day, and the rest of us looked on in envy or self-pity. I knew I'd never get on that stage to accept the local dignitary's handshake. I never felt remotely close. The guys who won the prizes seemed like another species to me, a gene pool equipped for playing the system. Then along came Johnny Roe, binning *English Four* and asking us to write about fear, and by the time the bell rang for the end of that first class I had written until my hand ached.

I wanted Roe to notice me, I suppose. His story had been insane, but he'd performed it like some Olivier on recreational drugs. Not only that, but in among the bluster and the bollocks there had been touches that had hinted at those tricky little depths – the ones that begin to whisper up from the tacky shallows of your adolescence. The story had been a whopper from start to finish, of course, but I fancied I'd cottoned on to what he'd really meant – that the baboons were an unexpected threat, and that they represented the first signs in a child's life that all was not well, that we're not invincible after all and that out there, among the cliffs and the rocks of childhood, you might suddenly find yourself alone, having to cope. I wanted to show him that I'd picked up on this, and so I took a risk and wrote about the first time I remembered my parents arguing, when I'd first feared as a child that they would separate or even abandon me if it continued. I would never have dreamt of revealing such personal stuff to the other teachers, but I knew that Roe wouldn't bat an eyelid.

I waited for the return of our essays like a little kid waits for Christmas. The interval was unbearable, but by the next lesson he'd marked the books. Ever his own man, he had a curious way of giving back the work, picking a single brown exercise book from the pile on his desk, glancing at the name then walking slowly towards the cowering author. He appeared to have pre-arranged the books in some sort of order because the first recipient, Ian Forrester, had claimed to us in the playground that he'd done a hatchet job on the essay because he thought it was 'daft'. It was a brave but foolish act. With the exercise book in hand, Roe began slowly down the aisle in his Hush Puppies then accelerated abruptly, as if he were unable to control himself. Arriving a yard or so from the small figure of Forrester, he braked, lurched slightly then hurled the offending essay at the pupil's head. As it bounced off the victim's bonce and slapped on to the desk, Roe whispered his logotype '*im-be-cile*' through drawn-back lips. The next few books were also flung at those who were deemed to have failed in the exercise, and the misery of their public execution was clear to us all. There was to be no way back for those who had dared to turn in defective work. You could see that he would never forgive.

Then, little by little, in the shoe-squeaking silence, the books further down the pile were returned in a more civil manner. He said absolutely nothing, but by throwing the books back in a less aggressive manner it was clear that he approved, sort of. As he came to the final batch, and began to deliberately place them on each desk like an indifferent but efficient waiter, I dared to dream that he might be saving mine until the last. Yet despite the feeling that I had turned in a half-decent essay, I was still terrified that I might have written too much about myself or something, and that I might be in for the last-but-not-least imbecile treatment.

Finally there was just one. Roe picked up my solitary exercise book from his desk, walked slowly across to where I sat by the windows, and casually skimmed the book to my hands from a short distance. As I caught the flapping object, he positioned himself opposite, looking me straight in the eyes. He raised one eyebrow and nodded – or at least I think he did. With the rest of the class watching me as Roe walked back to his desk, I opened the book carefully. There was no red ink on the work, no corrections. At the bottom of the fourth and final page he had simply written 'Brilliant'. I snapped the book shut as if it contained pornography, stunned by this unexpected praise. It seemed out of character from him, too unreserved. But it was a life-changing moment. As if I had suddenly been presented with a cheque for a million pounds, the sumptuous gift of acceptance was bestowed. The essay wasn't brilliant at all, and looking back it was a bit of a wild response to a new pupil's first effort, but he was not a conventional chap. The way he'd returned the books had been a vicious exercise in favouritism, dismissing those who were not prepared to tune into his wavelength. But I was extremely chuffed to have been singled out, to have been taken on as one of his apostates.

I took the book home that night and kept staring at the infamous word. It seemed an adjective that belonged else-where, but I was captivated by it. I kept closing the book then reopening it to check that it was still there. These were powerful emotions, and they changed me for ever. I began to enjoy school, for the first time I could remember. When it was a Johnny Roe day, everything seemed brighter somehow, and he hardly ever disappointed. The Lord only knows where he got his ideas from, or if he simply walked into the room every day and improvised, but it resulted in sparkling stuff. In amongst all the tales I can remember there was one where he wanted us to think about eccentricity, and told us the story of when he was a student, working as a porter on a provincial Rhodesian station. 'When we were on the night-shifts,' he said, 'the best way to pass the time was by playing cards. We would play all night around a small round table. But one of my fellow porters was convinced he was a *bat*.' I can still hear the word 'bat' across the years, given the tight-lipped sibilant treatment as if he were Olivier again, delivering a crucial speech. 'He would hang upside-down from the bare light-bulb above the table, casually playing cards. We got used to it in the end, and often forgot he was there. A curious man.'

Not all of his lessons consisted of daft stories, however. He was obliged to follow some sort of programme during that first year of the old O-level literature course, but had chosen well from the books on offer. In the previous years we had read the usual stuff in class – Conan Doyle, Jack London, Mark Twain – all thoroughly decent copy but with no obvious purpose. I never recall being asked to comment on the books, or draw anything as deep as a conclusion. We just read them in class, because that was the easiest option for the teachers. But after some three weeks of Roe's tales from the asylum, he suddenly presented us with a set of scuffed copies of a novel called *Lord of the Flies* by William Golding. This was to be our first 'set book'. It had a yellow cover the colour of diarrhoea, but inside I found treasure. As he read us the opening pages that same lesson it was as if someone had shot an electric charge through me. The tension in Roe's voice, the book's tight imagery, and the slow unfolding of a some-thing-nasty-in-the-woodshed feeling had me transfixed. I raced home on my bike that afternoon and read on to myself in the evening, understanding every word of it, picking up on everything. Where had this book been all my life? It seemed the key to everything.

Even more happily for me, after a couple more lessons of dramatic white Rhodesian renderings, he began to probe. Closing up the book one afternoon with about ten minutes to go until the end of the lesson, he put on the migraine expression: 'This shell – this conch that the boys are using. It's what we call a *symbol*. It's symbolic of something, a metaphor. What is it symbolic of? What does it represent?'

He floated as usual, up and down the central aisle. Most of us were still shy of offering up a quick answer, in case we got the 'imbecile' treatment. You could never be sure with him. But I really wanted to show him that I understood, to confirm my promising start. When no one raised their hand, I decided to risk it. He caught sight of my arm with a side-ways glance, lifting his hand slightly as an invitation for me to speak.

'It's a symbol of order, sir,' I announced, trying to sound confident. Still looking at the back wall, he waved his hand for me to continue. I'd been reading the study notes at the back of the book, and had come across this phrase. With the eyes of the class focused on me, waiting for me to continue, I added: 'The boys need something to replace the organisation that they had before. It's like the school bell or something.'

Roe waited his habitual few seconds, swivelled on his shoes and stared in the direction of the blackboard, way up at the other end of the classroom. '*Exactly,*' he hissed, still staring into space. 'Ball. You can go home ten minutes early,' and he wafted the air to his side, dismissing me. Some of the other pupils grumbled.

'But sir!' someone protested. 'That's not fair.'

As I grabbed my satchel and made for the door, grinning, all I could hear was Roe's swift response to the dissenter. 'Be quiet, you *imbecile.*'

As the year progressed there was some sort of silent covenant between us. Every week when the late-afternoon lesson came around he would ask a question from one of the set books and allow the winner an early home-time. But it became embarrassing to the extent that I began to pretend that I didn't know the answers. He knew this, of course, and one morning I arrived early to the tutor group, with no one else in the form room but Johnny Roe. The previous afternoon no one had been able to supply the end to a phrase from Shakespeare's *Macbeth*, our second set book, but I'd said nothing. Being in Roe's favour was one thing, but I couldn't let it go too far. Some of my mates were not so enamoured of him. As I passed his desk he piped up suddenly: '*No jutty, frieze, buttress nor coign of vantage, but this bird hath made his pendent bed and* … what?' I placed my satchel carefully on my desk.

'*Procreant cradle,*' I supplied, smart-arsedly. I hadn't the foggiest of what the two words meant, but they sounded good. He smiled.

'Why are you failing in mathematics?' he asked suddenly.

I shrugged. 'I don't know sir. I suppose it doesn't really interest me so much.'

Fiddling with his keys, he stared beyond me to the windows. 'It *can* be interesting,' he suggested. 'See if you can get a better mark this term,' at which he moved his head slightly to indicate that the moment of intimacy was over. Instead of taking the chance, in the empty room, to congratulate me on my nerdy knowledge of *Macbeth*, he decided instead to advise me not to put all my eggs into one basket – or at least that's what I think he was saying. It was a kind of indirect praise, I suppose, and the only way that he could bring himself to acknowledge the communion between us was to have a dig at me for being crap at maths. But that was fine. By that juncture I was happy at school for the first time in my life, and he was the reason for it.

Towards the end of the fifth form, Johnny Roe stood at the front of the class one morning and announced: 'I won't be with you next year in the sixth form. I'm leaving for Australia.' Out of the blue, just like that. I stared into my desk, stunned by the news. It was the most miserable moment of my school career – as the dusty old grammar school squeaked its final squeak and the new comprehensive giant trod on its head and squashed it for ever. I hated the pomp and circumstance of the place, but it had been around since the eighteenth century. In its death throes, I figured it deserved a bit of respect. But Johnny Roe was going a tad further. When someone dared to ask him why he was leaving, he replied, 'I have no desire to teach maniacs to tie their bootlaces.' So much for the egalitarian dream.

Fifteen years later, travelling around Australia, I looked him up in the telephone directory in Adelaide, the city that I remembered him saying he was headed for. There were two entries for Roe, both with the initial J. I knew that it was probably not a great idea, that he might not remember me, and that with the passing of time I might well see the cracks in his armour much more than I had done when I was a smelly youth. I preferred to keep the illusion intact, but it seemed a shame to pass through the city without looking him up. Uneasily, I dialled the first number and a woman replied, possibly his wife.

'Is John there, please?' I asked timidly.

'No – he's still at school, but he'll be back about five. Who's speaking please?' she answered. So it was him. Impulsively, in a moment I have always regretted, I decided to back off.

'Oh – it's just an old pupil of his. I was just wondering if he was at home. I ... I've got to leave this afternoon anyway, but never mind.' As she asked me to leave my name I hung up. It had suddenly seemed pointless as it dawned on me that I would have had nothing to really say to him – save *procreant cradle* perhaps. And there would have been nothing worse than realising that although he had been an important person to me, I had hardly registered on his consciousness. There would have been plenty of pupils during his long career who'd been half decent at English, and I preferred to save us both from embarrassment. 'Philip who?' I just couldn't face the phrase.

When I'd finally had to teach kids myself, the only thing I took from Johnny Roe was the engagement. Reasoning that if I could entertain them I would stand a better chance of controlling them would turn out to be an occasionally successful policy, but one that could backfire just as easily. I had neither Roe's poise, nor his timing. Another obvious problem was that I had never whistled at any baboons, and even if I had, it would have been difficult for me to have silenced my audience in the way that he had done. And yet something rubbed off, something stayed with me – which was the knowledge of how powerful the sensation of confidence can be.

I suppose I could have gone for tea that afternoon and thanked him for brightening up those couple of years, for helping to channel me down a certain path – but in truth I was afraid that if he did remember me, he might have asked me if I'd ever come to find mathematics more interesting. I would have been forced to tell him that I had never mastered logarithms, and that the only thing I had ever managed to do with an isosceles triangle was to spell it correctly. *Imbecile!* he would have hissed. I can hear it now.

5

BUMPING

The interesting thing about kids is that they have always thought the same things, at the same stages. Father Christmas and the Tooth Fairy get the push around the age of eight, just as other new concepts begin to kick in. One of these is the realisation that parents aren't quite as clever as they once might have appeared, and the other is that teachers have a life outside the confines of the classroom. The latter discovery is a startling one, almost as unnerving as the day that you realise your parents are still having sex. The teacher discovery usually happens in town, shopping with your mum. Miss Smith is upon you before you have time to hide, passing you both with a casual smile and hello as if nothing were the matter – as if the fact that she is arm in arm with a man were of no significance whatsoever. You stare incredulously into the ground, incapable of accepting this enormity. Miss Smith goes shopping. Miss Smith has a boyfriend. 'Wasn't that Miss Smith?' your mother asks, but you are lost in your thoughts. You were sure that Miss Smith lived at the school. You thought that at night she became part of the furniture and that in the morning she was transformed once again into a living being, magically restored to life by the school bell. 'Saw you on Saturday, miss,' you might venture on the Monday, should the teacher be a fairly sympathetic soul – but in truth you are hoping for confirmation by denial. You hope she will say that it must have been somebody else, and that she had been at the school all the time, morphed into a blackboard duster for the entire weekend.

Gradually you come to accept that teachers watch the TV, go shopping and even have children of their own. What you can never accept is that they are emotional beings just like your parents, and that they love, laugh and cry just like normal people do. Of course, it would be nice if the myth were really the truth, and as a teacher you could just get on with things in the classroom without the added burden of a relationship to contend with, but unfortunately it isn't the case. As with the rest of the professions, teachers have emotional histories. Miss Smith really was shopping in town that day. She had other things in her life apart from me, and several years later I had other things in mine apart from Alan Plant and Jim's loonies.

It all began one September back in the 1960s when I was ushered into my new junior-school class a little later than the rest. My mum had received a letter telling her that the new intakes were to be staggered throughout the morning, and as she finally handed me over to the new teacher at the classroom door I was shown into a room already full of new faces. As I glanced at the seated throng, a pair of blue eyes met mine. They belonged to a dark-haired lovely by the name of Beverly Dumbrell, whose olive skin stood out from the rest of the pale little creatures who sat there in their shy first-morning silence. Her eyes followed mine as I was introduced to the class and shown to my seat. Naturally, though I was besotted with her from that moment onwards, I did absolutely nothing about it. At the age of seven, your repertoire of chat-up lines is generally rather scant, for which reason I was hoping that she might be rather more forward in the initiative stakes.

After a couple of days she approached me in the playground and asked me where I lived. Happily, it turned out that her parents had a house about five minutes from mine, in a smarter neighbourhood close by. To my amazement, she asked me if I wanted to go round to her place for tea, that very night. To my further amazement, my mother consented and I wandered round at about five o'clock to my first date, all on my own.

I found her house and was given the standard orange juice and biscuits by her friendly parents. After tea, we were allowed to play in her garden together, and that was when it happened. Suddenly whispering in my ear that if we crouched down behind the bushes her parents wouldn't be able to see us, she led me to a clump of small hedges at the end of the lawn. I had no idea why she was suggesting this until we squatted down as planned and she planted a big smacking orange-juice kiss on to my skinny lips. Before I had time to recover she did it again, this time with an even greater hint of hidden passion. I was stunned. As with all reactive souls, I couldn't understand what I'd done to deserve such a wonderful thing. My head was buzzing with sensations I had no understanding of, but I wasn't complaining. Beverly seemed a beautiful and frightening thing, a promise of something beyond the everyday humdrum.

It only took a few months from that magical kiss for everything to go tragically wrong. When I went to play at her house one weekend she broke the news, before we'd even had time to snog. Her dad had got a new job, she said, and they were to move to Tasmania. Assuming this place to be just down the road, I asked if I'd be able to visit her from time to time. I can still hear her rather final 'No', spoken with the conviction of a wiser person. Her voice was like bubble-gum, all sweet and chewy. The news didn't seem to affect her in the same way as it did me, and the clipped announcement of our future separation blew over me like a chill wind. When I asked my mum that night where Tasmania was, she confirmed my darkest fears. I was now the tragic hero, and spent the remaining three months of our mayfly relationship staring at the ground. The folk group The Seekers had a song in the charts around that time whose lyrics only seemed to confirm to me that life was cruel and no longer worth living. '*Now the carnival is over, we may never meet again*' the singer wailed, and I truly believed that destiny had written that song and piped it out on the airwaves for me, so that I could gorge on its meaty sentiments.

So Beverly left, sending me one solitary postcard a month

or so later, thence to disappear Down Under for ever. Heartbroken at seven, the configuration of ill-starred lover was programmed to default. It took me years to recover from this little setback, and even at the age of sixteen, when people would ask me why I was looking glum, I would feign a winsome smile and reply, 'Oh, it's nothing. Just an old wound.' I finally decided to let it heal during the sixth form at school, but Helen, my girlfriend for those stressful but stirring A-level years, chucked me after we both went on to separate universities, finding herself an enormous physical education student 'with muscles in all the right places' (sic). Then again, I'd not been entirely faithful to her, since, like everyone else, I had gone to university hoping for a reasonable diet of debauchery, but the reality had turned out to be rather more difficult. It wasn't all doom and gloom, however. I tried my best to sow some wild oats, but as I'd noticed in earlier adolescence, the only way to achieve this was by actually talking to girls and maybe even getting to know them. The social events that were organised for us throughout my undergraduate years consisted mainly of weekly discos where, bumbling and blinking in the dark to a cacophony of decibels and garish strobe lights, you found it tricky to engage in meaningful conversation. All I could ever manage to holler in some poor girl's ear was 'What are you studying?' or 'I'm so glad that it's Saturday tomorrow!' when I should have screamed 'Do you fancy a fuck?' Other people always seemed equipped with a whole list of pick-up gambits at these events, walking off to sexual fulfilment while I trudged through the night back to my garret where, bent tragically over my guitar, I would launch into the latest wrist-slitter by Leonard Cohen.

When I finally did manage to be unfaithful to Helen, it was wholly through the initiative of my one-night partner – a red-headed Irish girl called Mo who had coincided with me a couple of times in the coffee bar and who was also studying English. She was witty and confident, and laughed at everything I said, whether it was funny or not. I found that strangely appealing. One night she'd strayed down with a female friend to my brick-dust college bar and plonked herself next to me and my friend John, ignoring him and making her intentions fairly clear. By the time John and her friend had disappeared (separately), I was gulping into my lager and lime, terrified.

'Fancy a coffee?' she offered, howling out a full-toothed shriek at her own joke. I shrugged and nodded. She continued 'Your place or mine?' at the top of her voice.

'Maybe yours,' I offered quietly, horrified at the thought of her siren blaring off down our corridor.

'Look here now,' she said, sensing my nerves. 'My mate Judy says that if a guy asks you up for a coffee, what he really wants is a fuck. Now what a guy will never ask you up for is a fuck. So I always say to Judy – if they say coffee they mean fuck, and if they ever said fuck they'd mean coffee. So my place it is.'

There were one or two other episodes, but nothing on the industrial scale of sexual conquest related by my ex-school friends when we gathered in the pubs at home over the holidays and compared notes. As they notched up the numbers, all I saw was a long droopy tightrope to walk across, one that swayed out over the big beyond. On the wobble across, I met Nancy. She was a first-year student at Lancaster, with whom I went to Greece during the graduation summer. At the beginning of my final year, she had come across, like Mo, and sat down next to my friend John and myself, at a table in the bar. She had a female acquaintance with her called Ted. Ted was black and rather exotic, and had taken an obvious fancy to John. She was chatty and funny, and within five minutes she was snuggled up with my best mate, as if it was meant to be. Nancy was pale, had a shock of ginger hair, and was beautiful in a freckly sort of way. She rarely spoke, but she seemed smitten, for some unknown reason. She looked after me that final year, cooking delicious meals and generally mollycoddling me, in a curious sort of silence. She was a Quaker, and seemed to like sex a lot, but I never found out if those two factors were connected. With Nancy, it was sex for breakfast, sex for lunch and sex for tea. It was an interesting dietary concept, called 'The F-Plan'. It was exhausting, and occasionally annoying, but it was gratifying to finally find someone who actually seemed to like me for more than one night.

Before we went to Greece that summer, on the notorious 'Magic Bus' from London, I had gone to stay at Nancy's house in a small village near Warrington. On the second day she took me to a Quaker service at the Friends Meeting House in the suburbs of the town. I knew nothing about

Quakers, but had expressed an interest in seeing what went on. We arrived at what looked like a small public library, at the door of which stood a tall gentleman in a duffel coat, distributing pacifist literature. Inside the hall the seats were arranged in two opposing halves, so that you had no choice but to sit opposite a decent swathe of folks. No one was speaking, rather like Nancy. As the seats filled up, I began to feel uncomfortable in the mute-button silence. No one was in charge, nothing was happening. I stared at the floor, attempting to avoid the gaze of the people opposite. After what seemed like several hours the hush was broken by an elderly chap in a raincoat who shot to his feet and began to deliver a speech in a loud, rambling voice.

'I was walking down the road yesterday afternoon,' he announced to the ceiling, 'and it suddenly occurred to me that the birds in the sky are something that we should take more heed of. What I mean is that when you focus on the sheer amount of them, it makes you think about some purpose, some greater pattern to things. I don't mean to suggest that there is any pattern, but you never know. All of which reminds me of another thing I'd like to share with you, regarding my sister who is having trouble getting up the stairs these days. It occurs to me that one day we will all have trouble getting up the stairs, and this is something I'd like to share with you,' at which point he sat down sharply, his points made. To my further astonishment, no one followed up with any further comment. It seemed par for the course. The service continued in silence, until every now and then someone would shoot up with a wholly unconnected point, which in its turn would receive no comment.

I was as taken with the meeting as I was with my calm and quiet girlfriend, Nancy. It set me up for years to come. It seemed a very civilised way of going about things – standing up when the fancy took you, talking nonsense then being allowed to sit down again, wholly unmolested. I almost signed on there and then. I think it was the lack of arbitration that I really liked – the absence of any verdict. Life was unlike that in general, on the more judgemental streets outside that Quaker Meeting House. I'd just finished university and was experiencing the kind of limbo that only the reactive set encounters, waiting for the next episode and what it might bring along. I'd seemingly taken a step forward, and had been given a place on my second-choice PGCE at Hull, but I was already feeling the weight of that decision. I was going to be a teacher, but in truth I had no idea whether I had made a sensible choice. A teacher. A transmitter of knowl-edge. I wasn't sure I had any. It suddenly seemed a better idea to be a Quaker, and to hang around the Meeting Houses of life. No one would sit in judgement on me there.

By the time I'd begun the PGCE, I was still lingering in the mellow shadow cast by Nancy – only she was in Lancaster and I was on the opposite coast. She had been over a couple of times during the first term, and after the Jomble-Wimping episode at St Peter's I'd come back hoping to ride out the rest of the term to the wholly appropriate chorus of Boney M's *It's a Holiday*. But things took a turn for the unexpected. It never rains but it hammers down, and I was simply swept away. I'd noticed the girl during the first two months – another redhead called Polly, who had been one of the movers and shakers of the English group. She was tall and mysterious, with piercing green eyes and lovely legs. I don't know whether I was getting a thing about redheads, or if it was some influence from a previous life, but I fancied her more than I'd fancied anyone ever before – or so it seemed. Hormones have a nasty habit of clouding your judgement, but there's not a lot you can do about it at the time. Despite the calm and lovely Nancy over in Lancaster, I decided to get proactive, for once in my miserable life. I would deal with the consequences later, or so I figured.

Like some sleazy private detective, towards the end of that first week I spent a couple of days observing her movements. Like me, she came to the university on her bike, and so it was merely a question of memorising its colour and placing mine next to hers for the Friday afternoon push into new emotional territory. Emerging with apparent coincidence from the coffee bar at around four that fateful Friday, I sauntered down to the bike sheds just as she was fiddling with her combination lock.

'Oh! Fancy meeting you here,' I joked, pathetically. She smiled back, but seemed more interested in her bike. 'Read any fascinating books this week then? Have you recovered from the three weeks yet?' I asked, desperate to keep her there for a few more minutes at least.

She sighed. 'The three weeks were just fine. They kind of got me away from here anyway.' Upon making this serious-sounding declaration, she cracked her code and the chain tumbled free.

'Oh', I mused. 'I thought you liked it here – in Hull, I mean.' She sighed again and looked at the floor. 'Is something wrong?' I asked, nervously. After a moment's silence, she looked up and cast me a tired glance.

'Just man trouble, that's all. It's nothing you'd want to hear about. But thanks for asking anyway.' This sounded promising, although I hadn't noticed her with anyone up to that point. But I'd suspected that someone as pretty as her might be spoken for. Figuring it was now or never, I went for the kill for the first time ever.

'If you want to talk – I mean just talk about, whatever – erm, why don't we have a drink together tonight? I've no plans,' I concluded, fairly pleased with myself for getting this into the air with a minimum of stuttering.

'OK,' she replied, to my surprise. 'Where? The King Billy?' And the King Billy it was, at eight o'clock. Whatever 'man trouble' she was having, it clearly wasn't getting in the way of her coming out on a Friday night with me. So far so good.

Polly, it turned out, was in a long-term relationship with a guy called Adrian, a PhD student at the university. She loved him but she didn't love him, she felt that he didn't understand her any more and, worst of all, he was violent. Up to that final point in the conversation that evening, I was smitten beyond smitten, but the sudden and unexpected mention of violence did give me cause for reconsideration. It lasted all of two minutes.

Adrian studied chemistry, and apart from spending two nights of the week at York University on some research project, he was also away from time to time on rugby trips.

And so the inevitable happened, despite the shadow of imminent death for Polly, myself, or both – and we began to see each other. I even got to meet the boyfriend, when he unexpectedly returned one evening to their flat because a rugby trip had been cancelled. Fortunately, I was reading the newspaper on the floor at the time, looking at the cinema schedules, whilst Polly was reading on the sofa. To give the man credit, he took in the scene with apparent calm, staring down at me as if I were some annoying but insignificant worm, in whom his girlfriend could not possibly have been interested. He was such a hulk, with an air of suppressed violence in his curling lip, that I seemed of no physical consequence. He sat down on the sofa and smiled half-knowingly at me.

'The rugby was called off,' he announced, smirking slightly. 'Too fucking cold. The ground's frozen. Going to make me a coffee then?' he suggested casually to a trembling Polly. 'I mean, I'd have thought you'd be pleased to see me.'

For the rest of that term, through the dark dead chill of an east-coast December, I fell in love with this woman, for woman she seemed – being two years older than me. The difference between twenty-two and twenty-four will always seem more significant than between thirty-two and thirty-four, between seventy-two and seventy-four and so on. Avoiding death at the hands of Adrian also added a certain spice to the affair, it has to be said. No longer did I spend my days travelling up and down in the university library lift to see if I could catch a glimpse of my poet hero, Philip Larkin, and no longer did I even pretend to be interested in the course. All I desired was to see Polly, in the coffee bar, in my bedsit, in her flat – wherever. I never gave Nancy another thought until a couple of Fridays before the Christmas break, when Adrian was definitely off for the weekend playing rugby. I arranged to meet Polly in the pub that night, with the warm thought of being able to stay over in her flat nestled into my bones. Literally five minutes before I left my bedsit, the phone rang. It was Nancy. My blood froze as I heard the unmistakably metallic echo of a station platform announcement behind the background hiss.

'Where the hell are you?' I snapped.

'On Leeds station,' she said, confused by my tone. 'I'll be in Hull in a couple of hours.' My silence said it all. 'What's the matter?' she asked, bewildered.

'Nothing,' I told her. 'But you'll have to let yourself in. I'm going out. I'll be back about midnight,' and I put the phone down.

It was beyond despicable, of course, but I was so head over heels with Polly that hurting someone else didn't even register. When I returned that night – close to midnight – it was pouring down. The wind was howling, tossing great sheets of freezing rain through the dark, like the beginning of a cheap horror movie. Arriving back at the large mansion that housed my bedsit, I looked up to the window to see that my light was off. More worryingly, the door to the house was wide open. Something was wrong. As I dumped my bike in the porch, the owner, a foul-tempered geography lecturer at the university, appeared like Norman Bates in the gloom. 'Where the fuck have you been?' he yelled. 'That fucking loony girlfriend of yours – she's flipped.'

'What do you mean? Where is she?' I yelled back.

'How the fuck should I know!' he shouted, his voice howled out by the wind. 'You'd better go and find her. She's been wailing all night, and now she's run out without a coat, and she hasn't come back!' At which point he pushed me out on to the step and slammed the door behind me. I ran into the empty streets, imagining Nancy frozen with hypothermia. The rain was still hammering down, bouncing off the pavements and glugging down the overworked drains. Rounding a corner about fifty yards from the house, I found her, sitting dejectedly on a garden wall, her wonderful mass of red hair a sodden line of black streaks over her swollen, tear-damaged face. I approached her with caution. Calm though she always seemed, I knew that I'd pushed her too far. I stood over her, waiting for some reaction. She was shivering.

'Don't you think you'd perhaps better come inside?' I tried.

'What's the point?' she managed, sniffling. She was right. There wasn't much point, but I wanted to save her from freezing to death. I gave her my coat and we walked back to the house, back to separate futures. She left in the morning as quietly as she'd met me, back in that Lancaster college bar. I never saw her again.

I don't know how long the average life-apprenticeship lasts. Cynics claim that it never ends, whereas happy middle-aged couples with perfectly adjusted children and handsomely paid-off mortgages tell you a different story. I'm somewhere between those two, sitting on the fence, as ever. Or maybe it's just a question of bumps in the road. Talking in the snug of the King Billy one night, Polly said: 'You learn by your humiliations.' By approving the phrase, I wasn't trying to salve my conscience over Nancy, but it at least helped me get the whole messy business into perspective. You drive along the road in the dark, too fast to avoid that sleeping policeman. You hit the bump and bang – you slow down, gather your wits and drive with more caution until the next bump, maybe miles or years down the road of life. Trite but true. And it's the destiny of those whom we can't avoid – teachers, parents and lovers again – to be those very bumps in the road. Up to that rainy night, the bumps had mainly been of the teacher variety. Nancy was the first big emotional bump, because she'd shown me with her quiet dignity what a shit I'd become. The trouble was, I was obliged to face the tricky challenge of the January teaching practice in the midst of this turmoil, added to the fact that Polly would be doing hers too, miles away. I wasn't sure I could do it.

6

BLUFFING/LEAVING

After a month or so of teaching practice I began to feel that what I needed most was some cold cream to remove the make-up at nights. It wasn't so much a question of choosing which mask to wear as coping with the daily dose of schizo-phrenia that accompanied my entry and exit on to the Lynton Comprehensive school stage. My basic intention every waking morning was to stride confidently to school and attempt to convince my audience that I was something approaching a fully fledged adult, whatever that is. Despite the growing evidence from the Dirty Corner that the weather, high up in the snowy peaks of maturity, was not as stable as it might once have seemed from below, I was nevertheless convinced that I had to try and scale the heights somehow. It was a bit like learning to walk. Despite the bruising you encountered, you had no choice but to go along with it.

It was this that made the teaching practice a rite of passage. So intense was the experience that everything else – save women perhaps – faded into the grey margins of every-day life. All that mattered was looking the part: to the teachers in the staffroom, to the pupils in the classroom, to the caretaker in the corridor and to some of the parents who gathered outside the school in the afternoons. It struck me one day, as a couple of chatting mothers cast me a wan smile as I passed them on the way to the sanctuary of home, that this was what really happened to you as you grew up. You found yourself having to assume some sort of identity that wasn't really you – only to find, one random morning, that you'd finally become that person. The ill-fitting jacket and the poorly knotted tie had made me look like I was trying – and failing – to be a real person, one who is up and running as society deems fit. But I realised that one day I would get there, whether I wanted to or not. It was a mildly depressing discovery. I knew that there would be no particular moment in which I would recall detonating the bridge that I'd finally walked across, but suddenly I guessed I would be there, on the other side – striding through the grass in the more mature meadow of life.

Meanwhile Geraldine, the deputy head of year, had asked me in for a chat. She wanted to know how I thought I was getting on. Alice Roberts, the tutor assigned to me at the university, was due to visit, and so Geraldine needed to be able to report that she'd spoken to me. She'd seemed a friendly enough woman from the first day, keeping her distance from the staffroom but apparently on good terms with the majority of its occupants. But now I was under the lamp, despite the welcoming smile. It was time to pretend again, to speak from behind the adult mask. Geraldine wore a sombre blue suit as a nod to her position, but there was some warmth behind the uniform. She sat up straight.

'So tell me, Philip. Four weeks and you seem to be coping! That's what Hamish and Jim have told me. They're very pleased with you. How would *you* rate things so far?' She continued to smile. It was nice that Hamish and Jim had said this, but I suspected that it had been a standard response. I got the impression that Geraldine and the Dirty Corner were a twain that rarely met, and I knew for a fact that Geraldine quietly disapproved of Hamish's pipe. At the first staff meeting I'd attended, she'd dropped a mildly caustic remark about the state of the carpet, particularly the section that coincided with the Dirty Corner.

'I'm quite happy,' I mouthed. Since her silence invited further comment, I added, 'All three classes are very different. It's good that I can have a variety of pupils.' In what ways were they different, she enquired, nodding her head slightly to one side as if she wanted to really hear me this time.

'Well, they respond to me in different ways. Hamish's class enjoys the reader, and they seem to have plenty to say. I think they're really responding well. Jim's class? Well, they're obviously more difficult, but I would say that I'm achieving my objectives.' Geraldine asked me what those were. I wanted to reply that it was to get the teaching practice over as soon as possible and get back to being a slob, but of course I told her that it was to 'involve' them. This was a buzzword at the university, and one with which Alice Roberts, soon to visit, had peppered her lectures. I thought it might impress

Geraldine. Besides, I *had* involved them to some extent. They'd participated actively in a debate, they'd told me what they thought about each other, and about me – so I had clearly given them a forum for involvement. One of them had even kissed me. They had also been involved in a project, mercifully set up by Jim before me, in which pairs of pupils had been obliged to choose an appropriate charity. Once they had made their choices, they had been required to brainstorm a three-pronged plan of action called 'PART' – which stood for 'Plan, Act and Report', or 'FART' as Plant had helpfully amended on the board one day. At least it proved he could spell. Anyway, I pretended to Geraldine that I had been helping them with the last two letters of the acronym, because I knew, with my shallow survival instinct still intact, that when Alice came to visit I could ask them to show her what they'd been doing. It was a cheap trick, but I suspected it would work. I only sought to clear the obstacles. I had no other long-term plan.

I'd still not been to Lincoln to see Polly, and the few telephone conversations I'd had with her were confirming the cooling of relations. She'd mentioned a teacher there by the name of Tony, who was 'pestering' her, to use her word. He'd asked her out for a drink and of course she'd refused, but during the last call she'd evaded the subject when I'd brought it up, following it with a tiny but significant silence. Perhaps I was getting perceptive in my old age.

The next time I saw her was months later, on the morning we were due back at university. I caught sight of her unmistakable red hair in the passenger seat of an expensive-looking car. It all seemed to happen at subliminal speed, but she'd seen me too. As if she'd been shot from behind, her head bobbed forward and disappeared, somewhere in the vicinity of the glove compartment. And then the car was gone, lost up the road in the heavy traffic. It was definitely her. Why had she ducked down like that? Why hadn't she just waved? We could pick things up from where we'd left off. We'd both been busy.

I tracked her down later that day. 'Sorry about that this morning,' she said. 'Sod's bloody law. I just couldn't pretend that I hadn't seen you. Tony *insisted* on bringing me.'

'Tony?' I replied, with a hint of horror in my voice.

'Yes, well …' she began, head bowed, avoiding my eyes. 'I didn't get the chance to tell you. Erm, it's a bit of a mess.'

So that was that. Another glorious relationship down the wastepipe. She wrote to me a year or so later, on pink note-paper, asking me to their wedding. I declined the invitation.

As I had suspected, Alice rang the school to inform Geraldine that she would indeed be visiting the school on the fifth Thursday. My fears having been confirmed, I approached the following lesson with Jim's class in a busier, more focused sort of way. For a change, there was a single concrete objective – of pulling the wool over Alice's eyes. Things hadn't been too bad of late, to be truthful, but there were certain individuals, quite apart from Alan Plant, who were still capable of explod-ing at any given moment, for no particular reason. I tended to start the class by lighting the touchpaper, then retiring to a safe distance. But in the lesson before the visit, I'd decided to come clean with the whole thing from the beginning.

I'd just begun to clear my throat to ask them to shut up when two of the surlier girls from the class walked in late. You could smell the cigarette smoke on them from yards away. Neither of them apologised, nor did they seek to explain themselves, but I didn't fancy a confrontation before I'd even begun. Class vigilante Kelly, however, was not feeling so generous. 'You're a couple of slags!' she announced from her habitual throne by the window. 'Aren't you going to apologise to Mr Balls?' This was now accepted as my surname. There was nothing I could do about it, except perhaps call an amnesty on it for the duration of Alice's visit.

'That's enough, Kelly,' I piped up. 'I can fight my own battles, thank you.' She chewed on her gum-cud and stared back at me with cold blue eyes. The two latecomers sat down, muttering imprecations under their breath. Plant was staring at a comic at the back of the class, seemingly absorbed. So he could read, after all. That was good to know, but at that precise moment I needed his attention more than anybody's.

'Well, now we're all settled in, can I just tell you that the next lesson will be rather special for me – for all of us?'

Kelly was immediately on to it. 'You mean there's an inspector coming?' she sneered.

'Not quite. She's called Mrs Roberts and she's coming from Hull University to see how we're all getting on. She wants to see what sort of things you're doing. She's not an inspector.' At the mention of the word 'inspector', Plant looked up from his comic.

'So she's coming to see *you* then,' he declared. Someone else quipped 'You'd better buy a new tie' and another added 'and clean your shoes', followed by Kelly's little aside to her neighbour, just loud enough for me to hear – 'and learn to fucking teach'.

I made no attempt to contradict that assessment of my skills, but the fact remained that I had no intention of actively teaching them when Alice came. They were going to do the work, and demonstrate their 'involvement'. This was more or less what I told them, after replying to Plant.

'Of course she's coming to see me too,' I said, in the direction of my friendless foe. 'For that reason, I would ask you to try to be on your best behaviour, and to show her some of the materials that you've been working on for the PART project. I think that would be a great idea, and you never know, she might even be able to tell some influential people about your work. The more people that see it, the better.' Plant had gone back to his comic by this time, but to my relief, the murmurs and shuffles that accompanied my suggestion sounded like reasonably positive ones.

Kelly spoke up: 'Who is this Roberts? She an old bag or what?' I asked her what the point of her question was. 'Cos if she's an old bag we'll have to do it in a different way like. We'll have to do it like speaking well and all that stuff.' I assured her that it made no difference, and that Alice was 'elderly' but not an old bag.

'What I think we should do is get into our project pairs and think about how we can present what we've been doing. Remember, if you all present your work, then Mrs Roberts will have to listen fourteen times – since there are twenty-eight of us. And she might want to ask questions, which you will have to answer. I can't answer them for you. But anyway, that would give each pair five minutes at the most. We might not get enough time to tell her about everybody's, but we can try.'

In that moment of idle delegation, my teaching career began, I suppose. If they'd decided to mess it up for me, they could have stopped me there in my tracks, and shoved me down some other path. But they got on with what I asked them, in a burst of unusual commitment. I knew that some of them had been putting in time out of school, and that Kelly and her friend, for example, had been visiting an out-of-town institute for Down's Syndrome children, engaging with them and writing up a report based on which of their activities seemed to work best. Two other pairs were doing similar things at retirement homes, another pair was working on initiatives for raising funds for cancer research, and so on. When asked to do real things, and to work with real people, I got the impression that Jim's charges were not so loony after all – but it was difficult to bring out this saner side of them in normal classes. Neither was there any guarantee that they would be able to present their work in an organised fashion to Alice, but I tried to give them some vague guidelines.

'Both of you must speak, at some stage. Try to bring in

something visual, that you can hold up or distribute around the class. And when you speak to an audience, what should you always remember?' I'd forgotten about Plant, of course. Looking up from his comic he casually announced that we should remember to fart. Grinning up at the class, his gassy little joke fell on silence.

'Shut it, Plant!' scolded Kelly. 'Just because you've done fuck all doesn't mean that the rest of us have.' Plant looked daggers at her, but then decided it was better to go back to his comic.

As the class worked on the presentations, I wandered over to the outlaw on the edge of town, drew up a chair and sat next to him. It was the first time I'd hinted at anything resembling a sustained conversation. His face looked ahead, but his eyes were fixed in a sideways stare like a dog ready to snap if you so much as moved. 'So, erm, what have you been doing in PART, Alan? Who have you been working with?' He kept his face rigid.

'I've been doing it on my tod,' he replied eventually. 'No one wants to work with me, do they?'

'I don't know. But if you say so. Whatever – what have you been doing?' I saw some pupils smirk in our direction, but I kept to the interrogation. Plant thought about the question, then pointed slowly at Kelly, across on the other side of the room.

'Fuck all. The blonde bitch over there just told you. Why you asking me again?'

'Because Mr Drewery must have given you a topic to

work on. What is it?' I could see him begin to sweat, and his right leg began to twitch up and down in a jerky manner. Just as I thought he might turn round and sock me one, he leaned closer to me.

'Aren't you going to shop me then?' he whispered.

On suddenly asking me this strange question, he had turned around to face me, like a gargoyle come to life.

'What do you mean?' I asked.

'You know. When I had you down, like, on t'first day. I never knew you was going to teach me. You gonna shop me?' So at last, he was coming to the boil. It seemed like a long time ago.

'It never occurred to me. As far as I'm concerned, it never happened.' His leg stopped twitching.

'You a puff or what?' he asked. 'You should have shopped me.' I admitted that I should have, but that I'd had a lot on my plate since then – that I'd been too busy. Then the *pièce de résistance*.

'You gonna make me do this bloody presentation thing then?'

'That depends, Alan. You still haven't told me if you've done anything. You can't present something that you haven't done.' He stared back into space.

'I have done summat. Drewery told me to do it. I an't done much, but anyway. Summat. It's about Flids.'

'Flids?' I asked.

'Thalidomide,' he explained, rather more loudly. 'It's their nickname, like. But I guess that's not too funny.'

'So what have you found out about the victims?' I asked.

He grinned. 'Some of them are pretty neat. There are some of them with no arms, like. And they learn to paint with their feet. Open doors and get dressed, like. All sorts of shit. Some of them ain't got any fucking limbs at all, poor bastards. But they get by, like. One of them won a competition for painting – and the blokes judging it didn't even know – till he came for the prize, like. Ha! That's good that. He's done it with the brush in his gob. And he's won. You feel sorry for the poor bastards, but anyway – some of 'em just get on with it, like. That's all right.' And as quickly as the torch had come on, its weak light snapped off again.

'OK – that's interesting, Alan. But if you have to present some of the things you've found next lesson, in front of the class, you'll have to mind your language. But look. Write down some of the history of all this – some dates, some basic facts – and be ready to tell us. If you do that for me, maybe I won't force you to speak.'

He looked ahead again. 'Nah. You won't force me to speak. If you do, I'd watch your back.'

Plant was waiting at the gates on the morning of Alice's inspection. As I approached the narrow entrance I could see him craning his head like a periscope above the mass, out from the push-and-shove of blue jumpers and brown leather satchels. He was standing to the left of the entrance, and over on the right, stationed just in case, I could see one of the foot-soldiers who had been a part of the welcoming committee back on the first day. Trying to look unconcerned, I joined the jostling line and stuck to the middle. As I passed the two guardians of the gate, my eyes were drawn inevitably to the left where Plant was now standing alert, his back against the lower steel pole of the arch-like construction through which the ranks jostled every morning. As my eyes met his, he lifted a finger to his lips and bulged out his eyes – with the obvious message that a failure to heed his warning might result in some kind of unfortunate death. Why hadn't he just stayed at home? I scurried past, head down. My idea for the lesson was to pretend that we'd already agreed on a selection of presentations, so as to avoid the issue of Plant and several other weaker projects. But what if Alice decided that she wanted to choose for herself? If I were visiting a novice teacher, that's exactly what I would do. Did Plant want to ratchet up the tension? As I reached the safety of the school building I recalled that he was already on a final warning for truancy. He must have used up his quota, which was a pity. Now I had to face the possibility that Alice might ask him to speak, after which I would have the expensive burden of hiring a team of bodyguards for what was left of the term.

Alice left Geraldine's office for the staffroom some five minutes before the class was due to begin – a tiny woman hidden beneath a large, shapeless woollen coat and a loud yellow bonnet that I prayed she would take off before the lesson. I was convinced that some wag in the class was likely to throw a comment her way, but try as I might she was oblivious to my hints.

'It's been bad weather for some time, eh?' I tried. 'But things seem to be brightening up now. It's much warmer.' This fell on deaf ears. Either that, or she couldn't hear from underneath the bonnet. Talking to her reminded me of those irritating conversations I used to have with my grandmother, when she was beginning to lose it. 'Gran. That was Mum on the phone. She says can you make the tea tonight?' To which Gran would reply, 'Yes. I can make breakfast tomorrow.' With Alice it was fairly similar.

'The first class is Mr Drewery's fourth years, Mrs Roberts. It starts in five minutes,' which prompted the response, 'Oh good. And which year is this class in?' As I was thus engaged, Alice's woollen back was turned towards the Dirty Corner, some of whose members were visible above the bonnet. Hamish, who as head of department should have known better, was playfully blowing kisses her way, whilst Jim made short little thrusting movements with his hips from a sitting position, simulating sex with the poor woman. I managed to keep a straight face as I explained that the lesson would consist of some of the pupils presenting the topic material 'we' had been working on. Jim was too busy thrusting away to catch wind of this little porker, and so I guided Alice out of the staffroom as quickly as possible.

Ushering her into the eerily silent class, I bowed slightly to allow her in first, as all good boys do. Non-regal though she was, I wanted to combine the sort of attitude you'd adopt when helping a granny across the road with the sort of respect you would show to a richer, china-cup pensioner who had asked you round for afternoon tea. Fussing one of the gum-chewers in the front row to fetch her a chair, I cast a glance at Plant. He smiled from the back, and repeated the raised finger to the lips. The classroom was so unnaturally quiet that I feared Alice might think that I'd paid them to be silent. She took the chair offered to her and sat to one side by the radiators, under the window. I saw Kelly look at her friend and point discreetly to her head, in obvious reference to the ludicrous bonnet. Perhaps Alice was bald under there? Trying to shake the vision from my mind's eye, I moved to stifle any possible change to my plans.

'Well, good morning, class. This is Mrs Roberts, whom I told you about, and she's going to listen to some of your presentations. Perhaps you'd like to start – Kelly and Jane?' And so Kelly and Jane walked confidently to the front and started.

'PART stands for Plan, Act and Report, and so we'd like to do the last part today,' began Jane, Kelly's tall and dark accomplice. 'We've done some work with Down's Syndrome children at the day centre in Caistor, and we wanted to find out what kind of stuff they liked to do best. I mean, what kind of *activities*, miss,' she corrected herself. Alice nodded and smiled, pleased to be thus addressed. The girls continued with a skill and seriousness that belied their normal behaviour. The common sense came through, the poise under pressure. They thought Alice was there to inspect them and their work, and so they handled it all with a seriousness I hadn't thought them capable of. The thought of Plant being asked to present his work – of which there was scant evidence on the desk – continued to terrify me, but as I listened to the procession of presentations and realised that they could easily pass muster with no help at all from me, I began to fantasise that even the man himself might be able to do it.

After a half-dozen presentations, with the lesson almost through, Alice suddenly sprang to her feet to announce that she would just like to spend the last five minutes looking at some of the projects herself – as I'd feared she might. Plant was to the left side at the back, conspicuously alone. He'd made no effort to even bring his comics. Alice shuffled to the back, to a pair who had not spoken. To reach Plant, she would have to pass a central pair, but they had already been up to speak. As the class began to murmur quietly amongst themselves, I dashed to the back and joined Alice. The project there was one of the poorer ones, and as Alice received a brief reply from one of the smoker girls whose work it was, I intervened.

'Yes, well – Sharon and Michelle have been looking at the problems experienced by elderly people when they first go into homes, and the difficulties of adjustment ... blah blah.' Just as I ran out of ways to stretch it further, the bell rang. Alice thanked the class for the presentations, and Plant stood up slowly and walked past me, brushing me slightly with his elbow. I never got to know if it was a thank you or a final warning.

As for the rest, I didn't imagine that they'd been trying to save me, although I fondly thought that there was a smidgen of affection somewhere in their unusually adept performances. I was probably kidding myself, but basically I wanted to be liked. I wanted Kelly to like me because I was terrified of her, I wanted Plant to like me because I wanted him to leave me in peace, I wanted some of them to like me because they thought I was maybe just a little bit hip, and I wanted others to like me just because I was me. In truth, I wanted that more than I wanted to control them, and I wasn't sure it was a good idea. But I felt it most acutely. I had no officer qualities, no gift of distance. The mask was slipping, but I was determined to fix it on more firmly if I ever got a job at the end of the year. All that was left was the damage-limitation exercise with Alice.

'I enjoyed the lesson a lot,' she enthused, sitting opposite me in the empty room after the class had left. 'You've obviously worked very hard on those projects with them. Most admirable in such a short time.' I smiled weakly. Her bonnet had flattened the side of her hair to such an extent that her ears stuck out and upwards, like a rabbit on alert. Only she wasn't on alert. 'You know, I recall Geraldine telling me that some class had been working on similar projects for some time now, right back to September – but that must be another class,' she concluded, incorrectly. 'How splendid that a school like this, with quite a difficult intake, can manage such a wide range of work. I do so like to see the children *involved*!'

'Yes – this group has been involved,' I repeated, 'and some of the projects that you didn't get to hear about were really interesting. Some have worked on the Thalidomide issue, others on cancer. I've found it quite uplifting. They've been – how should I say it – involved.'

And so Alice and Hamish wrote their reports, the time flapped by, and before I knew it half-term had arrived. The swots had kept on swotting and Plant had howled and farted, albeit a little less frequently than before. Only once, on the way home from school one afternoon, had I thought he might try something on again, out of the sheer anarchy that pervaded his soul. Walking briskly away from the school was my daily routine, and lost in thought one afternoon I'd failed to see Plant and his henchmen up ahead. They'd seen me, however, and had slowed to a dawdle. As I was almost upon them, the three pedestrians of the apocalypse turned sharply to face me and shouted 'Boo!', which made me jump absurdly, like a pensive rambler stumbling into an electric fence. Once recovered from the shock, I laughed pathetically, as if I wanted to be their mates after all. Maybe I did.

'Where do you live then?' asked the smaller of Plant's disciples, to which I pointed in a vague south-easterly direction.

'Well, it's my parents' house,' I added, hoping that this might end the encounter.

'That's the fucking posh part of Cleethorpes,' observed the other taller boy. They had begun to walk alongside me, but on the latter comment Plant stepped in to take control. 'Don't swear now,' he began, affecting a more neutral accent. 'Mr Balls doesn't like it – do you, Mr Balls?' Half relieved to be at least engaging them in dialogue of a sort, I returned Plant's serve with a fairly tame shot.

'It's not that I don't like it, Alan,' I began, 'it's just that there are rules in the classroom and I have to obey them as well. I probably swear more than any of you, but there's a time and a place.' At this, the three of them began to hop up and down as they walked, twirling around to face me and snickering like children half their age.

'Go on then!' laughed Plant. 'Show us how you swear! Drewery does. He swears like fuck.'

Speeding up slightly to imply that the party was over, I managed, 'I can't believe that Mr Drewery swears. I really fucking can't,' before checking out the traffic and crossing the road in the direction that I had previously indicated to them. They stayed put, guffawing. Before I disappeared down a convenient side street, Plant shouted across the passing cars: 'I can 'ave you for that! I can tell them what you said!'

On the final day of my TP there was a disco organised for the fourth years, partly in celebration of the week's holiday to come but also to acknowledge the efforts made by Jim's class regarding the projects. I'd not helped a jot in this success, and any further progress they'd made had been through occasional meetings with Jim and Geraldine. But I was invited along. The disco was in the school hall, and consisted of winking coloured strobes and a darkened dance floor packed with pupils whilst Jim, Hamish, McCall and myself stood around

awkwardly on the outer edges. Plant, out assaulting pension-
ers, was nowhere to be seen. With proceedings scheduled to
end around 6.30, the Dirty Corner diehards had promised to
have a subsequent and final pint with their apprentice. I
guessed that we might get away before that, but the disco
turned out to be something of a surprise. Pupils whom I had
thought completely indifferent to me were suddenly paying
me attention, and begging me to join them on the dance
floor. When Jim had playfully tried to join his temporary ex-
pupils, they had run screaming from him, scattering like
hunted gazelles. Apart from this, Hamish and McCall had
affected a few inelegant bends of the knee and a minute's
worth of ludicrous arm-waving to *Hi Ho Silver Lining*, all of
which left me to enter the congregation, should I have been
called upon to do so. Shrugging my shoulders and pretending
to be embarrassed when they called me to dance, it was Kelly
who finally persuaded me, walking out from the mass and
pulling me back in towards it. The girl who up to then had
treated me with open contempt was suddenly all friendly and
flirty. To the inevitable strains of 10CC's *I'm Not In Love* we
smooch-danced in the shadows as the class looked on and
applauded. I felt confused. Why be so cold when all the time
she liked me after all? I mentioned this, in the swirling lights.
'I never knew you cared,' I attempted. With her nose buried
in my chest she replied, 'I don't. It's just that Jane Sims bet
me a quid I wouldn't dance with yuh.'

In the pub that night I bade farewell to Lynton School
and to the commissioned officers from the Dirty Corner.

They'd all been pretty kind to me, truth be told, and informal beyond the call of duty. I wasn't sure whether all staffrooms were like this, or if I'd just happened upon a particularly quirky one, but the importance of having been adopted and cared for so quickly was undeniable. That was basically how I liked it, but you never really knew. Above McCall's flat nose sat a pair of eyes that saw through pretence for sure, and as for Hamish, I could never quite work him out. That was the way he played it, of course, but I harboured a worm of a feeling that night – as I went to buy my round of beers and escape for a moment from the circle – that despite appearances, these men might well have thought that I was yet another young apprentice on the conveyor-belt of easily forgotten incompetents that had passed anonymously through the school. Any excuse to go out for a pint. They'd probably been doing it year after year, student after student. I felt that the real me was in hiding, that I'd taught not a single convincing lesson, and that I had about the same idea of how to plan a term's syllabus as the average refuse collector.

'So, young apprentice,' coughed Hamish, just as he'd coughed on the first day back in January, 'do ye reckon you're going to be a teacher then?'

Settling down to the final pint, I decided to come clean. 'Oh, I don't know, Hamish,' I replied, trying to sound more world-weary. 'I'll go back and finish the course, but you never know. Something else might come along. I guess there must be another world out there.' Hamish cocked an eyebrow and McCall smiled his smile.

'Och aye, there's another world out there, for sure,' Hamish said. 'But don't ye start thinking that it's a better one. I'll be retiring in a wee while, I think, but I reckon it's been OK. No regrets and all that stuff. Tricky to begin with, but easy enough in the end. Mind you, if it's the money you're after, then ye'd best get out now. Right, Tony?'

McCall nodded.

7

SWEEPING

Peas grow in abundance on the rolling hills of the Lincolnshire Wolds, from where they are transported in small lorries to factories in the Grimsby area, tipped into large containers and frozen. They are then stored in large boxes known as palletainers, and put into cold storage until being packaged and sold under the name Findus or Birds Eye. The crucial point about all this, as far as I was concerned, was that these little green objects provided students like myself with employment every summer – one of the few advantages of living in the area. That particular summer, with my final student grant having expired sometime during the Easter holidays, the local Birds Eye factory, steaming and smoking in the northern summer like a Victorian workhouse, was a necessary destination.

In this particular workhouse, the word *peas* was off-limits, which is akin to working in a nuclear reactor and never hearing the word *radiation*. The vegetable whose presence ensured some much-needed money was either referred to obliquely as one of three things – *fuckers*, *bastards* or *cunts* –

or sometimes as a lively combination. This came as something of a welcome contrast to the academic year just gone, where, Plant and the Dirty Corner notwithstanding, one had dealt in curriculum philosophies, forms of knowledge (again), Piaget's genetic epistemology and the difference between *interpsychological* and *intrapsychological* – guff designed solely to take student teachers to the brink of suicide. The relief, therefore, to be told merely to 'Sweep them fuckers up!' cannot be exaggerated.

I'd worked in these factories each summer from the age of seventeen, and had more or less learned how to make the quasi-Dickensian experience as stress-free as possible. It was worth it, for the tax-free money we could walk away with. But there was a catch. Some of the regulars – the permanent year-round factory workers – were ill-tempered malcontents who viewed students with suspicion. Like the peas, we were usually described in less literal terms. The regulars resented our tax-free status, misunderstood our youth-gabble as pretension and, most of all, envied us our freedom. Teaching might have already seemed to me like hell on earth, but from the factory inmates' side of the fence, I was part of a group that was on its way up and out, into the mysterious world of professional salaries and social mobility that had passed them by.

Being thus unpopular, it was easy to be sacked. We were highly dispensable. Put a foot wrong and you were 'down the road', as the chargehands put it. This could have serious consequences for the financial year as we knew it, and by the second week of July I was wrapped up in my white overalls, carefully sweeping up the bastards and still unsure as to whether I was truly destined for the world of professional salaries. This despite the fact that from the three applications I'd sent off, one had surprisingly replied. This was for a grade one English teaching post in a secondary school just outside Hull, a school that I'd heard on the grapevine was OK, in a social-intake sense. If I was going to jump on this particular wagon, I didn't fancy any more howling Plants riding past bareback and shooting at me with stolen rifles. Anything that promised an easy-ish ride looked like my kind of school. But interviews were allegedly like driving tests. The folklore stated that you rarely passed first time, and that if you did, you were much more likely to be the sort of flapdoodle driver who had fluked his way through the exam only to sail haplessly over a cliff on the occasion of his first Sunday outing.

The interview was scheduled for the third week of my factory spell, so I needed to last at least until then without being sacked. I had a feeling that the chargehand on the night-shift disliked me, for no particular reason beyond the fact that I'd been promoted in the second week. This had been a huge stroke of luck, liberating me from the miserable torment of standing for eight hours in a dark, sub-zero pea tunnel to working on the quiet, soothing QC platform, courtesy of the one friendly red-hat on the day shift, an unusually humane character by the name of Nobby. QC (Quality Control) was the job dreamed of by only the blessed. With hardly a care in the world, you sat outside on a weighbridge in the sun, posing as the student girls filed by to the canteen.

Even better than this was my companion on the scales, a student architect called Steve. He was from a world that could have been intimidating to a bungler like me. The path to architecture seemed an altogether more considered and mature choice of life from where I was standing, and yet listening to the tales of how he had similarly stumbled his way along, I relaxed. 'Teaching's a cool idea,' he insisted, which was the first time anyone had ever said anything remotely like that to me. 'Cool' wasn't quite the word that I associated with my choice of profession.

The date for the interview approached. Donning a turd-brown jacket and a crusty tie, I hauled my bicycle on to the train at Cleethorpes station and returned, via the old ferry from Barton-Upon-Humber, to a school not far from the scene of my previous crimes, in the leafier suburbs of Hull. It was called Willerton High, and it took me almost an hour to find it, once I'd been deposited by the chugging steamer on to the northern river-bank. Since it was a bit of a scorcher, as hot as it ever gets on the Siberian east coast, I arrived at the school sweaty and flustered. Given the small number of vehicles in the car park, I assumed that the kids had gone home the week before, leaving only a straggle of teachers to tie up the year's loose ends. I parked the bike, undid my cycle clips and walked, bum-sore, to the secretary's office. The ample playing fields of the school shimmered green in the late-morning light, the leaves of portly oaks fluttered in the delicate breeze and something in the air announced the end of a working year. It looked quite a pleasant place, brighter and cleaner-looking than Lynton, although it could have been the effect of the sunshine.

Laura the secretary was blonde and slightly cadaverous, but friendly enough. 'Ah, Mr Ball. Hope you had a good journey. Did you come by car?' When I told her I'd come by bike, her face seemed to drop slightly, as if this were unbecoming of a teacher at her school, but I may have been mistaken. Everything in the empty school was slightly echo-prone, exaggerating the effects of anything said. 'The other candidates have been and gone,' she announced, rising up and ushering me down the corridor. 'You'll be interviewed by the headmaster, Mr Beacroft, and the head of English, Tom Lund. I think they're having a coffee and chatting about some matter or other, so why don't you just nip down there to the library and wait for me? Just knock and go in. I'll be down in five minutes or so to bring you back.' I did as instructed and knocked on the library door, entering when I heard a small screech from inside. The school librarian, a sprightly woman in her fifties by the name of Delia, bade me sit down.

'You must be one of the candidates for the English job. Oh, how super! Always exciting when new staff come along. Perhaps Mr Lund is going to interview you here. That's his office there,' she added, pointing to a small gloomy cubbyhole in a corner of the room. I'd understood from Laura that I'd be led back to the headmaster's office for the interview, but I quite fancied a bit of time to prepare myself, to whip up whatever mental adrenaline was left after the weeks at Birds Eye.

Once inside the silence of the cupboard-office, I looked around for hints as to what sort of thing my interviewer might be partial. On the small table in front of the chair into which I plonked myself lay a pile of unmarked essays and a couple of novels by DH Lawrence. *Sons and Lovers* and *The Rainbow* sat quietly to one side, both copies well thumbed. On the only wall space available to the side of a bookcase, a poster had been stuck up featuring the classic moody mug-shot of Lawrence, all skinny face and bushy beard, staring at the world like a folk singer tired of life. I hated Lawrence. I'd read both the books in front of me and I'd thought them dismal, full of over-serious people doing over-serious things, in seriously over-written prose. But it looked as though Mr Lund thought differently. Just as I was reflecting on this, Laura appeared at the door to the library and summoned me back – as I had thought I'd understood – to the headmaster's office. As I nodded goodbye to Delia, she handed me the standard 'Hope to see you in September!' line, which was kind enough, I suppose.

A middle-aged man with curly brown hair and a bright, confident face sat behind a large oak desk. I assumed correctly that he was the boss. 'Come in, Philip, come in,' he urged, wafting the air in a gesture of friendly impatience. 'Name's Beacroft,' he added, standing up and stretching out a hand. The accent was faintly public school, faintly Yorkshire – never an easy combination. Then, at the far end of his long table, perched on the edge of his chair, I spied DH Lawrence. 'And this is Tom Lund, head of English,' continued Mr

Beacroft, pointing an open palm towards his fellow interrogator. Lund stood up quickly and nervously, and offered a sickly handshake. He was dark and small, with the Lawrence beard and the same tense expression, as if he needed to go to the toilet.

'Glad you could make it,' he opened, in more grammar-school tones. He had what looked like a series of questions jotted down on a piece of paper, which he slotted between his knees as he sat down.

'Well, then,' began the headmaster, 'let's get down to business then, shall we? Philip, if I may call you that – you've applied for the post of grade one English teacher here at Willerton High. Now I won't ask you why you've applied to this particular school, but let me just say that you've made a damn good choice. Isn't that right, Tom?' he laughed, looking across at the brooding novelist.

'Absolutely,' came the reply, in a tone that suggested that Beacroft had just said exactly the same thing to the previous two candidates.

'Now then, I'll abuse the head's prerogative and ask you the opening question. Why teach? Why come back and lock yourself away here when there's a whole world out there waiting to be conquered?' It was a tricky question, as openers go. I got the impression that DH Lawrence thought so too, for he seemed to shuffle uncomfortably in his seat. I managed to clear the first obstacle.

'Well, I think that you could perhaps say the same to anyone starting out, in any profession,' I ventured. 'You take one path and erm ... you decide to go down it. I think I'm good with people. I'm not sure I see myself as a pen-pusher.' Beacroft seemed reasonably convinced by this.

'How did the teaching practice go?' he probed.

'Fine,' I returned. 'Some difficult pupils, but by and large they were OK. I enjoyed it.'

Beacroft nodded, his chin propped up by a fist and his face staring, across the table, into mine as if he were trying to detect the slightest rip in the mask. He gestured to his bearded colleague. Lund stared at the papers between his knees then suddenly looked up at me, almost melodramatically.

'Who's your favourite author, might I ask?' he began. Maybe he hadn't asked the others this question.

'Lawrence,' I coughed. 'Definitely Lawrence. Fantastic stuff.'

'Lawrence?' he intoned, sitting up and focusing on me more attentively. 'That's amazing!' he pronounced, looking down the table at Beacroft. The big man smiled back, indulgently. Lund went on. 'How nice at last to find someone who appreciates good literature!' he enthused. Perhaps the previous candidates had expressed a weakness for *The Beano*. 'We have things in common. Love him myself. Can't get enough of him, but of course the students don't always agree. Got a sixth-form class at the moment that can't stand him, but there's no accounting for kids' tastes these days, eh?'

Buoyed by this beginning, I scattered some more random thoughts out into the office air, hoping for further fortune. I suggested that with Lawrence, it might be a case of maturity – that with time they would come to see that he was a great writer. 'That's right!' frothed Lund. 'Much as I love him I wasn't sure that we should do him for A-level – *The Rainbow*'s a bit convoluted sometimes. But the rest of the department voted me down. Anyway, which is your favourite?'

'Oh, *Sons and Lovers* – definitely. I think that few books have captured better that bitter-sweet thing.' He nodded, whether the book was bitter-sweet or not. I thought it sounded good. I also recalled, in a moment's inspiration, my mother saying that Trevor Howard had been wonderful as Walter Morel, the crabby old miner. 'And Trevor Howard, of course – wonderful in the film,' I spouted, like some mature old sage. The fact that I was only three when it came out seemed to pass my interviewers by.

After that, the questions appeared to get easier. The two bowlers sent down a series of mild, medium-paced balls which I batted back without bluster, tickling shots here and there, taking a few modest singles. There were no spectacular boundaries in my repertoire anyway. Lund seemed to relax and began to describe the department to me, what they did, what they believed in, what the kids were like. I could only imagine that he'd decided to give me the job then and there, or that the gentle bowling was his way of winding things down before getting rid of me, unworthy as I was of any further searching questions. The only other tricky moment arrived with the mention of the burning issue of the day – mixed ability.

'During your teaching practice, Philip, did you get any wind of the policy towards streaming?' he asked casually, as if the question were an afterthought. This had me lean forward into a more defensive posture. Little though I'd learned about the whys and wherefores of this matter, I realised from the warring factions at Lynton that it was your views on this issue that marked you out, as surely as the newspaper you chose to read or the shoes you decided to wear. So which way should I lean? I looked again at my interrogator, and wondered there for an instant what it might be like to work with him, to socialise with him, to throw in my lot with him and this school, to set out through the valley of life with these two strangers as my shepherds – and it led me down to lie. I hit out at the question.

'Well, it was mostly banding, I think. In English the groups seemed to be separated, even before they got to GCE classes. I'm not sure that's the best way to go about things, but anyway.' Both men sat up. Lund invited me to go on. 'Well, it seems to me that you can get so much more from the weaker pupils if you have them in with the brighter, more motivated ones. It makes sense,' I tried, recalling the snowy pub debate.

Beacroft leaned over. 'But it's more difficult for the teachers, of course?' he suggested, eyebrows on the up. I hadn't the first idea of what he meant, but it seemed like the moment to agree.

'I can see that, yes. But that doesn't mean it's not right.'

That was about all I could manage. Pick'n'mix ability. Select at random, chuck them in a bag, weigh them and go home. Flagging under pressure, the last thing I noticed at that interview, apart from my fatigue, was the longish look the two men gave each other before shaking my hand. As we all stood up, Beacroft announced: 'Thanks very much for coming over today. It's been a pleasure. Um – tell me. If you were to be offered the job, we presume you would accept it?' Taking this to be a standard send-off, I gave them an affirmative. I figured I'd done OK, but I wasn't seriously expecting to work at Willerton High.

The next day I was back on Nobby's six-till-two morning shift. He was waiting for me at the weighbridge, throwing fish fingers to a cloud of seagulls. 'Ah – he's back!' He beamed. Steve was yet to appear. 'Just feeding me old mates from the fishing days, like,' he explained. 'They come back as seagulls, you know. Anyway – how'd the fucker go?' he asked. I hadn't expected him to be so interested.

'Fine thanks, Nobby,' I replied. 'Thanks for asking. I reckon it went OK.'

Later that morning, after I'd filled in Steve on the interview we decided to have a stab at the crosswords. The forklift drivers left their assorted tabloids on the weighbridge and would collect them before going up to the canteen, so we had the pick of the press when there was nothing better to do. Both of us being useless at crosswords, we would usually pick the *Sun* to do mid-morning, occasionally reaching for the more esoteric heights of the *Daily Express* or the *Daily Mail* when we wanted to kid ourselves that our combined reading age was creeping into double figures. Nevertheless, whenever we spread out a newspaper on the empty mound of unmade cardboard palletainers on the bridge, forklift drivers would appear like magic on their steeds, dismount and begin to watch us with a kind of wide-eyed fascination, as if we were sorcerers indulging in rituals of ancient magic. Most of these crosswords had already been started, tricky ones like 'It shines in the sky (3)' filled in, scribbled among tea stains and bacon bits from the drivers' early-morning break. As the weeks had passed and the drivers had got to know us better, some of them had approached us with the odd clue to solve, sheepishly in most cases, as if by acknowledging us as humans they were breaking the hate-the-student rules. It was mildly touching that they thought of Steve and myself as literary giants when in fact the evidence clearly suggested the opposite, it being a whole lot easier to continue a half-filled crossword than to begin one from scratch.

On that particular morning, we opted for the challenge of the *Sun*. Besides, one of the drivers was loitering with intent. He was a cocky young buck named Ray, an infamous show-off who would fizz around on his truck like he was at Silverstone, picking up and depositing the palletainers with Formula One speed and dexterity, never hitting the bridge, never dropping a single pea. The older drivers resented him, and you could sense that they'd closed ranks and frozen him out, unimpressed with the devil-may-care stuff, and jealous of his turkey strut and over-confident way with the ladies in the canteen. They would grumble about him to us, but they seemed to find solace in the fact that he was not so hot on the crosswords. 'You know he can't fucking read, that Ray. He makes out he can, but he's lying. Just like he lies about all the women he shags. He can't read, and he can't get it up. That's the bloody truth.' The target of this bile was dark-haired and tall, and could probably have made a more comfortable living from modelling if it hadn't been for his permanently unslept expression and his yellow-black teeth, the two front ones jagged and broken. He also appeared to sport a permanent black eye. But he seemed particularly fascinated by us, maybe because we tolerated him, gave him the thumbs-up when he performed some circus trick on his fork-lift and, more than anything, tried to help him with his crosswords. You simply couldn't work there as a regular and not attempt to do them. It was unthinkable. But Ray did have problems.

'You know they think I can't read,' he admitted that day, maybe suspecting that his colleagues had told us. 'You're a teacher, aren't you?' he asked me, lounging on the cardboard. 'Your mate here said you went for an interview or summin' the other day.'

'Yeah, well, I went for an interview,' I told him casually, 'but that doesn't mean much, Ray. It doesn't mean I'll get the job. Maybe I'll stay here and do QC.'

He looked suddenly horrified. 'Stay here? No, no. Don't do that mate. It's 'orrible in winter. There's nowt much to do, nobody much here. It's great when you lot come. Have a laugh with you and all, like. Teaching's good. I've got a little 'un who's at school. Teachers are important.'

'You've got a kid?' I shot back, amazed. Steve stopped measuring peas and looked up too. Ray looked too young to have kids. Maybe this was part of the fiction that the other drivers accused him of.

'Yeah,' he drawled, pleased with the effect of this announcement. 'She's seven now. Had her a few years back – well, the missus did.' I asked him which school she went to. 'Ah, well.' He paused. 'We live in Grimsby, like, but we got her into a good 'un in Cleethorpes. Called St Peter's.'

'St Peter's? Bloody hell. I did a few weeks' practice there, just before Christmas. Maybe she was in Mrs Howden's class?'

He looked slightly embarrassed. 'Hey that's brilliant. You were there? But, well, I don't know her teacher's name. Erm, she doesn't talk that much. Bit shy.' And then, as if to change the subject, he steered us back to the newspaper. 'I can't read that well, truth told,' he whispered. 'But you two could help me, couldn't you? I mean, what's that say?' and he pointed to one of the clues, the word *synonym*. 'That one's all over the place. There's always a lot of that one,' he insisted. I shot a glance at Steve, hoping he might take over, but his expression said the same.

'It says *synonym*,' I tried. 'It means a word that means the same as another word, like erm, whatever,' I muttered, unable to deliver.

'Like *shy* and *timid*,' said Steve. 'Like your kid.'

The next morning was Friday, which marked the end of the morning-shift cycle for us. Saturday off, then start afternoons on the Sunday. This meant no Nobby for a fortnight, and a different set of forklift drivers. Realising this, Ray was hanging round the bridge, looking more nervous than usual. When Steve went off for his break, Ray stepped up to the cardboard kingdom. Steve, as was his wont, had sketched an early-morning piece and had stuck it up on the back wall of the bridge. Ray pointed to the day's artwork.

'What's that then? What does it say under the picture?' I'd not taken too much notice of it up to that point, but even at a quick glance it was clearly one of Steve's better ones. He'd drawn a faceless, cubist-type businessman in a suit and bowler, standing alone in an enormous empty landscape. By his feet an attaché case was lying open, from which pieces of paper were fluttering away.

'It says, *Going nowhere in particular.*'

'What the fuck does that mean then?' Ray sniffed.

'I'm not sure,' I said. 'You'd better ask him when he comes back from break.' Ray sniffed again.

'Look,' he began, coming up close. 'Do you want to come round to my house tomorrow – for a cup of tea, whatever? I didn't want to ask, like, with your mate here. Come and say hello to our Susie,' he added. 'That's me kid. I told her last night that you'd been at the school, but she didn't say anything. But I reckon she might recognise you. Whatever … I'd just like you to come round. It's a shithole, like, but anyway. Never had a teacher in our place before. The missus'd like that. Will you come round, about eleven or something?' he pleaded, as if he expected me to turn him down.

'Sure,' I said. 'I'd be honoured.' And I was.

Ray lived on the dark side of town, near the football ground. I decided to take the bus, since I preferred not to have my bike nicked. I approached his two-up two-down terrace with a hint of a butterfly in my belly. Maybe it was all a set-up? He and his wife were serial killers, united in their hatred of student-kind. I'd noticed a tattoo on his arm proclaiming 'killer'. I rang the ding-dong bell. A dog barked somewhere inside and a lace curtain ruffled in the bay window of the house to the left. After an age, the door opened cautiously, and Ray's broken teeth grinned around the frame.

'Phil! Hey – come in. Come in. You came! I thought it was the fucking bailiffs.' The porch opened in to a small living room. There was a black mock-leather sofa in one corner and a television on the floor. The air smelled of wet dog. 'Well – this is it,' announced Ray. 'Not much here. Come into the kitchen,' and he led me through to the back of the tiny house. Standing nervously over a kettle was a small blonde woman of indeterminate age. Like Ray, she looked as though she hadn't slept for several months. 'This is my missus that I was talking about – Jane,' Ray disclosed, in case there was any misunderstanding. 'She's making some tea, aren't you, Jane?' Jane nodded, listlessly. 'Phil's a teacher,' Ray continued. 'He teaches little 'uns, and we reckon he might've taught Susie. Where is Susie?' he asked, a hint of impatience creeping into his voice.

'She's up wi' the dog,' Jane managed, jerking her thumb upwards to the ceiling and dropping a tea bag into a large mug with the other hand. Ray sniffed the air.

'It smells o' shit in here. What is it? ' he enquired. Jane began to pour boiling water into the mug.

'It smelled fine before you came in,' she replied, deadpan. I hoped she was referring to Ray. 'Sugar and milk?' she continued, looking at the floor. Maybe she wasn't so impressed by teachers. I asked for two sugars. Ray shouted up the staircase.

'Susie! You get down here now. Your teacher's here to see you.'

After a few muffled barks and a flurry of shuffling and stamping from upstairs, a small girl finally appeared at the bottom of the stairs. On catching sight of me, the stranger, she ran straight to Ray and hid behind his legs. So it was true. Susie really existed. Ray picked her up and I followed him with my mug of tea back into the living room. 'You sit on the sofa,' he ordered, as if I were the honoured guest. I hovered on the sticky black plastic as Ray sat down on the floor with his daughter still clinging to him like a koala bear. 'This is Phil. He's a teacher,' he intoned again, trying to get his family to appreciate the enormity of the occasion. 'He taught at your school,' he cajoled, trying to get her to look at me. Susie buried her head further into her dad's belly. Getting visibly edgy, Ray tried a different approach. 'Who was that teacher you said to me?' he asked, looking up at me.

'Mrs Howden,' I replied, taking a slurp of tea. At the mention of this magical name, the girl suddenly stopped squirming. Noticing the effect, Ray tapped her on the head.

'He said Mrs Howden. That your teacher? Tell your dad. Is that your teacher?' Suddenly, the girl's face emerged from the folds of Ray's clothes. She looked across at me and pointed, a tiny whisper accompanying her gesture.

'Jomble-Wimp,' she breathed, just loud enough to hear.

When I got home at about eleven that night and opened the front door, my dad was standing at the end of the corridor that led to the front room. This was slightly odd, since he spent most of the time rotting in his chair in the lounge watching TV or staring into space. He was an undemonstrative man from whom emotions crept unwillingly, if they ever crept out at all. Once, when we were watching *The Sound of Music*, his eyes moistened and he blew his nose – at that point when the Nazis run back to the car to give chase to the Von Trapps, only to find that the nuns had whipped out the rotor arm. Aside from that, and the odd scribbled poem I found in his drawer when I was looking for fags to nick, he kept himself to himself.

'What's up?' I asked. 'Everything OK'?

He broke into a nicotine chuckle. 'You got the job!' He beamed. 'They rang this afternoon. It was the headmaster.'

I stood there, nodding, as my dad waved at me to come down the corridor and accept a hug from my mum. They'd never made this sort of fuss when I'd scored a hat-trick for the school team, passed my A-levels or graduated from university. Everybody seemed more thrilled about it than me. Shit. I'd got a job. It felt good to have beaten the other candidates, but standing there with the mindless hum of the factory still burbling in my ears, I couldn't focus on the moment. All I could see was a vague vision of the next forty years – stacks of unmarked exercise books and howling Alan Plants.

'How does it feel, love?' my mum asked, clearly thrilled.

'Scary, ' I replied, and lit up a fag.

8

DETONATING

I'm thirteen, sitting in a gloomy high-ceilinged classroom. The geography teacher, 'Pud' Parr, stands at the front – an old bulldog in a black gown. We are being asked in turn to read out a paragraph from the textbook *The Continent of Africa*. When it gets to me, I dutifully begin to drone out the text, to which no one is listening. As we turn the page, the text leads to a black-and-white photo which breaks up the first paragraph. Remarkably, Pud is still awake.

'Read the caption,' he barks.

I do as I'm told. It reads: '*And almost everywhere you travel in Africa, you may observe the farmers washing their bullocks in the river.*'

I can't control myself. A burst of air guffaws from my lungs.

'What *is* the matter, Ball?' shouts Pud, staring over his specs like Squeers.

'Nothing, sir!' I gasp. But Pud isn't convinced.

'Is there something funny in that sentence?'

'No, sir, nothing at all.'

We hand in our geography exercise books at the end of

the lesson, and we never see them again – a dream come true.
Pud sells his old car to a scrap merchant but forgets to tell
him that our books lie scattered in the boot. He finally
explains this to us at the end of the academic year, after which
he finally hangs up his gown and retires. No matter. By that
time we are well acquainted with *The Continent of Africa*,
since there is nothing else we can read or do. Ah, the good
old days. Thank goodness I passed the eleven-plus, or I
would never have known what African farmers got up to in
their rivers. A continent of well-scrubbed bullocks. And talking of young bovine creatures, one is standing over me,
waking me from my reverie.

'You must be Phil!' the young chap says, all jolly and
matey. He hovers over me, hand outstretched, waiting for me
to get out of the armchair and shake it. It's still break time on
my first day in Willerton High School. I'm still a teacher. It
wasn't all a funny dream. And someone wants to talk to me.
The fact that everyone had previously been so absorbed in
their own business on the opening morning of the new term
had led me to the comfy armchair and the daydream. I jump
up and look keen.

'Mike,' he tells me. 'Mike Rix.' Mike is wearing a dark-
green rugby shirt, tight little white tennis shorts and a ginger
moustache, which goes nicely with his bouffant of flaming
red hair. He's short and stocky, like a Herefordshire bullock.
He has a mug of tea from which he takes a practised slurp,
looking quizzically over the rim at me.

'Where've you been then? We were waiting for you. We

just had the new teachers' meeting with the deputy head. He's over there,' he explained, nodding his head in the direction of a large senior-looking teacher over by the door. Something skips and wobbles in my intestines. The deputy head looks remarkably like Pud Parr, minus the gown. The omens are not good.

'Oh shit,' I manage. Dreamily ensconced in the armchair, Pud hasn't seen me. Perhaps he's looking for me now. 'Um – I didn't know there was a meeting. Who told you?' My fellow probationer, whom I presume to be a teacher of physical education, is all knowledge and action.

'Look in your pigeonhole, mate!' He grins, having finally concluded that I'm the clown of the new recruits. 'There was a note.' I had no idea that I had a pigeonhole, although it seems a fairly logical idea. 'Wakey wakey!' he laughs. 'You need a cuppa, mate. Haven't you got a mug either?' and he skips off, thumping another teacher on the arm and oozing matey charm as if he's been in the school for twenty years.

I decide that I don't like Mike, but in truth I dislike myself even more. Waiting until the little bullock has threaded his way through the rest of the herd, I make my way discreetly over to Julie Acklam, the English teacher to whom I was introduced by Lund two hours earlier, before registration. 'Excuse me, Julie,' I begin, leaning diffidently over her chair. 'Do you know where the pigeonholes are?' Her nose is in a paperback of *The Mayor of Casterbridge*. I can see things underlined, and there are little scribbles in the margins. She looks up.

'Where they've always been,' she snaps, returning to Thomas Hardy.

'Right,' I reply. 'And, um, where have they always been?'

'Well, they're not likely to be out there, are they?' she snaps again, faintly shifting her head to the right with the implication that where I am staring, out through the windows and to the school playing fields, will not be the location in which I will find the buried treasure. As she busily makes a further note to the side of the book's original print, I make as if to walk away. 'Outside the door, you daft lump,' she finally informs me, her eyes firmly fixed to the book.

'Right. Thanks,' I apologise, for being a daft lump. Friendly place this.

Once I find the pigeonholes, an enormous cupboard-like construction just beyond the door of the staffroom and actually rather difficult to miss, the note inside does indeed inform me of a meeting for the new teachers, all of whose names are helpfully written out onto the invitation. The memo bears the name Peter Gabriel, whom I now know to be the Pud Parr lookalike. He didn't look like a Peter when he was standing there earlier, more like a George or a Winston. He also failed to bear any resemblance to the charismatic lead singer of the group Genesis, a band I rather like, but none of this is helping my budding career. I figure I should go along and apologise to my new deputy head. His office is next to the headmaster's, a positional logic that even I can work out. The door is open, so I give it a timid tap. 'Come in,' says a deep fruity voice. The office is more adorned than the headmaster's, with pictures of wife, children and, presumably, grandchildren competing for space on every single surface of the room. On the wall behind Mr Gabriel's head, which still hasn't looked up at me, is a small tapestry, hand-woven by a member of the extended family, I guess:

> *If you can fill the unforgiving minute*
> *With sixty seconds' worth of distance run*
> *Yours is the Earth, and everything that's in it*
> *And which is more, you'll be a man my son.*

He still doesn't look up, so I assume that he's filling the unforgiving minute or his colostomy bag. Maybe he's writing another note to me personally. It seems a trifle unreasonable at this stage of the game, but I know I'm not going to like him. Kipling's trite little maxim I know only too well, since it stared down at me from the back of our upstairs toilet for some eighteen years, before I flapped my wings and fell out of the nest. The rest of the poem makes me ill, both for its smug little sentiments and for its inevitable association, in my particular case, with the act of defecation – but this is the verse for which I reserve a particular loathing. He finally looks up.

'Mr Ball, I presume?' he begins, taking off his glasses.

'Yes, I'm sorry about missing the meeting.' I squirm, adopting a diffident stance. 'It's just that I didn't know about the pigeonholes,' I offer, hoping that he'll accept this peace offering. Mr Gabriel smiles across the several miles that separate us – me starting out, him winding down.

'That's all right,' he says, smirking. 'It wasn't a very important meeting, at least not in terms of useful information. But it's the same every year,' he sighs knowingly. 'You always find out who the organised ones are.' This is a punch aimed way below the belt, but I figure it might be unwise to fight back. Sensing a knockout, he goes for bust. 'Your fellow probationers are Mike and Eileen. I suppose you'll bump into them in the staffroom or somewhere. Well, good luck with the rest of the day,' and with that he returns to his memo writing, or whatever he's doing.

Up to this point, my first day has gone reasonably well. A lush green September morning forms the backdrop to my professional debut, as I drive through the gates of Willerton High School. I say 'drive' as opposed to 'ride' because I've blown part of my Birds Eye takings – 125 quid to be exact – on an old second-hand six-volt Beetle whose chipped light-blue paint and chug-chug engine throb cannot quite mask the other competing sensation that I have of entering the world of adults, tax and National Insurance. It's a mildly positive feeling, bolstered by the fact that Henry, my landlord from the previous year, has agreed to take me back into his mansion again, and has moved me from the tiny room I occupied to the wonderfully spacious attic flat now vacated by the previous tenants. It's more expensive, of course, but I'm earning a salary now, a mysterious word that I've only previously associated with Roman soldiers and mid-life parents. Now I just have to earn it, at the same time as convincing my new head of department that I really do like

DH Lawrence, a pretence that I may have to continue for the next thirty-odd years before he retires.

Slowly threading the Beetle through the stream of purple-uniformed pupils winding into the grounds for another year at the mill, I feel like the goldfish in the proverbial. Pupils stare back at me through the windscreen, comment and point. 'I'm the new guy, OK,' my phoney smile tries to tell them. Some of them chortle and giggle, and a hand slaps the roof. Hey – I thought this was a good school! Then it occurs to me that it may be the old Beetle that they find amusing, and that their largely middle-class peepers have already singled me out as a member of the proletariat. Next morning I resolve to drive to work in my Guevara beret.

Tucking in apologetically between the more senior cars of longer-established staff, I see in the mirror that my new leader is waiting at the staff door entrance for me. As I duck out from the car he bounds up to me as if I were a long-lost son. He's all arms and action. 'Welcome to the madhouse!' he fidgets, laughing into the school-dinner air. 'Right!' I grin back, surprised by this welcome. Apart from the beard and the smallish physical aspect, the contrast with Hamish couldn't be greater. By 'madhouse' Lund means that it really isn't one. I can tell this somehow, behind the forced irony. Hamish would have said 'Welcome to paradise!' from which I would also have picked up the converse meaning.

As we approach the staffroom I can hear the buzz of conversation, of catch-up lines from the holidays, of some sort of bonhomie. We walk in through the door and the immediate impression is of a more homely, oak-beams-and-fireplace sort of room, with none of these things, of course, but with a less tatty air than the one at Lynton. The school is also a state comprehensive, a few years older but basically from the same era as the Cleethorpes building – square, functional and flat-roofed, the sort of job given to architects whose sight is failing. Nevertheless, some attempt has been made to give it an air of bookishness. Two male teachers are puffing on pipes and a striking, middle-aged woman with her hair in a bun and sporting a long hippy floral skirt is knitting on a high-backed armchair in the middle of the room. Lund looks around for someone to present me to, and picks on the knitter.

'Ah – let me introduce you to Tessa. Should have met her last week really, but she was on a CND march.' He says this without irony. 'Tessa's my right-hand woman, as in deputy head of English.' As if on some sort of slow-motion pills, Tessa looks up, settles her knitting to one side of the large chair, smooths down her skirt and rises all stately and shimmering, like a Pre-Raphaelite heroine. I imagine I've seen her somewhere before, on aprons in over-priced gift shops, or on tasteful birthday cards with *No message inside*. She's autumn, she's Keats, she's got a slightly masculine, handsome face – but she's like nothing I've ever seen in the flesh before.

'Well, well,' she purrs, looking me up and down as if I'm new flesh to devour. 'What *do* we have here?' Lund, hopping around now like a demented jumping-bean, attempts to stop her from asking me any further questions, like 'How big is your dick?', for example. He then appears to say, 'Don't worry, it's the menopause,' when in fact he has said, 'Don't worry, it's just men, of course,' adding helpfully, 'Tessa came here several years ago, straight from a convent. She's been making up for lost time ever since,' which seems to be slightly risqué territory for him. As if he lives in terror of this remarkable thing in front of me, he drags me over to the windows where sit a pair of glum-looking men, in their late twenties, I would guess.

'John Butler and Steve Blacktoft, mainstays of the department,' Lund announces. 'This is Phil Ball, the new recruit I was telling you about.' Butler and Blacktoft, far from looking at my genitals, hardly look at me at all. 'Right,' sighs one of them, and lifts his hand in a tired wave. The other, who sports a natty little moustache, merely nods then goes back to staring out of the large, three-quarter-length windows. To their immediate right, a younger woman is busily writing something in a notebook and blinking from the smoke rising from the cigarette dangling from her lips. She looks up and gives Lund a hard stare.

'I was wondering when you'd get round to me,' she pouts in a broad black-pudding accent, the fag dancing on her lips. 'Julie Acklam,' she announces, standing up and holding out her hand to be shaken. 'I'll present myself then,' she scolds Lund, who defends himself with a minimal protest.

'I was getting round to you. Keep your hair on. It's only the first day,' he quips – but I sense some tension. Julie is also youngish, her hair tied back to one side with a clip and, in opposition to Tessa, a large grey pleated skirt – the sort some might wear to hide a big bum. She's as blunt as a rubber cosh, and my immediate feeling is that we're not going to get on. But it's too late for any further impressions. That's the main bulk of the English department, and the bell is ringing for registration. Reminding me that I have a tutor group to meet, Lund offers to take me down to my classroom, and we scramble with the other teachers to find the new register among an unseemly pile by the door. It's time to meet my new flock, to bless them with my fresh-faced wisdom. Apart from the standard twenty-five-hour teaching load given to new inductees, I've been handed a tutor group of fifteen-year-olds, lost lambkins to whom I will be entrusted to guide down the moral pathways with which I am so thoroughly acquainted. It should be fun.

My room, rather like the loonies' room at Lynton, is down at the end of a long L-shaped corridor, the foot at the end of the boot. I'm at the terminus, at the end of the line, where any ill discipline can remain a dirty secret. Lund hands me the register before we get to the door, and bids me good luck. I'm beginning to regret lying to him about Lawrence. He's been kindness personified so far, and I know he's decided to not come into the room because that might be misinterpreted by the kids. I'm not altogether sure what's required of me as form tutor, but I'll have a go. It means I have to fill twenty minutes every morning, and at the moment the only thing I have planned is to fill in the register.

The air isn't so bad on walking in. First impressions are not unfavourable. In general, the pupils are large, and the low growl of broken voices floats on the still air. Some are already sitting, some are standing around in clumps as I open the register on the desk. 'OK. Can we all sit down, please?' The clumps disperse, the holiday chit-chat subsides. 'I'm your new form tutor, and my name is Mr Ball,' I announce, waiting for the titters – but nothing happens. It's almost disappointing not to be made plural.

'Erm, I'm going to read out your names alphabetically, as they are here in the register, and I want you to just identify yourselves, please, so that I can learn your names.' Unknowingly, I've stumbled upon a sure-fire method of identifying the troublemakers. Halfway down the register, I almost see it coming. This is because the pupil is called Wayne, a name that represents a sure-fire genetic condition. 'Wayne Stark,' I pronounce. Up to this name, everyone has simply replied 'Sir' and raised their hand, some more enthusiastically than others. Now there's a silence. 'Wayne?' I try again, looking around the room.

'He's absent, sir,' explains a tall, gawky youth almost under my nose. His attempt at a moustache and his thin, lank hair make him look like a wind-torn scarecrow.

'That's odd,' I tell him. 'There are twenty-five names in the register, and I've just done a head count. There are twenty-five pupils here. I'll count again,' I attempt, in the silence.

'Aw, I'm just mucking about, sir,' pipes up the scarecrow again, as if this were the joke of the century. Several of the class laugh with him, others at him. 'Wayne Stark at your service,' he adds, and grins down into his desk.

'If you think that's funny then I don't!' I bawl, making him jump. The effect is most odd, sending a spooky surge of power into the usual 40-watt bulb. 'I'm not here to be mucked around with. I'm here as your form tutor, and everything that that involves. So cut the funny stuff, thank you, Mr Stark,' I rant, unstoppable. All this spews forth from someone else, as if I'm speaking in tongues. I've no idea where it's coming from, and I have to check myself to stop, just before I pronounce the deadly word *imbecile*. The boy crumbles; the class looks scared.

I pause, then continue on down the register until I reach the equally resonant name of Tracey Thompson. On pronouncing it, a husky voice, slightly advanced for its years, answers to the roll-call with a cheery, 'Hello, sir.' It invites a glance up from the register, and I take the bait. There in the middle of the room is a large smiling blonde, halfway between Dick Emery's 'Ooh you are awful' and a young Barbara Windsor. She smiles and waves. At Lynton the girls kept their distance, but they would seem to be made of different stuff north of the river.

'Good morning, Miss Thompson. I'm pleased to see that you're so happy to be back at school. Now perhaps we could finish the register.'

Remarkably, this seems to work too. Tracey huffs, turns over a hand and inspects her nails. Towards the back, two girls sitting together have raised their eyes to the ceiling, in apparent disgust at Tracey's forwardness. One of them is called Julia, because she is the next to reply to the register call, but other girls in the class sport equally revealing social-caste names such as Clare, Vanessa or Vagina. So it would seem that a fair percentage of the girls in the class don jodhpurs at the weekend. It remains to be seen what the other ones get up to. But I've got them quiet anyway. Never smile until Christmas, as the old teaching adage goes. Well, never smile until nine o'clock in my case, which I do when it's time to let them go to class.

I teach a class of first years (eleven-year-olds) before morning break, the first time I've taken this age group. As official baptisms go, it's hardly one of fire. None of the little things says boo to a goose, and they hang on my every word before beginning a composition on the exciting topic of 'My favourite person' with apparent enthusiasm. I walk around the class as they write, pretending to inspect their opening paragraphs.

They sit in pairs, but no one speaks – heads bowed in a furious scribbling, as if their future lives depended on pleasing me, on getting it right. All I see are the tops of heads, some of which shine with Brylcreem partings. The English exercise books are brown, exactly as they were when I was at school. I recall that biology books were orange, French were blue, and geography were a deep crimson – subliminal associations that still affect, in theory, my views of those subjects. When someone says 'maths' I see custard yellow, and feel slightly queasy. But English is the colour of mud. Maybe that's significant. Mud sticks.

The next day I come in earlier, check for memos (there are none) and on entering the staffroom, place my new floral mug and small jar of Nescafé on the large communal table. The mug gleams out among its brown-stained neighbours, all older and harder-bitten, chipped at the edges. As I wait to be spoken to, Tessa comes to my rescue, patting the chair to her side and indicating that I am to be handed the privilege of an intimate chat. Her soft Yorkshire accent flows and billows like her skirt, over and around the cigarette that she keeps in her mouth as she knits. The entire staff seems to smoke furiously, although in Tessa's case the Rothman's King Size clashes somewhat with the Pre-Raphaelite look. She tells me that she is knitting a jumper for her twelve-year-old daughter. 'So you have children?' I ask her.

'Of course,' she replies, removing the cigarette. 'Just had time for the one.' Her back is as straight as a Roman road. 'You heard what Tom said yesterday, about the convent. The funny thing is that my husband, Nicholas – well, he used to be a monk. So, a couple of fallen angels, you might say. Paradise Lost!' she cackles into the air, turning around to face me.

'Or Paradise Regained,' I quip, pleased with my little rejoinder. I think Tessa might be worth cultivating, not because I anticipate any visceral sessions in the library cupboard but rather because there's some warmth here. She'll tuck me into bed with a glass of Lucozade and murmur, 'There there. You're not such an incompetent prick after all.'

'How were the classes yesterday?' she asks, switching

into professional mode. I'd taught my third-year class after morning break, and a GCE literature group in the afternoon.

'Just fine. But I was exhausted last night when I got home. Does it get any better?' I add. She thinks about this one, pondering over the question as if I've asked her something terribly important.

'Oh it does,' she purrs eventually. 'It gets much, much better. It gets ...' and she pauses and closes her eyes, preens out her bosom and sighs out the climactic word '... wonderful!'

This is dramatic stuff for 8.35 in the morning. I happen to glance past Tessa to the windows, under which are seated the misery twins, Butler and Blacktoft – the two that showed such enthusiasm to meet their new colleague yesterday. As Tessa continues to savour her early-morning orgasm, I notice that the two men's eyes have met in silent dialogue. Butler's then lift, ever so slightly, to the ceiling, expressing the unmistakable *Why doesn't that silly old bag give her arse a chance?* It would seem that I have caught sight of a possible Dirty Corner. I shall have to investigate this one further.

Tracey paints her nails during registration, but Wayne avoids my eyes. I can think of no moral lesson to impart, so I allow them to mutter quietly among themselves. They seem to like this. Besides, the session is to be cut short by the term's first assembly. On the earlier bell, I lead my new charges up the corridor to the central hall. Since they know the routine, I leave them at the entrance and make my way around the back to where seats have been allocated to us on stage, behind the headmaster. I rather like this, since it reminds me of the old grammar school, of hierarchies and orders, of looking on from the ground-level perspective of childhood. As I settle into my chair under the bright lights I recall seeing the hairy creatures on stage as impossibly wise and frightening people, as a distant community of elders. Now I wonder what they think of me, sitting there in full view, with my beige socks and M&S brogues.

Beacroft walks on with a melodramatic swish of his gown and immediately whips himself up into a frenzy about the theme of 'friendship'. From behind, the black gown makes him look like an oversized bat. 'I do not intend to tolerate either bullying, insulting or exclusion this year!' he shouts, as if all the pupils have been guilty of this. He increases the volume in measured stages, waving his right arm in an unfortunate manner, like the Führer. 'Friendship and tolerance are the two great human virtues,' he roars. The pupils blink. Hundreds of heads, thinking of something else. Beacroft cranes his neck and stares out threateningly over the throng. No one so much as twitches. Beacroft runs a tight ship, and keeps the decks swabbed. I wouldn't want to get on his wrong side.

Hamish told me in a reflective moment back in the Dirty Corner that it was never a headmaster that you needed to get on with anyway but rather his secretary, with whom he would be inevitably having an affair. As Beacroft begins to read out some administrative blurb, my ex-head of department's words float back into my head.

'That way you know that if you drop some pearl in his secretary's earshot, something that implies that you're deserving of a promotion, you know it'll get back to the headmaster that night in bed, or in some car park in the back of his car. They're all shagging. It was enshrined in the 1948 Education Act.'

The vision fades, the crowd disperses, and I head up to the library. I have a double free period and I want to know how to sign stuff out, and so on. At break I proudly make myself a coffee and stand to one side of the table, occupying new territory. Allowing my daffodil-patterned mug to steam into the staffroom air, I try to look as if I am getting the hang of things, integrating into the culture. To help this along I take off my jacket and roll up my sleeves, since I've noticed several teachers doing this the previous day. It seems to lend them an air of industry and know-how. These are the airs that I need to adopt. Lighting up a fag does no harm either, not that you need to do this to get your nicotine fix. Most of the teachers smoke like chimneys at a steel foundry. Cigarettes hang from every orifice, filling the staffroom with the sweet fog of irresponsibility. I want to share publicly in this ritual. I want to step on to the first rung of the ladder of acceptance.

So as I puff away and work on the hard-bitten-but-casual professional look, my two fellow freshmen burst through the door. Well – one of them is a woman, and one so fresh that she shines through the fog like a lighthouse beam. Mike Rix, the jolly-come-lately whose path I have already crossed, is laughing and preening with her as if he's known her all his life. He has an annoying habit of thumping everyone on the arm, even beautiful women. 'Hey Bally!' he chuckles, punching me and causing my coffee to spill. 'This is Eileen, you *nummock*,' he honks, like a horny goose.

'What's a nummock?' asks Eileen, tittering as if in love.

'Someone like Bally,' roars Rixy. I smile weakly. I don't understand what nummock means. The Hull dialect is strange and exotic. Washed up on this foreign shore, perhaps the voluptuous Eileen can help me.

'You must be the other new teacher,' I begin. 'Sorry about yesterday. I've found the pigeonholes now.' But Eileen doesn't seem to hear, so taken is she with the Herefordshire bullock at her side.

'She's the new Environmental Science teacher!' the bullock bellows. Eileen giggles. Rixy continues, unstoppable. 'She's got green fingers. If your prize marrows are in need of a stroking, just take them to Eileen's garden shed!' I grin to please him, then steal a glance at Eileen. Her breasts are enormous, but her waist is alluringly slim. She looks like a ripe orchard, blooming and heaving with fruit – from which Rixy can hardly keep his stubby little apple-scrumping hands.

'Don't you get ideas now!' she simpers, thumping him playfully. Perhaps this is an ancient East Yorkshire ritual. Then the devastating news. 'I only got married three months ago!' Rixy already knows this.

'Ah Bally!' he replies, with a wink of solidarity. 'They're always the best, the married ones, eh?' I wink back, keen to agree. 'Makes the chase more exciting,' he concludes. The lovers bound off.

Seating myself on the edge of the huge wooden coffee table and trying to recover from the vision of Eileen's orchard, my ears begin to pick up on a sliver of *sotto voce* from the terrible twins, Butler and Blacktoft.

'Did you see that?' asks Blacktoft.

'Yep,' replies Butler.

'You know what? If the opportunity were to arise, dear fellow, I would fuck that up hill and down dale.'

'I would do the same and more, my friend,' replies Butler, nodding gravely. 'I think, however, that the surname Johnson is rather unbecoming for such a prime specimen. I rather prefer *Over* – Eileen Over,' upon which the recipient of this wisecrack, Blacktoft, suddenly leans forward and spits his tea into his mug, desperately attempting to prevent the liquid from staining his slacks. His tall body shakes until he can contain himself no more, letting out a final roar of approval like a sated lion climbing from his mate. I've found the Dirty Corner for sure, but should I take up the membership?

After break I have the first years again. I've decided to help a little more with their composition by feeding in some anecdotes at the beginning of the lesson about why my new friend Steve from Birds Eye is one of my 'favourite persons', the idea being to give them some criteria to hang their choices on. Then I'm going to tell them about my mum and get them to list for me some reasons why you would choose someone as your favourite, which I hope will give them more hooks for their writing. After that, I've planned to have a rest and let them get on with it. Everything sounds fine. There are no potential rebels in the class, as far as I can make out.

The introduction to the lesson goes swimmingly, and the kids get on with their task. After about forty minutes of traipsing around the silent classroom trying to look interested, I retire back to my desk and contemplate taking out the *Hull Daily Mail* from my bag, to check on the films on offer in the city centre. Just as I'm about to lean down, the door flies open and in marches Pud, aka Peter Gabriel. The children shoot up, like little soldiers on parade. Since Pud wears a suit and looks the part, the kids have responded in kind. He waves impatiently at them to sit down. My bum twitches slightly, but thankfully I manage to remain seated. He comes close and leans down to the table, as the kids resume their work in silence.

'Where were you?' he hisses.

'Erm, I told you,' I whisper, assuming that he's referring to the previous day. 'I was in the staffroom ...'

'No, no – not yesterday. Today. *To-day,*' he pronounces slowly. 'You were supposed to be on substitution before break. For Stan Greendale, the physics teacher. The kids were left on their own for half an hour, before one of them came to tell me. Good job some people are responsible in this school.'

I look down at the desk. 'I didn't know,' I whimper.

Pud moves away, and in full earshot of my junior soldiers replies: 'Substitution board. Look at it in future.' He then storms out and half slams the door.

Substitution board? What the hell is that? Nobody has explained this worrying concept to me. It must be a roster to check on, in case any colleagues go absent – but I've neither imagined that any of them will be away on this second day, nor even less that I'd be chosen to fill in for them. Almost in tears at this sudden intrusion into the tranquillity of the morning, I acknowledge to myself that it's a mistake on my part, but I'm not so sure that it's given Pud the right to come barging into my room to belittle me in front of my new class. They are still scribbling in silence, but it must have been obvious to even the dullest of the little things that I've just been given a bollocking. Something indignant wells up inside. Normally a pacific creature prepared to accept a ticking-off if justified, I've nevertheless inherited two things from my mother. One is her unfeasibly big ears, the other is her dislike of overweening authority. It's already got me into several scrapes down the years, and it will get me into several more. Sitting there in a blind rage, I decide that I don't like Pud, and I decide that honesty dictates that I should tell him so.

Reaching back for Johnny Roe, I look out of the window across the pupils' bowed heads and recall another of his stories – one of the more plausible ones about his first night as a rookie soldier in the barracks, back in Rhodesia. His fellow privates, already knowing each other, had planned a welcome for him and had soaked his bed with a collection of their own urine. Johnny Roe lay in the dark, listening to the sniggers of his new army pals. 'The only way to survive,' he told us, the migraine look fully engaged, 'was to fight back immediately. Any sign of weakness and they'd do it again, night after night. I knew that. And so I rose slowly from the cold soaking sheets and picked up my rifle from the side of the bunk. They could see me in the moonlight, which was shining through the barrack window. I walked calmly across to the nearest bunk, flung off the sheets, and jabbed the rifle butt hard into the backside of the sniggering incumbent. He stopped sniggering, of course. After that, no one bothered me again.'

I wait slightly longer than Johnny Roe, until the afternoon to be precise, just before the bell sounds for the beginning of lessons. After lunch I've hung around the senior staff offices, and am now sure that Pud is in his room, alone. As when you hold the poison-filled letter in the mouth of the postbox, wondering whether to send it or not, knowing that what you have written is guaranteed to drop you into deep and irre-deemable shit, I hover for a moment outside Pud's office, but I'm too incensed to pull back. I knock on the door and stroll in, replicating his little act some hours earlier. He's reading the sports section of the newspaper. Before he has time to protest or pretend that he's doing something more becoming of a deputy head, I launch into a practised little speech.

'I'm sorry,' I begin, looking him in the eye, 'but I really think that you should try to be more professional in future.' He splutters something and drops the newspaper. I push the rifle butt in a little further. 'I don't think you should barge into my classroom and make me look stupid in front of my pupils. I have to teach them all year, but you don't.' Having made this announcement with steely precision, I pull back the rifle and walk out of the room. As I do so, Pud continues to splutter, as if he is having a heart attack.

In case he comes looking for me, I head straight for the loo, walk into a cubicle and close the door behind me. There are a couple of minutes' grace before the classes start up again. I lean against the door with my heart thumping and the testosterone letting off fireworks in front of my eyes, and try to calm down. As I do this, the slow realisation that I have seriously messed up begins to seep into my brain. It's my second day. I might as well have literally shoved a rifle butt up his substantial arse, since it would have been no less serious an act of assault. Reason begins to return, coldly but surely. This is my second day in the complex arena called adult life, and I have just accused a vastly experienced deputy head of a large comprehensive school of being 'unprofessional'. Neither have I chosen the word idly. During my brief internment at Lynton I'd picked up signals to the effect that it just might be the biggest word on the teacher agenda. People used it sparingly, but even back in the Dirty Corner I'd sensed that it was not a word that one applied lightly to one's colleagues. You could call them idle bastards or perverts, you could accuse them of stealing your wife, but rarely could you call them unprofessional. I've thrown that particular dart at Peter Gabriel knowing full well that it will cause him some sort of convulsion. Checking that the coast is clear, I flush the loo and bound down the corridor to my classroom, twitching like a hunted gazelle.

After the class and afternoon registration, I reason that if I open one of the windows and climb on to a desk to get out, I can make a direct beeline to the friendlier air space of my Beetle, without having to face Pud or anyone else for that matter. If they sack me, I'll ring Birds Eye, ask for Nobby, and tell him I'd like to do QC for the rest of my life. But it seems a little cowardly. If Pud is waiting for me, I'll continue to stand my ground. I've gone beyond a certain stage with him now, so I see little point in backing down. I prefer him to think that I mean it – which would be true.

Pud isn't waiting for me, but Lund is. He is positioned strategically in the corridor so that he can collar me before I reach the staffroom. He looks a trifle unhappy. As I approach him, walking as casually as I can in the circumstances, he jerks out an arm and pulls my jacket slightly, indicating that we should step outside of the French windows that give on to the car park. He looks like DH Lawrence again, but closer to the version that died of tuberculosis.

'What did you say to Peter?' he snarls, through clenched teeth. His eyes dart around and about, as if he were an MI5 officer with ten seconds to get the vital information. Without giving me a chance to tell him, he asks, on a rising tone, 'Did you *actually* accuse him of being unprofessional?' I make a movement with my lips, and raise my eyebrows in confirmation. 'Oh God!' he moans. 'I was hoping that it might have been the headmaster's imagination. Of course Peter's told Beacroft. What the hell did you accuse him of *that* for?' he cries quietly, as if in some sort of agony. I go for broke.

'Because that's what he was being,' I retort, as calmly as possible. 'He came into my room and started bollocking me in front of the kids.' To my relief, Lund backs down slightly on hearing this.

'He didn't tell Beacroft that. He said he'd taken you aside.'

'Took me aside? No way,' I insist. 'He gave me a ticking off, right there and then. I was in the wrong about the substitution thing, but I didn't know,' I appeal.

Lund looks over at the trees. 'It's not a good start, Philip, it's not a good start. You can't just go in, guns all ablaze. For God's sake!' he whispers. 'Why didn't you come to me first? I'd have had it out with the old sod.' I say I'll try to be more careful in future. Lund then signs off with the more than reasonable, 'If there is a future.'

In the days that follow, I sense people avoiding me. It has obviously gotten around the staffroom, and people are undecided as to how to approach the problem. Maybe they think I'm a madman, or maybe they want to slap me on the back and congratulate me. I'm not sure, but I also keep my distance for a while. I pass Beacroft twice on the corridor in the next couple of days, but he deliberately avoids my eye, once pretending to look in his gown for something, and on the other suddenly veering off to the right and engaging a pupil in some meaningless banter. What sort of bomb have I detonated?

9

MARVELLING

My old friend John Cutts rang me from London for the first time in ages, telling me that he'd got himself a job on a new national motorbike magazine. He asked me whether I fancied trying my hand at writing short monthly stories, for the fiction section of the magazine, and when I asked what this might entail he turned a little vague. 'A bit of chain-oil, and maybe a bit of shagging,' he managed, eventually. Being unqualified on both counts, I said that I'd think about it. But when he suggested I hop on the Friday tea-time train for London I jumped at the offer.

He met me off the train at King's Cross, his biking leathers resplendent beneath his long blond mane. Despite being inseparable friends during our undergraduate years at Lancaster, we hadn't seen much of each other since. He looked exactly the same – six-foot four, streetwise and quietly cock-sure. 'Want a pint?' he asked, at which I nodded enthusi-astically. In a small backstreet pub behind the station, we settled down to a comforting session of catch-up.

'So you're a facking teacher then?' he opened, settling the

pints down onto the table. 'Can't quite see you doing that, old son. Naffin' better on the horizon? You going to do that story for the mag? You should concentrate on that. The money's all right. I could get you some more work,' he added, supremely settled in life's faster zone.

'It's like being back at the uni. No one tells you very much. I've already got under the deputy head's nose, and there's not much sign of a decent drinking club.'

'Well, son, I would say that you should just hang in there. Something'll come along. If not, write some facking stories like I've said. Any decent talent in the staffroom?'

'Nah. The best one's just got married. There's an ex-nun in her fifties who's making up for lost time, but I don't think I'm her type. Perhaps I'll just work on chastity. Good for the soul.'

John took out a small tin of Old Holborn tobacco and opened it to reveal a whole array of life-defining objects. There were cigarette papers of various shapes and sizes, a tiny pair of scissors, several discarded filter tips and a handsome silver lighter, one of the old Zippo flick-tops with a thumb-wheel for the spark. Everything occupied a designated space in the tin. It was more evidence, as if I'd needed it, that everyone else was organised, and that everyone had a life plan apart from me.

'Fack chastity. And what did you say to this geezer, this deputy head?'

'I told him that he was being unprofessional. You're not really supposed to say things like that to senior teachers.'

'Why? What does unprofessional mean?'

'Well, now that you come to ask me, I don't really know. He bollocked me in front of the kids.'

'Stick one on him,' advised John.

Much as I respected John's opinions, *sticking one on* the deputy head seemed an implausible solution. Rather I decided to look into the Thursday night five-a-side scene which I'd heard mentioned on the staffroom air. I'd understood that after these football games, the gathering would retire to a local hostelry to loosen their tongues. That sounded quite promising. It also looked as though it might help me to find out the impact that my clash with Mr Gabriel had had on the staffroom underbelly – something that was bothering me, because nobody really talked in the staffroom, not in an open way. Since it was unclear to me how the teachers really regarded one another, I wanted to know some of their secrets, to share in the gossip.

Before this outing, however, I experienced my first departmental meeting. It was clear that nobody talked very openly during these gatherings either. Still confused by the sound of silence surrounding the rifle-butt episode, I thought this newsworthy event might come up on the agenda of our opening meeting, with Lund formally inducting me into the group with a swift, 'And just to welcome Phil, the new mentally unstable member of our department brought in to swell the ranks of those already resident,' but no such luck. Rather he acknowledged my presence with a brief and pointed 'Phil seems to be looking after himself just fine' before getting down to the meatier issue of how many copies of the book *Kes* were missing from the stock-room. The only point of interest arrived during a pause in which Lund was forced to flick through a mound of papers, having misplaced some vital information that he wanted to convey to his largely silent audience, who were seated around a circular table. Uncomfortable in the quiet, Tessa looked across at me. 'How is Andrew Marvell then?' she asked, mysteriously. 'Has he written anything for you yet?' No one seemed to bat an eyelid at this one. The English poet Marvell had died at the fag-end of the seventeenth century – which would make it a bit tricky for him to write a letter to me. Perhaps Tessa was referring to some other Andrew Marvell?

'No – I can't say that he has,' I tried to reply, as lightly as possible.

'Oh, just wondering.' She smiled serenely.

Before this little episode could be cleared up, I made my Thursday night debut. Walking into the cold and cavernous air of the gym that evening, a whole sub-stratum of the male staff seemed to be there, many of whom I didn't know. There was another small staffroom in a separate building in the school, close to the science labs, and I'd yet to meet any of the white coats who hung around over there. Some of them were in the gym – but not in their white coats, of course. Both members of the Dirty Corner were also there, and they shot little glances at each other as I was invited to play on the opposite side by Stan Burns, one of the friendlier members of staff whom I'd heard talking about the five-a-side in the first place. It all turned out to be jolly but competitive, in a revealing sort of way. And of course, men being boys, adults are prone to viewing one another in sporting terms. When I was at school, the academic boys were never rated, but the footballers were. If you made it to the school team and you played regularly for the house, it meant you were left alone. It was the only sure-fire way to avoid getting beaten up every day. I was no great shakes at football, but I was competent. I was still hoping that this might be a way of gaining some cheap approval.

So sitting in the steamy changing rooms that night after the game – the stage where everyone has made his sporting point, rubber-stamped his place in the pecking order, showered and begun to talk about work – my colleague from the department, John Butler, fixed me with an ironic smirk. It was the first time he'd bothered to speak to me, and the first time I'd seen him vaguely smile.

'Hear you've been making a name for yourself then?' he remarked, pulling on his trousers. Various people in various states of undress and talcum-powder mist appeared to guffaw. Someone grunted, 'Fucking Gabriel – he'll never be the same again,' and another added, 'Unprofessional! Classic stuff.'

'So what did you *really* say to him?' asked Butler, clearly the unspoken leader of the gathering. Small and slightly frail, I'd neither expected him to be such a good footballer nor the quiet leader of the pack. People carried on dressing, pretending not to be interested but listening nevertheless.

'I told him that he shouldn't speak to me like that in front of the kids,' I explained. 'I don't know what he said after that because I went and hid in the toilet.' This earned me a little ripple of laughter. Encouraged, I added, 'As I was going out of his door I could hear a sort of gagging sound, like he was having a heart attack or something.'

'That'll make him turn up the pacemaker a few notches,' concluded Butler, whereupon I was invited out for the post-match drink.

That first night we retired to The Bell, a pub in stagger-ing distance of the school. The landlord had already prepared sandwiches for us and joked that he'd ordered some extra barrels too. For the rest of the night the noisy crowd got noisier and more indiscreet as the pints glugged down the plug holes. Butler seemed to have decided that the twin virtues of confronting Gabriel and playing football half-decently had earned me a chance to join the Dirty Corner. This honour had been bestowed upon me at Lynton with no effort at all, but here you obviously had to earn your beer spurs. Mike Rix was out with us too, but was taking some flak for his over-confidence. This made me feel much better.

'You shagged her yet then, Rixy?' quipped someone. I assumed this referred to Eileen.

'Nah,' said the bullock. 'Married women and all that.'

'Call yourself a man! You useless bastard!' howled the gathering. So Rixy's matey arm-punching habit hadn't gone down quite as well as he thought it had. But he was an excel-lent footballer. He'd survive.

Halfway through the night one of the scientists, a tall, fat, senior teacher referred to only as Jonesy, piped up with, 'Have you taught that kid yet? The one who thinks he's a poet or something?'

Someone burped. 'What do you know about poetry, Jonesy? Been doing *Ode to a Bunsen Burner*?'

Butler took over. 'It's true. We got some reports through on this kid from the junior school. They only send them when it's something a bit serious. Apparently he thinks he's the reincarnation of Andrew Marvell.' This got the table's attention, and the noise quietened down. Jonesy confirmed the news.

'It's true. I was doing some stuff on the basic elements of life – the usual crap we give them during the first few weeks – and after a while I notice him, at the back. Kid with one of those oversized heads. I'm talking away and he's writing something, under the bench. So I tell him to stop and pay attention, and he does. He sort of shoots up to attention. But twenty minutes later I'm still talking, and he's at it again. Scribbling something. This time I watch him as I'm talking – and he's looking around, like there's no one else in the room. He looks like he's really concentrating on something. Anyway, after the class when the kids are filing out, I call him over. What were you writing? I ask him. I don't think you were taking notes about the basic elements of life, I say. He says no, he wasn't taking notes – but in a serious sort of way. He talks like an old man. So I ask him to show me what he's been writing and he says he can't show me, for *various reasons.*'

Jonesy slurped back the remaining beer in his glass and fixed his audience, now listening more carefully. 'An eleven-year-old, and he says to me *various reasons* like a fucking Oxford don or something. But when I ignored him and insisted on seeing what he'd written, he started to shake like a maniac and I thought he was going to burst into tears. All right, all right, I say to him. You can keep it in your satchel. But if I catch you again ... and he's gone, straight out the door, without a word. I had a chat with Brian, his tutor, and he says the same. Like Butler's just said, only it's weirder. He lives with his dad. The old lady ran off with the insurance man a few years back. Apparently the old man thinks it's true. Not that his missus has run off but that his kid is Andrew fucking Marvell.'

This seemed to set off a whole new buzz. 'So who's Andrew Marvell?' asked Rixy's head of department, a fair-haired physical god by the name of Ian Bridge.

'Bridgey –' began Butler, putting down his glass. 'You are an ignorant shit of mountainous proportions, but I forgive you. What God left out, Man cannot put back into PE teach-ers. Andrew Marvell was a Civil War poet, born in the small hamlet of Winestead some fifteen miles east of here, in the godforsaken flatlands of Holderness. Brought up in this very city, he went on to be its MP, via Trinity College and a career as a metaphysical poet. Died 1678 of unknown causes, but possibly poisoned by his physician. Controversial character, and turncoat. Supported the royalists, but changed over to Cromwell. Better class of warts on the republican side.' This earned Butler a round of applause. Someone asked what we were supposed to do with this strange child. Butler extended an arm in my direction. 'Ask Bally. He's the man entrusted to teach him poetry.'

What made this news all the more shocking was the fact that I hadn't noticed this boy as yet. This is what Tessa had been referring to in the departmental meeting. What had this child with the oversized head been up to for the past three weeks? Whatever he'd been doing, he'd been keeping it to himself. Then again, it wasn't for me to suppose that Andrew Marvell went around showing his work to everybody.

And so, on the morning after my five-a-side debut, with the first hangover of my teaching career firmly in place, I resolved to look into the little issue of Andrew Marvell. The thing that was worrying me was that I had corrected all the first year's essays on 'My Favourite Person' and put the marks into my register. But now I remembered that one essay had been missing, and that I'd forgotten to chase it up. During registration, as I tried to hide behind the conveniently tall book which contained the names of my tutor group, I focused woozily on the smaller mark book located some-where below me on the desk. Sure enough, one of the essays had not been handed in. The space beside the name read Samuel Holdsworth. Could this be the poet?

At morning break, I approached Butler in the staffroom. He looked worse than me, if that were possible. 'Erm John,' I ventured, moving for the first time into the Dirty Corner air space. 'Can I just have a word about that kid?' After a lengthy silence, I received a decisive, 'No. Fuck off.' I understood how he felt, so at break I sought out Lund, in a rare rush of professional concern. He wasn't there in his library garret, but Tessa was – knitting, of course. 'Tessa,' I asked, from outside the small cupboard room, partly because of her predatory eyes but mainly because I wanted to spare her my six-pint breath. 'About this Andrew Marvell character. Any advice on what to do about him? I mean – do I encourage him, or do I treat him like all the rest?'

Tessa smiled. 'Impossible to say, my love,' she pronounced, clicking away at her knitting needles. 'Just follow your instincts. By all accounts, it won't make much difference what you try to do. Which is why we haven't really bothered to tell you.' And with that, she dismissed me with a long slow nod of her head.

I was intending to start a reader with them that morning, a book called *Walkabout* in which a couple of posh white American kids get stranded in the Australian outback and have to find their way back to civilisation, as it were. They meet an Aborigine boy on his tribal walkabout, and the book goes on to describe the dynamic between them as the white kids try to persuade the boy to help them. Of the list of probable and possible readers that Lund had given me, this seemed the most promising, and besides, since I'd already seen the film, it saved me from having to read the book. Distributing the readers around the quiet class, I asked casually for Samuel Holdsworth. One or two kids tittered quietly. A small boy at the back raised his hand, all the time looking down at his desk.

'Ah, Samuel,' I began, continuing to give out the books. 'I don't seem to have a mark for you for our first piece of work. Did I forget to put in the mark, or did you forget to hand the work in?' Samuel finally looked up. His forehead was curiously elongated, like Frankenstein. He kept his arm half-raised.

'I have the work here sir,' he piped up, with a slight suggestion in his voice that I was to blame for not asking him before. I sat down at my table, the books given out.

'Well, that's fine, Samuel. But everyone else handed the work in when I asked for it. If I allow everyone to hand it in when they like, it's going to make my job impossible.' I was just about to add that I would give him the benefit of the doubt – since it had been their first assignment – when he replied:

'It took me a long time to finish, sir, for *various reasons*.'

I told him that he could explain those reasons to me at the end of the class, so that we could launch into the book without any further delay. I also wanted this class to be my relaxation class, the one in which I could walk in tarred and feathered and nobody would react. The kids were all remarkably well behaved, and like Hamish's class at Lynton, all bright as buttons. Mixed ability? Well – there had to be some chaff in there somewhere, but I didn't see any particular need to run around catering for their every need. None of the essays had been exactly poor. I also knew that their good behaviour might stem from the fact that they were still new to the school, but despite my inexperience in such matters, I couldn't foresee any major problems. Just as long as Andrew Marvell was prepared to play along.

After closing our books at the point where Peter and Mary sleep their first night in the outback after the plane crash, the kids packed up their satchels and left the classroom. The resident poet was about to do the same when suddenly I remembered to call him to order. 'Er, Samuel – I thought you were going to explain those various reasons to me,' I ventured, just as he was reaching the exit.

'Ah, yes!' he bumbled, like a forgetful old intellectual, too concerned with the higher things in life. As he walked across to my table, his satchel strap cut a diagonal strip across his body, creasing into his white shirt and purple blazer. 'It's here somewhere,' he gasped, strangely out of breath. As he fumbled in his satchel, which was still hanging across his little body, I asked him for the reasons. 'Ah, well, sir, you can't always produce this sort of stuff just like that,' he explained, clicking his thumb and forefinger together to accompany the word *that*. He seemed to be sweating, and yet his face betrayed no emotion. He had a flat little nose and goofy teeth, like a rabbit. Scrabbling about in the satchel, he finally produced a single piece of paper. What appeared to be verses had been scribbled down in tight, scabby handwriting, with something akin to notes in the margins. There were small asterisks at the end of some of the lines, and arrows pointing in various directions. It was almost illegible.

'Two things, Samuel. This is a poem, and I asked you for

a composition. Also, it's not in your exercise book. Everyone else handed in theirs as I asked them to.'

The boy considered my objection.

'It's a *draft*, sir. I thought perhaps I could show you it like that, and then maybe work on it some more.'

'Well, that's a reasonable point, Samuel,' I conceded. 'But I didn't ask you for a draft. I asked you for the finished article, and besides, I showed you some ways in which I thought you might do the composition, if you recall. This looks like a poem.'

The boy sighed, as if I really hadn't got the point. 'I know that you asked for a composition, sir, but this has taken me just as much time. I find that poetry expresses things in a better way.'

Nothing could have quite prepared me for this – sitting in an echoing classroom arguing the toss with a tiny eleven-year-old about whether or not he should have submitted his homework to me in poetry or prose – and losing the argument. 'Look,' I tried, as he stood his ground with a little pout and a frown on his Frankenstein brow. 'I'll read your draft and I'll give it back to you tomorrow. And if I think it would have been better as a composition, then you'll have to do it like everyone else. If the poem works, then OK – this time. But you must understand, it's a different skill. We're going to do some poetry this term. But not yet. I want to work on composition writing first.' He seemed to accept this compromise, but his body language was still disagreeing with something. Then suddenly he was gone, leaving me alone with the draft.

The lunchtime bell chimed and I began to salivate at the thought of fishcake, beans and chips. For a growing lad like me, the school canteen had quickly become my favourite haunt. But the scrawny scribble in front of my nose was an issue as yet unresolved. I squinted down at the small white page, splattered with black ink. I'd heard that the myth about poor handwriting was that it often denoted genius. Neither wishing to have this confirmed or denied, I nevertheless imagined, as I clambered slowly over the jagged edges of words and smudges, that I saw a great opening line, followed by another great line. Ignoring my grumbling stomach for the next five minutes, I blinked in closer. Among the crossings out, arrows and myriad alternatives, I definitely saw something like this:

My favourite person

Oh but for a thousand heartaches lost and gone
I would remember thee, as strong as Fate,
And know how Love hath bound my soul
To cobweb chambers, chained my eyes
From those who dream in silent prayer
For what they cannot have.

A cankered time is all my age,
A mother gone, no kith and kin for comfort now.
You see me whole for what I am
Where others mock and feel no pain
For those that they have slain, and who
With backs turned to a distant sun
Go running from themselves.

You see me as I am, to never judge
The things that I should say and do
According to the rules of thumb
That others seem to follow to
A grave of their own making.

I read it again. There was no explanation possible, other than the obvious one that he had copied it from somewhere. And yet that would have been a pretty stupid thing to do in the circumstances. Besides, all the notes, the scribbles and the suggestions came over as utterly genuine. Would he really have gone to such lengths to fool me? And who was the poem about? His father? Jonesy had said that he lived alone with him, and that the mother had left. What was I going to do? The poem was wonderful, in a tortured sort of way. I found it difficult, but it said something. How could an eleven-year-old possibly have come up with this? It wasn't just the control of the metre, but the difficulty of the images. A soul bound to cobweb chambers. Bloody hell. Sitting in the still air of the classroom, the playground across to my left filling up with shouts and games, I stared at the piece of paper in my hand and suddenly began to feel frightened. The poem was so far removed from the day-to-day of the kids who I could now see running around outside that it seemed almost supernatural. On an impulse I walked out of the room and along to the library, to see if Tessa was there. She'd understand. I needed to show this to someone.

Tessa wasn't there, but Julie was. She looked up from an encyclopaedia as I hurried in, and she could see that I was flushed and excited about something. I didn't really want to show it to her, but it was obvious something was up. I hopped around in front of her, as if I had a piece of pornography in my hand.

'What's up, you daft ape?' she asked. 'What have you got in your hand? Something a little bit hot by the looks of it,' she remarked, perceptively.

'It's a poem,' I whispered, looking around to make sure there was no one else within earshot. A couple of sixth-formers were studying quietly at the back. Julie took the piece of paper and immediately frowned. Although she wasn't much older than me, she had a pair of specs that hung from a cord around her neck. When she put them on they lent her an air of wisdom that she otherwise seemed to lack.

'Did you write this?' She scowled. 'You could do with improving your handwriting. I can't read a bloody thing.' I told her that I hadn't written it, but I held back the identity of the author. 'Just as well, because it's crap,' she announced. 'What's this ... *Oh but for a thousand heartaches lost and gone?* Who did you ask to do this? The GCE group?' I told her that it wasn't them. 'Well, what are you trying to tell me?' she snapped, looking irritated at this intrusion into her morning.

'It's by one of the first years. I asked them to do a composition and he gave me this. I don't know what to do,' I confessed. Julie picked up the piece of paper again from the table.

'Well, the first thing I'd tell him to do would be to go home and write a bloody composition, because in case you hadn't noticed, this is a poem. Then the second thing I'd do would be to tell him – this must be a boy – to work on his handwriting and to hand things in when he's come up with a neat version that his teacher can read.

'And the third thing I'd tell him,' she continued, unstoppable, 'is that he shouldn't copy published poetry and pass it off as his own work. Now if you'll excuse me ...'

I picked up the poem from the desk. Maybe she was right. 'Do you know who the poem's by then?' I asked, hovering over her as she went back to her encyclopaedia. Not bothering to look up she snapped: 'Not a bloody clue. But if you've got that degree you claim to have then you can tell from the first couple of lines that it's seventeenth or eighteenth century. Let me look again,' she grumbled. She snatched the poem back and read on a little further, squinting with the effort. She sniffed. 'Well, OK, it's quite good. Sounds like John Donne or someone. I don't know. The title's modern, but it's too self-conscious to be Victorian. Whatever – put him in detention for not doing his work properly. Who wrote it?' she asked. I paused.

'That first-year kid Tessa was talking about. The one who thinks he's Andrew Marvell.' At this, Julie took off her glasses and placed them carefully on the table, the gesture pointing to the fact that she intended to read no further lines.

'Holdsworth or someone, isn't it? We got a report on him from the junior school. Look, the kid's a weirdo. Maybe he did do it. But it's just bits stuck together. He doesn't know what he's saying. He needs bringing back into the real world. Tell him to do the composition.'

I decided to leave it at that. I took the poem home that night and decided to have a longer look at it. If he had written it himself, he at least deserved some sort of feedback. I could correct his poem, then tell him to do the composition, as Julie had suggested. Bring him back into the real world? Well, I could see the point in that, but I didn't feel qualified to do it. The only thing I really felt capable of doing was to give him some observations on the poem. He'd given it to me, in the end, so what was he expecting – a mark out of ten and a 'Good, but must try harder' sort of comment? I made a mug of coffee, put on some quiet music and sat down on the comfy sofa of my new flat-cum-bedsit. It was turning dark outside, and a stiff breeze was blowing on to the high attic window to my right. The street below was stained with leaves and the air was chilly. The gas fire was hissing to my left. I looked at the second stanza, '*A cankered time is all my age*', and I could see the point that Julie had made, in her stroppy dismissal. It was a bit melodramatic. But the next line, presumably about his own mother, with the sudden change to focus on the 'Favourite Person' theme, struck me as wonderful. '*You see me whole for what I am.*' This must have been a jibe at his classmates maybe, who mocked him only because they '*Go running from themselves*'. That was the line that got to me. I knew absolutely nothing about child psychology, but my instinct told me that the average eleven-year-old could not possibly understand what that line meant.

Maybe he'd just 'stuck bits together' then, as Julie had said? I looked again and it seemed to me that if he'd really done this then he'd stuck it together very well. The last verse seemed to be saying that his favourite person, whoever it was, occupied a place in his heart because he or she believed in him, unlike all the rest. And the whole poem seemed to be confirming this, if I'd understood it correctly. It was oddly old-fashioned, and it was indeed self-conscious, but it was a pretty strong statement. Most of the other kids had written opening lines to their compositions along the lines of: '*My favourite person is my dad. I like him because he can fix my bike and because he has a good sense of humer.*' Fine, thank you, eight out of ten, and be careful with your spelling in future. What was I going to say to Holdsworth?

'Samuel. This is a decent attempt to write in the style of the metaphysical poets, although certain phrases come over as a little too modern, such as the post-Freudian *running from themselves*. Eight out of ten and try to be a little less self-consciously miserable in future. Oh, and by the way, next time do it in PROSE!'

In the staffroom the next morning, over pre-registration coffee, Lund made a rare appearance. 'I hear that our poet has added to his works,' he quipped, smiling but waiting to see how I responded.

'Well, yes,' I answered, over my mug. 'The problem is that it's brilliant,' I decided to say, which was a way of gauging what Julie might have told him.

Lund looked into his beard for inspiration. 'That may be true, and I'd like to see it. But by all accounts, he's not to be encouraged. I mean that at the other school they simply couldn't get anything else out of him. Apparently he drove the child psychologist to distraction. I think she's still under-going treatment. Be careful.'

At this point, I thought it reasonable to complain. 'Why didn't anyone warn me about him then?' I asked, as casually as possible. Lund frowned, picking up on the hint of criticism.

'Because it's too bloody weird!' he hissed. 'You're going to have to cope with it. He really thinks he's reincarnated. He knows everything about Marvell. Right down to the socks he used to wear. At his previous school they couldn't dissuade him. Apparently he used to tell the other kids to call him Andrew.'

So I was going to have to cope with it. Funnily enough, on the way to teaching the first years that day I almost bumped physically into Pud, as we both hurtled around a corridor corner. Both applying the brakes, it was incumbent upon someone to say something, and to Pud's great credit he managed, 'Oh hello, Mr Ball. Hope you've been professional today!', before moving to the side and carrying on his way. He wouldn't forget, and I knew that he'd exact some kind of revenge. It was just a matter of time.

If I was capable of nothing else, I thought it important to be professional with Samuel. But that would have required me to ignore his poem and tell him to do the work properly. I wasn't up to it. During the lesson we read *Walkabout* again, but this time I stopped the reading more frequently to check understanding. Deliberately picking on pupils to answer each question, it was only natural that I should try one on our poet. He seemed to be reading with the rest, but I wasn't sure.

'Samuel,' I asked suddenly. 'Why do you think that Mary is pretending that everything is all right?' The boy twitched slightly from behind his book. He had it propped up in front of him. Receiving no reply, I tried to help a little. 'I mean, why doesn't she just tell her little brother the truth? That they're stranded miles from anywhere.' At this, various pupils shot their arms up into the air, some of them straining to answer. After what seemed like an age, Samuel looked over his book as if he were staring into some other strange, alien world.

'I don't know, sir,' he announced. The other pupils became more desperate to answer.

'You don't know?' I repeated, disbelievingly, but he failed to take the bait. I asked another pupil to tell him.

'It's because Peter's little, sir, and he doesn't understand the dangers, sir. So if Mary tells him, sir, he's going to be upset!' gabbled another tiny boy, flushed with the excitement of telling me.

'Yes, good – that's right. Understand now, Samuel?'

'Yes, sir. Thank you, sir,' replied the metaphysical poet from another century.

When the class ended, I made sure he couldn't escape by walking over to him and telling him to wait until the others had gone. His little face dropped, and his buck teeth seemed to nibble on something. This time I took the work to his desk, at the back of the class.

'I liked this a lot,' I began. 'When I managed to make out what you'd written, of course.' He stared ahead, like a rabbit in the headlights.

'It's a draft, sir.' I told him I knew this. Then to the heart of the matter.

'You know, I've tried to write poetry too. I've been trying for years actually, Samuel. But I've never written anything as good as this. I'm not really sure how to mark it either. You say it's a draft, but to be honest, I'm not sure that you can make it much better. Perhaps the only thing that's missing is the aspect that I asked for. I mean that I still don't know who your favourite person is. It's not entirely clear from the poem, is it?'

He chewed on this one for a few seconds. 'It's about my father, sir.'

'Well, of course it's not my business now to ask you why your father is your favourite person, but you were supposed to tell me in the composition. And if you remember, I asked you to write down some examples of that person's behaviour, or virtues, or attractive features, whatever.' It wasn't strictly true that he'd neglected this, of course. He'd said in the poem that his father didn't judge him. It was the line that I liked the best.

Suddenly, as if someone had pulled a lever and the illuminations had come on, he began to babble. 'It's because he takes me everywhere, sir. On 16 August every year in the summer holiday he takes me down to St Giles-in-the-Fields – that's near Tottenham Court Road, sir – and we stay overnight near Bloomsbury, near Great Russell Street where he lived, sir. And on 31 March we go to Winestead, sir, but it's nothing now. You can't see his birthplace, because the rectory's been demolished. But we go to St Patrick's in Patrington – that's close by, sir, and the spire is one of the best in the country. He liked it there too.'

'Who? Who liked it? I'm sorry, I don't understand.'

At which point he drew breath, and pronounced the name as if he were talking about a famous footballer that I should have known about.

'Andrew Marvell, sir,' he pronounced proudly, without so much as a hint of discomfort in his voice.

'Your favourite poet then?' I enquired. For the first time since I'd become aware of this strange child, he looked up and gifted me some eye contact. Something must have worked.

'Ah!' he breathed, like an old man. And then he smiled at me, as if he were giving me some kind of endorsement. 'He was a good poet, but there are others that I like too. No – it's much more than that. Much more.' At this he looked down again, as if to signal the end of the confession. I nodded, pleased to have established this much with him.

'Well, look, Samuel, it's time you went to break now. Why don't you write it out for me, in neat? And next time, I'd like to see how well you can write a composition.' His face had gone blank again. 'The poem was good stuff, really. I liked it a lot.' Beyond the boy's head, out in the autumnal playground, eleven-year-olds were starting to play, running around, setting up goals with jumpers, thumping each other, shouting mild obscenities – doing what kids do.

According to the rules of thumb, that others seem to follow.

'We'll do some poetry later in the year, OK? But if you want to show me some more, any time, I'd be honoured,' I finished, laying it on a bit thick. If he really was bloody Andrew Marvell, I didn't want him thinking I was a prick. There were too many already who thought that.

I looked up some stuff about Marvell, went to see his statue in Hull, and one weekend even drove out east in the Beetle to the flatlands of the Holderness peninsula to find the church of St Germain, where Marvell was baptised. It was a godforsaken landscape, windswept and depopulated, like a Pacific atoll that no one could use for the next 3,000 years because of nuclear testing. As a kid, playing on the beach at Cleethorpes, I'd grown accustomed to the sight of the Spurn Head lighthouse opposite, a couple of miles across the grey tide and mudbanks. On a clear day you could see the skinny leg of land whose toe it sat upon, but it seemed like some sort of faraway mystical kingdom. Before the Humber Bridge, it would have been a four-hour drive around the river inlet and on past Hull to get there. Not that anyone ever tried.

And now I could see why. Philip Larkin, my own personal hero, whom I had resolved to ask to sign my copy of the *Whitsun Weddings* every day when I was at Hull University – and to whose office I would take the library lift every morning just to catch a sight of his famously bald pate – had said that he moved to Hull because he liked living 'on the edge of things'. I understood him more now that I had seen Holderness, and other lines started to make sense too:

Hull, with its face half-turned towards silence

There were occasional hamlets with dreary modern pebble-dashed houses, surrounded by flat fields of cabbages and lettuce. There was nothing at all. I had never seen any place so sombre and so silent. There was nothing here to attract a normal child, nothing that could have seriously moved Mr Holdsworth and his son to come along at the weekends, to sit in dull musty churches side by side and get some sort of kick out of it.

On my first outing to the peninsula I carried on driving, right to the end where the lighthouse stood. The road fizzled out into a track, at the end of which stood some high dunes. These led over to the thin end of the spit. I parked the car and scrambled up on to a hillock of sand. On one side, in the distance across the flat water, I could make out the faint beige of my childhood beach, and to the other the wilder North Sea. Some ships were queuing at the mouth of the river, waiting for the tide to swell. I guessed there was someone in the lighthouse but there was no one else around. It was like being at the end of the world. As the early winter wind gusted across the dunes I wondered for a moment what the hell I was doing there – and why in God's name was I so interested in this kid? Maybe because professional life was turning out to be a little lonely, and anything seemed like a welcome distraction.

I even read some of Marvell's poetry – finally getting round to it four years after my tutor at Lancaster had asked me to read a selection – and I noticed that his most famous poem *To His Coy Mistress*, contained two lines I'd heard before but hadn't known were his:

> *But at my back I always hear*
> *Time's wingèd chariot, hurrying near*

No need to worry about the chariot, though, if you could rely on reincarnation. I was also hoping to meet Samuel's father at the first year parents' evening, but he'd failed to show. I'd quite fancied meeting him, but had suspected he wouldn't come.

Meanwhile, his son had almost completely ignored my peace treaty and done very little of the work I'd asked him to do. He avoided my eye, sat alone at the back and paid no attention, and by Christmas I'd given up on him. When we finally did some poetry, and I asked them to write me some blank verse describing their sensations as they came to school (through eyes, ears, nose, mouth etc) he handed in a piece of paper with the following two lines written on it:

> *I cannot respond to bland pronouncements*
> *What I see and hear are too far away*

As with Plant, I felt that I'd failed, albeit for different reasons. And it wasn't just me. All the rest of the staff were tearing their hair out. Almost every week for PE he turned up with a hand-written note signed by his father, to the effect that Samuel had not been feeling well and could not do sport. In physics he had handed in the results of an experiment about melting ice with a short poem about how nothing could really disappear, because of the infinite sub-division of cells, and in maths he'd practised the daily art of staring into space, completely disconnected. There was talk of calling in a psychologist, or of even suspending him, but he was no trouble in the conventional sense of the word. The other kids seemed to view him as an eccentric to be avoided – not that he bothered them with his presence. Once, sitting marking some work in my room, I heard a noise outside and saw one of the older boys pull off the poet's satchel, undo the straps and turn it upside down, emptying out all the books and detritus onto the ground. I thought about intervening, then stayed put as the bully and his mate marched off, leaving Marvell to pick up his things in a stoical sort of way. I decided not to get involved.

I saw no more of his major works, which was a shame because I'd thought the first one wonderful. I copied out the neat version of the original poem that he wrote me, and kept it in a scrapbook. But I got no closer to that strange and difficult child that year, although his presence at the back of my class continued to spook me. There were other matters to deal with, above and beyond reincarnated poets, and some other interesting children at the school, but very different ones. Very different indeed.

10
CONNECTING

My fifth-year CSE literature group had begun to cause me problems. Despite the mixed-ability policy of the department, a line had needed to be drawn somewhere, and I'd inherited a group of ne'er-do-wells, sitting out their final school year in a fog of fear and loathing that was threatening to engulf me as well. They'd been OK for a while, but things were beginning to stir. It was the darker side of the school, the part that the sun rarely lit. I'd expected something of a sub-culture under the polished surface. But in amongst the shadows lurked something that I'd not been expecting at all.

I discovered it by chance. This was because one of the things that I did remember to do was dinner duty. The roster was printed up on my timetable, so even I was aware of it. When the weather was fine, the strictly observed rule was that no pupils were to be found inside during dinner hour – since unwatched children can get up to unspeakable things inside empty classrooms. Dinner duty involved the teacher patrolling the school buildings jangling keys with an air of authority. I'd seen several colleagues doing this, and I quite fancied having a go myself.

Things were going fine on my debut. It had been a long wait, but at last I was to get the chance to jangle some keys. It was a clear day, and no one appeared to be inside breaking the rules. Until I started hearing the noises. Quiet but insistent at first, they sounded like the tiny squeaks of a small animal or perhaps a door hinge. As I halted my steps and cocked an ear to work out which direction they were coming from, the noises stopped. Perhaps I had imagined it. But when I carried on down the whispering corridor they immediately started again. Heading in their vague direction, I arrived at the end of the corridor where a left turn took me to the foot of a staircase. To my horror, I came upon the cause of the noise. What seemed like a small tribe of pygmies was swarming on the stairs and banisters, sliding and frolicking in a curious semi-silence, totally absorbed in some happy ritual. As soon as they spotted me the squeaking noise morphed into a higher-pitched whooing and burbling, like a group of agitated owls. 'What are you doing here?' I blurted. 'You're supposed to be outside!' Momentarily cowed, they froze. They were all tiny, with the same shocks of black hair and olive-coloured skin, and they appeared to be drowning in their purple blazers. One of them was hanging from the banister above, suspended in mid-air over my head. 'Get out now!' I insisted, my voice faltering as I took in the scene. On this, the pause button lifted and the freeze-frame returned to 'Play'. The burbling re-started and they shot up the stairs. I gave chase, but it was hopeless. They were too fast and nimble for me. They knew every nook of the building far better than I did, and they flew down the corridors ducking and swerving, opening and closing doors to confuse me. Whenever I got close to making a capture they scattered from my grasp like mercury from a broken thermometer. Deciding to rescue my dignity, I gave up the ghost and walked back defeated to the staffroom. As I did, I could hear the strange music of their burbling begin again.

Worried that I would be taken to task for allowing some children to stay inside, I looked inside the staffroom for a confidant. Sipping on a mug of coffee by the window sat Stan Burns.

'What's up?' he asked, reading my face.

'Oh, nothing really,' I gasped, still out of breath. 'It's just that there was a group of tiny kids swarming all over the stairs. When I told them to get out they just took the piss and disappeared upstairs.'

Burns let go a guffaw. 'Ah, Bally! It's the bloody gypos! Don't worry about them. It's against their religion to go out into the fresh air at lunchtime. And anyway, they'd get the shit beaten out of them, so they're better off inside. Exception to the rule.'

I sat down, relieved. 'Nobody warned me,' I complained.

'Wouldn't have made any difference, mate,' replied Burns, cheerfully. 'They're a law unto themselves. They only listen to me, and then only on a good day. Do you want me to kick them out?' I told him no, and to finish his coffee. Just so long as I knew. Despite making me look daft, I'd no wish to subject them to the perils of the playground.

I liked Burnsy, as he was called, of course. There was no side to him. Like a good northerner, everything was up front and he'd already told me his life history. He was the kind of bloke you would have wanted on your side. Raised amid the tatters of post-war ration books and bulldozed, bomb-damaged Hull, he was part of a generation of the working class who had grown up to understand the importance of mates. You did a favour for them – because you could fix the plumbing or you knew someone who could – and then your mates would return the favour, sooner or later. The service industry was a distant fantasy, and this was the way that neighbourhoods used to work, before Rottweilers, out-of-town hypermarkets and the flag of St George killed them off for ever.

Burnsy was in his early forties and wore the look of an ex-boxer. He was squat and powerful, with a quiet menace, when he needed it, in his pockmarked face. His cheeks sagged slightly, lending him the doleful air of a basset hound, and his eyes were kind and alert. He was somehow reassuring the minute you met him. You wanted him to look after you, to soothe you with his unpretentious chat. He'd been friendly from the off, where others had been more cautious. He was all firm handshakes and a lack of bluff. Back in September he'd asked, 'How are your kids?', answering his own question with, 'They're smashing, most of them. You can't go wrong' – which is exactly the kind of thing you want to hear over those first lonely mugs of coffee.

He hadn't always been a teacher. He'd started out as centre-forward for York City in the early 1960s, and it had all begun with great promise – scoring on his debut. He still had the faded cuttings from the *Yorkshire Post* which he brought in to show me after I'd expressed an interest. But in his second season things had begun to go wrong and he was ousted by another young-ster who went on to become a legend at the club. Cycling to training one morning, an elderly supporter had flagged him down from the pavement. 'Listen, lad,' the man began. 'Take it from me. You're never going to make it. Don't waste your time around here. Get yourself another job. Get yourself a trade, lad, while you can.' And he did. After another year of occasional appearances and further humiliations he signed up for night classes back in Hull, eventually passing enough A-levels to allow him to take the old Teaching Certificate.

At the time I joined the school, he was working in what they used to call the Remedial Department, back in the days when they still thought you could remedy things. This was the most feared assignment among the staff, even in a school like Willerton. Though the classes consisted of only a dozen or so kids, there was always a hint of trouble involved. But it wasn't just about hard-line peacekeeping. One of the better days I remembered from the PGCE course had been when a remedial teacher had come in to give us a talk, in case there'd been anyone interested in taking up such a post. So I under-stood that certain kids had learning difficulties, which I supposed required a softer touch and a dose of patience. At Willerton, the remedial groups spent most of their time separated from the mainstream classes, forming their own small society within the school – a little sub-set who needed to trust the teachers assigned to them.

Burnsy was obviously cut out for this kind of thing, and was the only person with whom the gypsies had managed to set up some sort of working relationship. The notorious McFee clan lived in a corral of caravans on the edge of the city, where the fathers had managed to scrape some sort of living from the used-car-auction business in Hull. A couple of years later, when the Beetle finally died, I went to a night auction and saw them all there, all the pygmies I had tried to catch back on that first day – but when I tried to acknowledge them they just looked through me, as if I didn't exist. Their parents barked orders to them and kept them close, as if they mistrusted the whole world. I can still see them, huddled together in the frosty northern night.

Burnsy asked me the following week if I would like to go to one of his classes, 'to see how the other half lives,' as he put it. The class that I was to observe was with the gypsies and the lesson was what he called 'word extension', which he apparently did every Wednesday. The idea was to enrich their vocabulary with standard word-building exercises, using synonyms and antonyms – moving on to ground where children from these backgrounds rarely trod. That was the theory anyway. I sat at the back of the room as the class got under way and surveyed the scene. Almost all of the extended family was there, ranging in ages from thirteen to sixteen. The largest of the platoon and leader of the pack was the interestingly named Elvis Presley McFee. Weighed down by the weight of his name, he was slumped in his chair, pubescence sprouting wildly from every visible orifice. The class was oddly quiet, not what I'd expected at all. But as Burnsy gave out some books and chivvied them into life, Elvis suddenly nodded in my direction and mumbled, in the burbling tone I remembered from the staircase:

'Who the bugger is he then?'

Burnsy ignored the bugger bit. 'That's Mr Ball, the new English teacher. He said he was interested in seeing the class, OK? Now shall we make a start?' Elvis shuffled in his seat and scratched his head, seemingly satisfied with the answer. To my left, one of the older girls, Marion, was beginning to burble too. Burnsy had warned me that she had taken a fancy to me, but I wasn't quite sure what to make of this privilege. Only a couple of days after the original dinner-duty incident she had scuttled past me in the corridor with her younger sister and murmured 'Ooooh, Mr Bollocks'. Having learned my name from some unknown source, she had decided to take the piss, even though apparently smitten. Small and dark with a sadly weathered face, she was warming up again, avoiding eye contact by staring down into her desk. 'Ooooooh Mr Bollocks ... ooo ... ooo,' she warbled, too low for Burnsy to hear at the front. I decided to smile at her personal example of word extension, at which she appeared to go into small convulsions, still staring at the desk and wailing quietly, like an ambulance in the distance.

When the class finally got under way, it all seemed

frighteningly efficient. Blessed with the confidence and experience that a rookie like myself could only dream of, the bluff
working man seemed transformed. Much more articulate
than he had bothered to be in the staffroom, he rolled down
his moveable blackboard at every opportunity like some
enthused professor, tossing new words out into the air as if
they were gifts from another world, gift horses that the pupils
should not look in the mouth. And talking of horses, one of
the featured words was *stallion*. As the ten pupils gawped in
silence at the show, Burns decided it was question time.

'Elvis,' he began. 'Can you tell me what a stallion is?'
Elvis could not, or at least would not, and remained silent.
'Come on, Elvis. What's a stallion? We've just had a list of
words that describe certain types of animals, haven't we?
We've had *ewe* and *vixen*. So, stallion?' The apparent logic of
the explanation was not apparently logical to Elvis, but he
murmured something unintelligible and stared at the desk,
like my new girlfriend Marion. Most of them, in fact, had
spent the class staring downwards, as if they were being
punished. It was a diffident look, one that seemed to indicate
a congenital reluctance to look the world in the eye. After an
awkward silence, Burnsy brought me in. 'Mr Ball knows what
a stallion is, don't you, Mr Ball?' Nobody seemed impressed
by this. As I nodded, the ten faces continued to stare at the
floor. Suddenly, Elvis shot back in his chair as if he had been
electrocuted and shouted:

'What you asking me that for? Everyone knows what one
of them is!'

Stan Burns walked over to Elvis and grinned in his face. 'Well, come on then. Just in case they don't know, you'd better tell us. What is a *stallion*?'

Elvis began to rock back and forth in his chair in an alarming fashion, muttering a string of bubbling sounds in rehearsal for the big moment.

'It's the 'oss that fucks the mare!' he blurted out, as if Burns were an idiot. 'It's the 'oss that fucks the mare! What you ask me that for?'

As that first year trundled by, I could see that Stan Burns had one of the toughest posts – not because the gypsies were particularly threatening, but because you could tell that behind the tough-bloke humour there was a guy with a vocation, to use the word that the *Daily Express* had been bandying about when talking of the teaching profession. Burnsy wouldn't muck you up. Far from it. You could see that he believed that he had a duty to a group of youths, but that it was all as hopeless as trying to get Plant to behave or Andrew Marvell to do his homework. The gypsies could never really come over to his side, however much they might secretly have craved the touch of social acceptance. Their culture permitted them to attend school and pay lip-service to it, but they only understood survival. They trusted Burnsy, but they weren't allowed to show it. So they came to class, at least – and participated in its baffling rituals.

This makeshift relationship worked well enough. The one recurrent problem that vexed Burnsy, however, was the fact that the gypsies never came in on Fridays. They also stayed away when it rained. Various teachers in the staffroom would offer their theories as to why. One was convinced that it was linked to some superstition, whereas another thought that it was because it was easier to catch fish in the river when it rained. But the Friday absence was the most baffling. All Burns's enquiries and entreaties to the class on this subject had been met with silence, the gypsy *omertà*. The school could have kicked up a fuss and insisted on their attendance five days a week, or demanded some kind of justification for the kids' absence, but Beacroft was a pragmatist and knew it wasn't worth it. Some of the other remedial kids had protested. If the gypsies didn't have to come in on Fridays, why did they? But that first year I was there seemed to pass by without the problem coming to a head. It was just that Stan Burns felt bad about it, as if he'd failed somehow. 'It's thirty-eight days,' he pointed out, one night in The Bell. 'All those Fridays add up to thirty-eight days of the bloody school year, when Elvis just might have picked up something useful, the poor bastard.'

What added to his woes that year was that Burns's marriage appeared to be under threat. This was unsurprising, given his alleged appetite for bedding a sizeable chunk of the female population of Hull. From the beginning of the Thursday night drinking sessions to my gradual acceptance in the Dirty Corner, it had become clear that Stan was the Man. Since I thought that at the age of twenty-three it was all downhill from then on, it came as something of a rude awakening to find that a squat, flat-nosed remedial teacher in his mid-forties with a pockmarked face and a sumo wrestler's belly, was up there in the Lothario stakes with Warren Beatty. As was the case with Nobby at Birds Eye, women apparently found Burnsy irresistible. It was a new lesson in life, for men in their twenties are still sadly convinced that women are interested in looks. Stan Burns was the perfect example of a different type of anthropology. You could see it in the staffroom, in the pub, with the dinner ladies, anywhere you went with him. He had the chat, the instinctive touch. Women liked the fact that he took a real interest in them, that he was funny, that he was polite, but above all that he would look after them if they asked him to. He wouldn't let you down if you were in trouble. But polygamy has its limits in the modern world, and Burnsy's wife had probably had enough of him looking after everybody else.

Fast-forward to the summer term, and as the final week of term approached, Burnsy had gypsies and marriage on his mind. Added to that, it was his birthday on the last Wednesday. He had let this slip to the Dirty Corner, and also to the remedial class one day during a lesson on the zodiac signs. Apparently, Elvis had hung behind after the bell. 'I see him standing by the door,' Burnsy began one lunchtime, 'and I ask him why he's not going off to his next lesson. He looks at the floor and then he tells me that he's leaving at the end of the week. Shan't be coming back, he says. I know that, Elvis, I say to him. You're sixteen now. It's time for the big wide world. Anyway, haven't you got reading now with Miss Barmby? – and he shuffles. He only shuffles when he's worried about something, or when you ask him what something means. After a moment or so he mutters to me, can't buy you nowt, sir. I'm relieved, and of course I tell him that the last thing I expect is for the class to buy me a birthday present. "It's not a problem, Elvis, really. But thanks anyway, mate," I tell him, trying to end the matter. But Elvis stands his ground. "It's a problem for me," he says. So I ask him in what sense it's a problem and he mutters into his chin, "Can't go without paying respects".'

At this point in the tale Burnsy seemed to get embarrassed, but it wasn't really necessary to carry on explaining to us. It was well known that he'd been kind to Elvis and his clan, so that the elder was honour-bound to repay him in some way. But he had no money. Burnsy told us the solution. 'Look Elvis,' he said to the boy. 'Do you really want to do something for me, something for my birthday?' Presley McFee did. 'Well – it's this Wednesday, OK? But you can do something for me this Friday, on the last day.' The boy had looked up, as if he knew what the teacher was going to say. 'You come in. You all come in. If you do that, it'll be the best birthday present I've ever had.' Presley McFee said nothing, and slid away.

Through that final week the drama of it all was getting to everyone. Some were even taking bets on the outcome – offering odds on all of them coming, on some of them coming, or on simply Elvis turning up alone. Burnsy was mildly amused at the fuss, but something in his manner told you he was taking it more seriously inside. It was Elvis's last day. Would he or wouldn't he break the code? He'd never been in on a Friday for five years.

On the Thursday, Elvis turned up for class, but said nothing on the way out – which was par for the course. On the Friday, I watched Burnsy walk to morning registration like a man condemned. In his fonder, more foolish moments, I guessed he'd really believed that he'd got across to them in some way, that he'd made some impact on their secret lives. To him it was important, and I was impressed. It had made an impact on my secret life at least. But I'd seen by then that he was no mug, and that he was hardbitten enough to know that most of his attempts to connect with them had been a waste of breath. Yet as he walked into the classroom, there was Elvis, sitting at the front with two of his younger brothers. The rest had stayed away. Burnsy had said nothing. There was no need.

11

INSPECTING

'Do you smoke dope as well, sir?' asked Gray as I tried to focus the class on the delights of Stan Barstow's *Joby*, a standard book for CSE groups, I assumed, because its main character was a kid who was threatening to go off the rails. All the books that they were expected to read on their two-year course had a grimy-northern-truant-problems-at-home feel to them, as if the only thing that non-academic children would want to read about were broken homes and failure. You almost expected them to smile at you one day and ask, 'Are you trying to tell us something, sir?' But they didn't, of course. They asked you if you took drugs, if you had a girlfriend, if you liked fish and chips – anything to avoid doing what they were supposed to be doing.

'What do you mean by *as well*?' I asked in answer to Gray's question. I thought a lighter approach might work with this pupil. 'Do I smoke dope as well as *what*?' I repeated, recklessly. The class reading was going nowhere. We might as well have a break. Phil Gray sat at the back, of course. He was blond and blue-eyed, with cheekbones perfectly chiselled around a disarming smile. Around him sat his harem, a small coterie of gum-chewing girls to whom he referred cheerfully as 'my slags'. They seemed to like this. The rest of the group was scattered thinly around the classroom, some slumped over their desks, some with their feet up on nearby chairs, others staring into space. There were about fourteen of them, none of whom could strictly have been described as troublemakers. They simply couldn't be arsed. Come the summer and they'd be out of there, into the world of apprenticeships and jobs that some of them were already doing on a part-time basis.

'What I mean, sir,' explained Gray, 'what I mean is … What do I mean, Mandy?' he laughed, turning to one of his girls. Mandy swooned slightly and chewed on her cud. 'He means, sir, do you do drugs like Mr Tapley did?' The group had been taught by the previous English teacher for the first year of their course, but he had abandoned them in the summer, leaving them to complete their final year with over half of their project and essay work still to do. The only information I'd managed to gather about my predecessor was that he'd 'gone back down south' where he had 'other interests' to pursue. Until the CSE group began to open up and talk, I'd never thought to enquire why I'd been employed at such short notice, but now it appeared that my predecessor had done a runner for reasons unclear. The only thing I could get out of the Thursday night crowd was the refrain 'Don't talk about that cunt', and so I did as I was told.

I sighed and placed *Joby* down on my desk, spine up. 'I'm

really not sure you should talk about other teachers in that way,' I ventured, half-heartedly. 'Anyway, what makes you think I do drugs at all? Do I look so bad?' I appealed, deciding to take a break. It was the last week of September, I took the group only once a week, and up to then they'd been fine, in an idle sort of way.

Gray smiled. 'You look great, sir – don't worry about it. I was just wondering, though, that if you did do drugs, like – well, I could sell you some for half price, that's all.' At this, the harem exploded into a collective cackle, some of them leaning over and slapping their hero on the back in congratulation at this latest pearl of wisdom. 'Sir,' he resumed, as one or two of the others around the class began to stretch and yawn, 'how much do they pay you for doing this? I mean, really, sir?' Mandy and the harem sat up straight at this. This was a question they could relate to.

'Ah, well, that would be telling,' I replied. 'Perhaps we should get back to *Joby*.' But Gray was not to be deflected from this one.

'No sir, really,' he intoned, trying to sound serious. He looked like a less intense version of James Dean. 'It's just that next year I'm starting out doing some building with the old man, like, and I'm going to be on about eight grand.' The harem melted. Visions of sports cars, soft tops, wind in the hair. Gray continued with his lecture. 'What's the point in all of this anyway?' He shrugged, for a moment becoming philosophical. 'What's the point in wasting time at university, like you did? All those years, sir, and you end up sitting at that desk teaching us. And you're not even on eight grand, I'll bet.'

He was absolutely right. I wasn't earning anywhere near that figure, but I thought it wise to keep him in the dark, just as I thought it equally wise not to ask him how much he was selling his dope for. But the point about university needed answering.

Besides, I thought it might wake up the rest of the class. 'Why was it a waste of time? I mean university?' I asked, looking around for an answer from someone else. Gray tended to dominate proceedings, to say the least. The other boys in the class accepted him as the chief lion in the pride, and quietly accepted their role as the losers. They watched the lionesses from afar, pushed out from the inner circle.

Getting no response, I reformulated the question. 'If you go to university, or college, whatever – you get the chance to move to another town, see how the other half lives. You get time to think about things, to read, to talk about things. It can be exciting,' I lied. 'There's plenty of time ahead for working nine to five. And besides, money isn't everything.' I watched Gray as I said this. He possessed an uncanny ability to do several things at once, none of which were related to the matter in hand, and yet still take in exactly what you'd said. If it interested him, he would respond. Deciding to stop tickling one of his lionesses, he looked up, stuck up the two-finger peace sign, and with his free hand pretended to draw deeply on a large joint.

'Yeah man,' he drawled. 'Peace and love and everything

else. So you get a university grant, sod off for three years and talk about what?' His slags agreed, chorusing a loud 'Yeah!' in solidarity. Before I had the chance to argue back, he supplied the *coup de grace*. 'You know what my old man says about students? He says they're a waste of taxpayers' money.' At this he swung back on his chair and casually announced, 'If you're going to buy dope then I reckon you have to earn it. I don't think the taxpayers should be buying students' drugs for 'em.' The slags applauded, some of them wolf-whistling. The scraggier lions looked up, distracted momentarily from their belly scratching. They seemed vaguely interested in seeing how I was going to respond.

'Well, that's a fair point,' I conceded, sitting up on the edge of a pupil's desk and assuming a slightly higher position. I'd found this posture a useful one. It made you look more relaxed than if you hid at the front in your official chair, and it also raised you above the level of your charges. It also signalled that you'd had enough of the official programme for the day, and were prepared to talk about something real. 'But aren't you closing down your options?' I tried. Immediately to my left someone asked, 'What does that mean, sir?' This was Paul Baker, a small cherubic lad whose voice had yet to break but who defiantly did all that he was asked. He'd read the books, handed in the work, and was probably in the wrong group. Vaguely resentful, he clung on desperately to the notion that every class was worthwhile, and that he would pass his exams. I could see that he hated these distractions because he was still dreaming of university.

I walked back to the board and wrote up the phrase, then I wrote up the word *options* three times.

'If you close them down, this is what happens,' I illustrated, smugly. 'You decide at sixteen that you want to do what Phil says he wants to do. Well, maybe that's OK,' I said, but crossed off one of the option words. 'Then you buy your house, settle down happily ever after, let's say at the age of twenty-one, and maybe that's OK,' I repeated, crossing off another of the words. 'And then you're left with just one. That's what closing down your options means.' Baker scribbled down some notes in his exercise book.

Gray wasn't having this at all. He rose up from among his throng. 'That's crap, sir,' he announced, pointing at the blackboard. 'You mean that if I've got myself a job, found myself a woman and bought a house I've done summat wrong? I don't get that.' I shrugged and smiled, as if my little example had won the day. He sat down again, but he hadn't finished. 'It's *you* that's closed down your options,' he barked, squinting slightly and reading the phrase from the board. It was the first time he'd ever looked in its direction. 'And now you've got to teach tossers like us.' He grinned, returning to his normal self.

'Speak for yourself!' piped up Baker's little voice to my side, clearly tiring of the debate. At this act of defiance he was howled down by the pack, Gray almost sending out one of his lionesses to hunt him down.

'OK, OK! Quiet!' I shouted above the din, but I'd lost it. Gray went back to his harem and left me with five unforgiving minutes to fill. 'Right,' I asserted, pathetically. 'Let's just finish this page of *Joby*.'

The problem was that I liked Phil Gray. The other problem was that he'd done absolutely none of the work that he was supposed to have filed away for the November progress inspection by Lund. After each book read, the pupils' job was to write up a kind of report and summary of the story, the characters, the author's biodata and so on. As part of the rubric they even had to write a couple of lines about the theme of the book, and finish it off with a vague opinion. It was hardly a doctoral thesis – more a kind of routine to keep them occupied, but Gray had still failed to produce evidence of a single line. This was fairly serious, since there should have been a year's work already accumulated. At the end of that second year of their course the files were to be sent away to the CSE examining board and assessed. Since Gray had his job on the building site waiting for him, he wasn't exactly bursting with enthusiasm to write up these summaries – but the twin responsibility of pressuring him and gathering all the group's work together was making me panicky, even though June seemed far away.

However, in the fish and chip shop queue that Saturday evening, as I was scanning the deep-fried goodies on offer, in skipped Gray, splendid in black leather biking jacket. Mandy from the class hung on his arm, gnawing ferociously on her chewing-gum entrée before the salt-and-vinegar delights to come. 'Hey sir!' he greeted me, squeezing me affectionately on the arm. The silent queue shuffled slightly and pricked up its ears. 'Spending that massive salary of yours on good grub, I see!' Mandy continued to chew. 'Haven't you got a missus back home to do the cooking for you then?' he joked. As with the queue at the doctors, people in fish and chip shops prefer to guard their dirty secrets and stay silent. But there was no way out of the trap.

'Ah well,' I replied, as quietly as possible. 'I don't believe in closing down my options' – at which Mandy took no offence, engaged as she was in the tricky task of reading the menu. Fish and chips, or fish and chips with mushy peas? Back in those far-flung days in the north, curry sauce was as futuristic as the internet.

Out of politeness, since Gray seemed genuinely pleased to see me, I waited for them to get their chips and walked a little way down the road with them. 'Where do you live then?' asked Gray, blowing chip steam from his mouth, out into the cold night.

'Down Hull Road,' I decided to reply, as vaguely as possible. He already knew.

'Yeah, you live in that big house, don't you? I've seen you going in there after school. I live further down, like, and I go past on me bike. You're not from round here, are you?' I told him I was from Grimsby. 'Yeah well, you can't help that,' he laughed. 'We'll forgive you. Do you like teaching then? I didn't mean to be nasty, like, the other day. Just that I thought you were saying I was doing the wrong thing, or summat. I mean if you really want to teach, well, I suppose that's all right. Some bugger has to do it.' I hugged the warm wrapping of my fish and chips – destined to be eaten at home – close to my side. It was freezing. Gray had Mandy for warmth. All of a sudden I felt sorry for myself, walking down a street I didn't know, talking to people I didn't really know, all on a Saturday night.

'Teaching's OK,' I managed, speeding up slightly. 'It's just where I've ended up, I suppose, Phil,' I continued, charmed into opening up. Cars whizzed by. 'You've decided what you want to do, and I respect that. I never made that kind of decision. I'm sorry about the other day too. I guess what I was trying to say was aimed at the rest of the class, that's all. Maybe some of them aren't so sure about what they want to do. But if you're happy to go into the building trade then that's fine. I would have been useless at that kind of thing. The only thing I was ever any good at was reading books and writing essays – but you're right. It's probably not the be-all and end-all. And anyway, this is my first year. I'm not exactly an old git or anything. And you're right by the way – the pay's crap.'

The happy couple walked along a little further with me, then turned down a small dark side street which led to Mandy's house. 'See you then, sir,' they both chorused. 'What you gonna do?' asked Gray. 'Watch *Match of the Day*?' I nodded, then made another mistake to add to the burgeoning list. The intimacy of the moment seemed to encourage an attempt at softening Gray up over the CSE work issue.

'Hey – don't forget though. You said you'd show me some of that work you did last year, remember? And you've still got the one to do on *Kes*. So when are you going to hand it all in? Mr Lund's going to check up on you next week – you know that.'

This stopped the couple in their tracks. Gray looked over his chips at me in the dark street.

'Hey, sir! Unfair call!' he groaned. 'We're not talking about school. Sending-off offence!' He smiled, returning to his jollier self. He wagged his finger at me. 'Now you go home and enjoy *Match of the Day*, and forget about those files. It's the weekend!' he quipped, and disappeared into the night. But I was to come to regret that brief encounter, as subsequent events turned out.

This was because I was a probationary teacher, and these poor players do not yet have the job for life until they are officially deemed competent at the end of their debut season. Rixy, Eileen and myself were to be inspected by the local authority educational officers who specialised in our particular subjects. These inspectors were to visit us twice in the year, or more often should we be deemed problem cases. It seemed to me that this was more like the real thing, and that pulling the wool over an inspector's eyes might not be quite the cakewalk it had proved to be with Alice. For all Lund's apparent friendliness and support; I sensed somehow that really he was unsure about me – and that the rifle-butt incident had contributed in large part to his doubts. He'd also dropped into a conversation that the English inspector, a chap by the name of Clive Gibb, was big mates with Dr Mortlock, the director of the PGCE course at Hull, and not one of my admirers. All happy families together then. I wasn't exactly looking forward to his visit, and the mess that the CSE course had become was making me nervous. Besides, the one teacher who was slowly turning into an unlikely friend, John Butler, had summed him up in his usual literary way: 'Be careful, Bally. He's a nasty twat.'

Butler was becoming a friend because like a moth to a blue zapper lamp, I was always attracted to the wrong characters. Unable to find any easy-going types to copy maths from in the more complicated world of the workplace, I latched on immediately to anyone whose attitude seemed to be vaguely against the system, to be vaguely dangerous. My mother wouldn't have liked him, which still seemed a good reason for cultivating him. Instead of finding someone who could sit me down and show me quietly how to play the system and get over the inspector hurdle, I chose the person who had referred to him as a 'twat'. But Butler was an established teacher. He could afford to think like that. He could also afford to play the clown, in his quiet deadpan manner, and get away with it. One day before Christmas, as I was teaching my quiet and worryingly conscientious GCE literature class, the door creaked open and Butler's head appeared in the gap. 'They're back together again.' He frowned, disappearing into the school morning. The class looked up as one from their *Julius Caesars* and raised a communal eyebrow. I shrugged.

At break I walked into the staffroom to a buzz of questions and answers. 'Where's Butler?' someone was saying. 'What's all this shit about some couple being back together again?' Others shot back affirmatives as they poured steaming water on to their Nescafé grains. 'Yeah – he came into mine as well. He said *they're back together again*. Who's he on about?' Butler failed to appear and the speculation continued. No one could think of anyone at the school who had been recently separated, or of any famous people in the news. At last, Butler appeared. He walked across to the coffee table in silence and picked up his mug. Then the questions erupted. 'Butler! What you on about? What did you mean *they're back together again*?'

Butler filled his mug, and walked casually across the gauntlet. 'Norman Scott's buttocks,' he replied, easing himself into his Dirty Corner armchair. The staffroom exploded, dropping their mugs of coffee and sending text-books flying. Butler was the wag, the one that kept the spirits up, in a perverse sort of way.

The Liberal Party leader and his lover aside, the lesson Gibb was timetabled to see was the opener of the day with my first-year group, Andrew Marvell et al. This came as some-thing of a relief, since the thought of him watching me with Gray and his harem brought me out in a cold sweat. Not because they would have misbehaved, but because it would have revealed the fact that I had no resources to deal with them. Maybe he suspected this anyway, and chose to watch me with the little ones. Maybe he figured that a class with them would tell him more. Agonising over what kind of lesson to teach, I sought out the nun, a couple of days before my trial by fire. She was still knitting, this time a woolly hat for her husband, the rampant monk, to keep his tonsure warm. 'Sit down, my love, and calm down,' she opened, high up in the still air of the library where she spent most of her time. 'Now then, he's not the nicest of chaps, that Mr Gibb,' she twittered, unusually critical. This made me feel even worse. 'Now knowing your reputation ...' and at this she winked, 'I wouldn't cross him, my love. Just nod at everything he says, and always agree with him. I don't think he's very bright really – inspectors seldom are – but that's not the point here, pet. The best thing to do is to distract him a little. I mean do lots of things, and never give him a chance to say that any one of them wasn't good enough. That's my advice. Get the little things talking if you can. Gather them around you like Jesus and show that you're in control. But most of all,' and here she paused for effect, closing her eyes again in that pre-orgasmic way that she had, '... use a visual! Put something on the wall and refer to it, my love. Inspectors always like that. Suffer the little children to come unto you. Think of something that you can gather them around.' And with that, she went back to her woolly hat.

I had no idea what she was talking about, but it represented advice. Back in my flat I had a large poster of Renoir's *Dance at Bougival* on the wall, up there to impress potential visitors with my aesthetic tastes. In truth, I'd got it as a free gift when I'd bought my mum a mock-leather pouffe in a clearance sale the year before. Nevertheless, I thought it might work for the class. It was the usual Impressionist stuff, with people sitting around in some French village or other half drunk, whilst the painter homed in on someone having a deeper little moment on their own – in this case a couple of revellers dancing in the foreground. The chap, his face hidden by a large yellow peasant's hat, looked a little bit too enthusiastic, whilst the beautiful pale-faced young woman he was leading seemed to be having her doubts – or maybe not. You could neither tell what she thought of him, nor really see what he thought of her, because of the yellow boater. Perhaps they were strangers, or like Scott's buttocks, they'd just got back together again? I decided to use it for the big day.

Gibb met me as I was scurrying off to registration. As Lund introduced us I held out my hand for the shake, but it was unforthcoming. The inspector was enormous, with large glasses that curled up slightly at the top edges of the rims, in a slightly feminine touch. His hair was thick and full, and he held himself aloft like a man who meant business. He didn't like me. Call it instinct, but the vibes flooded over me right there and then. Looking down at me from his majestic heights, a voice rolled down from the mountains: 'I'll come along in ten minutes or so.' Then he turned his back on me to continue talking to Lund. Fine. I had the poster rolled up in my bag. I would have time to put it up on the wall. If I'd done so the day before there had always been the chance that Wayne Stark or some other bright spark might have decided to add some modernist touches to the canvas.

When I walked into the classroom it was raining outside, a phenomenon guaranteed to make my tutor group annoyingly lively. 'Sit down!' I screamed, to no avail. Tracey was busy recounting some sordid tale to her minions in the far corner, whilst two of the larger male members of the flange of baboons were jumping up and down as if in the latter stages of some mating ritual. I thought about whistling, but went for the simpler, 'Sit down!', at which one of the flange commented, 'All right. Keep your hair on!' They scattered and allowed me to take the register. Leaving them to murmur among themselves now that they were safely seated, I decided to dispense with any moral lesson for the day (I usually did anyway) and took the poster to the back of the class armed with blobs of Blu Tack. Dismissing the class slightly earlier than the bell, so that I could prepare myself for the ordeal to come, I moved back to my desk. As ever Tracey was the last to go, on this occasion, it seemed, because she'd dropped her nail varnish. As she wobbled past me on her unfeasibly high heels she began, 'What's up wi' you this mornin' then? Get pissed up last night again, did yuh?' As she teetered past me, I was about to return the wisecrack when to my horror I saw Gibb standing inside the door. Even worse, Tracey continued. 'Oh hello,' she said, beaming at the frowning inspector. 'Who are you then? You a mate of Bally's?' Gibb strode into the room and past her, without so much as a word. 'Charmin'!' said Tracey, and click-clacked out of the room.

Gibb walked slowly across to me like a dark executioner, but as his mouth began to open the first of my little cherubs began to flood in through the door. I smiled weakly and fussed my way past him, pretending to usher them in. When they had all sat down, I introduced our visitor to them. 'This is Mr Gibb,' I announced, 'and he's come to watch the lesson today. He's a very special visitor, so I want you to be as polite and helpful as possible.' As ever, the little dwarves remained silent, a look of expectation on their morning faces – all except Marvell, of course, who was looking down at his own lap – on which, I suspected, he already had the first stanza of his latest epic penned out. I'd thought to provide a chair for Gibb, but for some reason he looked even more annoyed as I ushered him into it. I was hopping about, hyper with nerves. After some poorly gabbled preliminaries I explained the theme of the day. 'Now we've been looking at the topic of character for the last few weeks, haven't we?' The cherubs said nothing. 'That's right,' I concluded, uselessly. 'We've looked at the characters in the book *Walkabout*, and we've talked about our favourite persons, and ... yes, erm character,' at which point it became fairly obvious that we hadn't been studying character at all, but never mind. Push on. 'I thought we might try to do some prediction today, some speculation. I thought we might try to see if we can work out what people think and what people are like just from looking at them. Do you think we can do that? Anyone?' I asked desperately, appealing for hands to go up. None did. I glanced nervously over at our resident poet who was, of course, paying no attention. I hoped Gibb couldn't see him there at the back, and that his curly glasses were for short-sightedness.

One of the pupils, a boy by the name of Brian Frobisher, was bright and could usually be relied on for a good answer. I decided to pick on him. 'Brian. Do you think that you can tell what someone is like from their appearance?' Little Brian suddenly glanced at me and then across to Gibb, as if he'd understood that I'd wanted him to speculate on the inspector's personality. Realising my mistake too late, there was no time to stop him.

'I think he's very important, sir. He probably reads lots of books and is very patient.'

Searching for a spade to dig myself out, I laughed. 'Ha yes! Very good, Brian.' There was nothing else for it. I turned to Gibb, whose towering body was squeezed painfully into the tiny chair I'd provided for him. 'Is that true, Mr Gibb? Would you rate yourself as a patient person? We know that you're very important.' Gibb looked across at me as if he were witnessing the ravings of a complete imbecile. It was fair enough. There are times in your life when all the wrong things come spewing out of your mouth, at precisely the wrong moment. This was one of them. Pointedly, Gibb straightened his back and looked away from me to his tiny assessor.

'It depends,' he began, in a bored sort of voice. 'It depends on the circumstances,' at which he looked back at me over the top of those curly glasses. From that point onward I had two choices. Tell him to loosen up or fuck off, or get on with the lesson as I'd intended it. I decided to give the teaching profession one last try.

Suffering the little children to come unto me, we walked to the back of the class and formed a circle around my nondivine presence, close to the colourful poster. I wanted to look as Christ-like as possible, on the advice of Tessa. Gibb hung back at a distance, scribbling notes, probably about my halo. He was scribbling far too many for my liking. 'Now this is a painting by a famous French painter called Pierre-Auguste Renoir. Does anybody know when this picture was painted? I mean not exactly. Which century do you think?' Silence. No problem. I knew that Andrew Marvell would know, and now he couldn't hide, exposed as he was in the circle.

'Samuel?' I asked. Some of the pupils tittered. The poet looked around wildly, then realising that there was nowhere his eyes could hide, he answered, 'Nineteenth century, sir. Impressionist.' He twitched and looked at the floor.

'Exactly. Good. Now what do the rest of you make of the picture?' upon which I asked a series of rather more mundane questions, which prompted replies from a range of the urchins gathered. I hoped Gibb would take note of this, that I could get plenty of them to talk, not just the cleverer ones. In fact I began to turn things around. The lesson was work-ing. Good old Tessa. We could celebrate by having wild sex together in the library.

'Do you think the dancers know each other?' I asked, to which a girl answered: 'No. He likes her but she doesn't like him.' When I prompted her further she offered, 'Well, you can tell. I don't think they know each other, and she's moving her face away from him.' Someone thought that it was just the dance. Another thought that she 'fancied him' but that she didn't want to show it. I'd got them talking.

'Maybe he's got smelly breath,' I joked, since the woman

appeared to be intimidated by the proximity of the man's face. The kids tittered. I tied it up by ushering them back to their places and asking for adjectives to describe the two characters, writing them on the board and dividing them up into positive and negative.

Then I asked them to write an introductory paragraph to a potential story, one in which the character of their choice – from the painting – describes how he or she came to be at the dance. By the end of the paragraph, I asked them to begin introducing the other character, as a lead-in to the eventual story. They got on with their task and I walked around busily, instead of opening the newspaper as I normally did when they were working. Being little first years, they didn't dare to comment on this change in my behaviour. From disaster to triumph. I'd pulled it around. I felt that I'd taught a decent lesson.

Even when the last child had gone Gibb continued to write notes, stiff and officious in his chair. I hovered around my desk, fiddled with some books, sniffed a couple of times and waited for the verdict. Eventually, he rose in judgement. Still keeping his distance, as if I might contaminate him with my incompetence, he spoke his first words to the wall behind me. 'Do other members of your tutor group address you as *Bally*?' he asked, with the rising tone of an accusation.

'No, of course not,' I bit back, trying to show him I wasn't to be stamped on completely. 'Just Tracey. You know – nice kid an' all, but there's not much you can do about it, ha ha.' The Lord High Executioner seemed unmoved by this, save a slight twitch of those flighty specs. I noticed they had a vaguely pink tint to them.

'Oh, I would suggest that you *can* do something about it,' he announced. 'You simply make it clear that you're not prepared to put up with such familiarity, and from that day onward she stops it.' Of course he was right, but only in the ideal sort of world that I had never inhabited. Not for the first time in my life, I was more affected by the tone than by the message. Tessa's voice echoed in my head – *Just nod at everything he says* – but I couldn't.

'Maybe that's true,' I began. 'But I don't think she means any harm. She's no trouble really, and the point is that ...' Suddenly he jerked his gaze from the wall behind me and looked me in the face.

'The point is clearly that you have let her get away with behaving largely as she wishes to behave, and I put it to you that as class tutor you are failing in your duty to make her understand the rules of engagement with adults. Do you see what I'm getting at?' he asked, seemingly exasperated.

'Um – yes.' I shrugged, deciding to back down. But there was more.

'Now let's look at the *lesson*,' he began, a hint of amusement in his voice. Maybe I'd entertained him. Some praise at last. 'I suppose you could say that the objective was clear, to elicit the language of character and to work on description, but wasn't it all rather complicated?' he drawled, as if I'd just stepped on a booby trap or done something so obviously wrong that it was hardly worth talking about.

'Well, I thought they did rather well,' I countered. 'I thought they offered up some good speculation as to the dancing couple.'

Gibb sighed like a deflating whoopee cushion. 'Well, *some* of them spoke,' he sneered, 'when they could get a word in edgeways. But I would say that it was a reasonable lesson until the little joke about the gentleman's breath.

'It's all very well making that sort of wisecrack,' he continued, coming closer to my desk, 'but if you were to do it with a more difficult class you might find yourself unable to get the pupils' attention back. You'd risk losing them, and with it your authority too.' Shuffling my feet and looking at the cold wooden floor, I tried desperately not to hit back, but to no avail.

'But it wasn't an older class!' I snapped. 'I wouldn't do that with a more difficult class. And anyway, they liked the joke. They got on with the work just fine!' I appealed, my voice beginning to crack and quaver. Gibb leaned down to his chair, picked up his heavy leather briefcase and dropped his notes inside. He looked up and smiled.

'Well, it's clear that *you* enjoyed your lesson, but I'm afraid I didn't. There were some good points, but next time I'll expect you to be more consistent in your behaviour towards the pupils, and perhaps less complicated in your approach. I'll submit a written report to Mr Lund and he'll no doubt meet with you soon to discuss these issues. Good day,' and with that he was gone, ducking his head slightly as he went out of the door.

The memory of Alice, with her absurd woollen bonnet and her gently bumbling comments came back to me as I gathered up the detritus from my table – the remains of yet another feeble lesson in the long yawning history of the curriculum of mankind. What was I doing there, arguing the toss with some inspector who clearly hadn't had sex for the past six years? Bastard. I hated him. Glancing out of the windows to make sure no one was looking, I aimed a two-fingered salute at the door under which he had just ducked. If they wanted to sack me, if they didn't want me to sow my seeds of wisdom into the ploughed-up fields of their fucking lousy local authority, well then they could stick it up their proverbials. I was through with it all.

Lund took his time, but when the judgement arrived it was brutal and swift. It was a couple of days after Gibb had been, and we met on the corridor after classes. Walking in opposite directions we both came to a halt and exchanged pleasantries, but it was obvious that I wanted some feedback and equally obvious that he'd been waiting for his moment. The more nervous he became, the more he resembled DH Lawrence after a bad day at the typewriter.

'So erm ... did you get to speak to Mr Gibb?' I asked casually, dropping it into the flow as if it had been the last thing on my mind. 'I was wondering if I'd received the thumbs up,' I added, upon which Lund did the most curious thing. He slowly turned his back to me, bent down slower still, like some old man in a state of collapse, then suddenly sprung around to face me. His face was red, and spittle was already bubbling from his lips. He jabbed a finger in the direction of my nose.

'The trouble with you,' he rasped, 'is that you can't take criticism. You can-not-take-crit-ici-sm!' he bawled, his face coming up closer and his voice echoing past me down the empty corridor. 'What is your bloody problem?' he continued relentlessly, twirling around manically in a *Swan Lake* death throe. What was my problem? That was a good question.

'What do you mean I can't take criticism? Of course I can.'

Lund looked up at the ceiling in despair. 'Well, I suggest you go home tonight and think about it,' he advised, still volcanic but ceasing to spew lava. 'It's nothing to do with the lesson itself!' he seethed. 'Gibb actually told me that some of it was very good. He says you have the makings of a good teacher. But you can't spend the rest of this year confronting everyone who disagrees with you.

'Just go,' he moaned, 'and think about it. We'll talk, assuming that you'll listen,' and he stormed off in the direction of the library.

Radiators and drains. This was one of my mother's favourite sayings. 'There are two types of folk,' she would say, whenever a problem had been caused by someone outside the family circle. 'One warms you up and makes you feel better, and the other just takes it all out of you.' I sat beside the radiator and sought some warmth that evening, staring out of the high window that looked down onto a wintry Hull Road. 'You can't take criticism!' The phrase rung in my head pitilessly all evening. No one had ever said that to me before.

Not only that, but it seemed that I'd missed the point completely. Gibb had liked the lesson, for God's sake. What he'd really wanted to see was how I would react to a little bit of negative. He'd cast out the line and I'd bitten on the bait, then flapped around wildly on the deck instead of just allowing the hook to be taken out quietly. Now I was in trouble again. I was a dull shit of mountainous proportions. Would I ever get it right?

What made things worse a few days later was the news, delivered to me with a trademark punch on the arm from Rixy in the staffroom, that his inspector had been 'a great bloke', a veritable radiator. Apparently he'd loved Rixy's lesson, which had probably consisted of the complex challenge of how to throw and catch a medicine ball. 'Hear you had a few problems with yours then?' he said, smirking. I deflected the comment by asking about Eileen. 'Oh, hers was great as well,' he confirmed. 'Apparently the inspector spent the lesson staring at her tits. It helps. Maybe you should grow some.' As he thumped me and moved away I wondered who had been drumming out the news that Gibb had been less than enamoured of my lesson. I guessed it was John Butler, and that it had leaked out on the Thursday night drinking session to which I'd not gone because I'd been feeling miserable. Lund was too discreet to have said anything, but this sensation of being in the public eye – for all the wrong reasons – was beginning to get me down. But I couldn't have a go at Butler. He was about the only friend I felt I had. But it seemed like a betrayal somehow. I'd thought it would remain in-house. Instead, further confirmation of my madness was spreading through the two staffrooms like a virus – a mutation destined to infect everyone else with the feeling that they were relatively competent. It would be nice for them to know that there was someone more useless than them.

At least my career as a writer was blossoming. John had accepted the article and had rung me from London to deliver the good news. 'Yeah – it's all right. You've even learned how to facking spell. Cheque in the post for fifty quid. Next month make it a bit sleazier.' The magazine came out a few days after the Gibb visit. The sensation of taking the noble publication down off the shelf, of opening it onto the page to see my name at the foot of the story – of seeing my ideas transformed into glossy print, with an artist's illustration – was a powerful one. I felt absurdly important, like I was at the centre of things, standing there alone in the murmur and the mutter of WH Smith. I stood by the magazine shelf for what seemed like hours, with the page open at my story, moving it around, chuckling and smiling as if I were a casual shopper who had just come across a classic of fiction. I wanted to show it to the whole shop. 'Look! This is me. They've published my story!' All this despite the fact that the cover featured a semi-naked woman draped across a Harley-Davidson and a header that announced 'BIRDS AND BIKES. THE FACTS'. And next month I had to 'make it a bit sleazier'. It sounded like more fun than discussing classroom management with local authority inspectors.

This temporary triumph turned sour soon enough. A week or so after my first appearance on the nation's magazine shelves, I walked into the CSE class ready to wrap up the tale of *Joby* and outline the task that they would have to complete for their files. Grinning at the back was Cheshire-cat Gray. 'Great story, sir!' he began, waving a copy of the magazine above his head. I froze in horror. Of course. He was a budding biker. The leather jacket in the fish and chip shop should have told me that. Not unaccustomed to bullshitting, I recovered just in time. 'What are you talking about, Phil?' I managed.

'Don't give me that!' snorted Gray, casting me a laddish glance. 'That's your name, innit? *Phil Ball*? How many of those are there then?' I walked across to where Gray sat swinging on his chair, surrounded by the harem.

'Let me see,' I asked, feigning curiosity. Gray swung away.

'Oh no you don't! You ain't confiscating it.' And he began to read an extract. As I tried to lean across and grab the magazine, the harem closed ranks around him. There was nothing to do but grit my teeth.

'*As she eased herself into the soft leather pillion behind, I knew she was mine,*' he read, hamming a breathy voice. The harem cackled as one. '*Call it the instinct of the predator, but the way her legs gathered slowly around mine, the soft squeal of leather on leather … sent sparks into the night.*' I crossed my arms in mock annoyance.

'So you can read after all, Mr Gray? Congratulations. OK, that's enough,' I half shouted, half laughed. If only Gibb could see me now. 'It's another Phil Ball – OK? Do you seriously think that I would write that sort of tripe?' I appealed. Gray chewed on that one for a moment.

'I dunno,' he said, fixing his eyes on me all the time, waiting for me to break. 'But I'll tell you what, sir. It's much better than that *Joby* crap.'

12

BULLYING

It's late February of the probationary year, and I'm walking past one of the prefab huts on the outskirts of the school complex. I've got a free lesson and I've decided to spend it with Howell in the drama hut. I have heard about Howell from time to time, a rare bird seldom spotted in the staffroom. This is because, I have since found out, he spends his time in his hut on the edge of the playing fields listening to obscure music, smoking exotic cigarettes and generally keeping himself to himself. He has very few classes because he is on a part-time contract, which is all that he appears to need. Rumours are that he's a wealthy man who merely seeks to top up his National Insurance contributions. Whatever, he's a very funny man with a bushy beard and a mind-boggling knowledge of contemporary music, and since telling him that I was rather partial to Captain Beefheart he seems to have taken me under his wing. At the very least it gives me an alternative to the Dirty Corner.

As I approach another of the huts, still some twenty yards from my final destination, I hear a noise that sounds like a bunch of pupils having a good time. The problem is, I can hear chairs crashing, throats jabbering and guffawing, and somewhere beneath this riot of sounds the vague squeaks of what can only be a large mouse suffering the horrors of its final moments of existence. But this is the music hut, I'm sure. I've only been out here a few times, but I can't be mistaken. As I come to the first window at the back of the small structure, I stop and take in the scene. It's a cold and clear sunny day, with the light reflecting off the windows, but I can more or less make out what's going on inside. Perched on a high cupboard, his tiny legs swinging and flailing about, sits Paul Sherburn, the curly-haired and moustachioed music teacher who plays the hymns so beautifully in assembly. Down below, a cluster of bulky fifth-formers appears to be dancing around him, howling with laughter. I can see Phil Gray, and one or two of his male accomplices. Some girls are dancing too, the problem being that they are doing it on the desks. How Mr Sherburn has come to be so perched like the fairy on the tree-top is not my concern, but the classroom looks seriously out of order. Gray is one of the more reasonable members of the school's few hooligans, but some of the others are allegedly less kind. I watch furtively as the tiny man twists, dangles and dithers on the high cupboard from which he clearly cannot get down without breaking his bones. 'Let me down I say!' he squeaks again, at which the class responds by dancing around his flailing feet and shouting ever more loudly. It looks like a scene from *The Wicker Man*. Howell is nowhere to be seen – probably with his headphones on listening to *Love* and smoking a Gauloise. Besides, he would be the last person to intervene. I'm not sure myself what to do.

Keeping my body almost flat against the hut's structure, like an SAS soldier assessing the situation, I realise with the cold logic of the jungle that I cannot save him. Even assuming that the pupils will allow me to break up their little ritual I can see, despite my inexperience in such matters, that to walk in and help Sherburn down from the cupboard is going to make matters worse for him. The only flimsy thread of dignity that he can rescue from this situation is the knowledge that none of his colleagues have actually seen it. There's no way to get to Howell's hut except by passing the windows, and on being seen I will be obliged to act, so like a cat burglar leaving the scene of the crime I turn back and leave poor Sherburn to his demons.

Since Gibb was due to revisit at any time, I'd had plenty of time to think about how I might present myself to him, but on witnessing this hellish scene I'm ashamed to say that I was perversely buoyed. Lund had said that my problem didn't really stem from the lessons themselves but rather from my style and attitude – the two aspects that needed working on. I'd partly taken this on board, even though I continued to feel, deep down, that Gibb had overdone the hard-man bit with me. Whatever, I was beginning to think that I should stay in the profession for at least another year, if for no other reason than to prove to myself that I could, and then we'd see. But what of Mr Sherburn? How had he wriggled through the inspectors' net? He was a wonderful pianist – anyone could see that – but how would he have responded to an inspector's question about the farcical scene that I had just seen through the windows? Apart from Plant on that distant first day, no one had mugged me since. It seemed a cruel thought, but if Sherburn had got through his probation, what was I so worried about?

The oddest thing about the incident was that later that day in the staffroom, Sherburn shuffled in as though nothing untoward had happened at all. As I watched him from my pew in the Dirty Corner, he seemed completely unmoved, chatting with all and sundry as he always did. He was one of the oddest-looking people I'd ever seen. Youngish, about five foot two in height, both his jacket and trousers were far too long and wide, painfully emphasising his pygmy body. He sported a wild, curly hairstyle with a touch of the bohemian, but the pencil moustache below rather spoiled the effect, like mixing Salvador Dali with Hitler. Above the neck he was a cheap-flick porn-star stud, but below it the professional limitations became manifest. He walked exactly like Chaplin's tramp, his feet waddling along in series of penguin-like jerks, and to really round off the likelihood that he would succeed as a teacher, he was possessed of a serious stutter. Apart from all that, he was fine. His piano-playing was divine, and I'd heard him improvising at lunchtimes in the assembly hall, banging out concertos like they were very small beer – probably to keep his sanity. One lunchtime I'd crept into the hall to have a tinkle, and thinking that no one was around (the kids were outside) I'd begun to sing a catchy pop song that was doing the rounds at the time. I rather liked it, and was trying to turn it into a slower piece, to make it sound more serious for the piano. Plodding away in my amateurish way, I suddenly noticed Sherburn standing by the curtains of the stage listening. Embarrassed, I immediately stopped playing. 'Oh no, Paul,' I groaned. 'I'm really sorry. I play like a blind amputee. I didn't know you were there.' He waddled over, trying to mouth something through a vicious attack of the stutters.

'N-n-no no! Don't stop for me!' he finally blurted out, in an unfortunate Eton Rifles accent. 'I thought it was rather g-g-good,' he corrected me, and he seemed to mean it. He hovered over the keys. 'L-l-look. If you just m-m-modulate that chord there … to a f-f-fifth, like that,' he managed, 'it sounds even b-b-better!' and he suddenly played the chord sequence that I had been struggling with for the last ten minutes with such dexterity and beauty that it took my breath away.

'Oh God – do that again!' I pleaded, hoping that no one else was overhearing our little love-in, and he obliged like the kindly genius he was.

It would have been difficult to have found an ounce of malice in him, which was probably why he was having such a hard time. I knew he was struggling before I came across the music hut incident, because he'd come up as a topic of conversation on several Thursday nights. The first I'd heard of him was when Francis 'Franny' Clift, another wag from the science staffroom, roared out over his pint, 'Did you see Sherburn the other day? He looked like a fucking dwarf on acid. When's someone going to cut his barnet and burn his clothes?'

Someone replied, 'He lives on his own, down by the church in one of those little terraced houses. The kids put bangers through his letterbox on bonfire night, the poor bastard. His folks have pegged it. Can anyone explain to me how the fuck he got into the teaching profession? He should be on stage, earning his mint as a concert pianist.' There was a murmur of agreement.

Not long after the Sherburn incident, my tetchy English colleague Julie Acklam threw a house-warming party, to celebrate her new relationship with a mortgage. Julie was single and proud of it, and the party seemed to be a way of announcing to all of us that she was quite happy, thank you very much. The football crowd were all terrified of her waspish tongue, but almost every week speculated relentlessly on her sexuality. 'There's nowt wrong with her,' pronounced John Butler one night. 'Nowt that being strapped under a bull wouldn't help.' The only way to be sure that you yourself did not become the topic of these conversations was to turn up most Thursdays, but I could see that it was equally crucial to attend any parties thrown by members of staff.

As the beer flowed and the fag smoke began to hang thickly in the air of Julie's newly wallpapered lounge, the hostess gestured across to me for a dance. I hated dancing because I was no good at it, but I tended to dance even worse in the company of acquaintances. To my further horror, on came a smoocher. As we inched around the lounge in an awkward clinch, the male members of staff who were seated for that particular number came into my view, one by one as we turned around. In the gloom I could make out their gestures, several mouthing 'Give her one!' and other sundry phrases. Appalled that Julie might notice one of them, I tried to stop her turning, fixing my gaze on the far wall where none of the Thursday crowd was gathered. And there he was, sitting glumly with a bottle of beer, his curly hair seeming to creep up the white wall behind him. He looked quietly drunk, but all the less jolly for it. I continued to look at him over Julie's shoulder as she rewarded me with a little forward thrust of her hips. It was the closest I'd been to a woman for months, but it all seemed wrong, there in her dark little house, with Sherburn drinking himself into oblivion. I felt like just one more victim.

Later in the evening, as the first revellers began to drift away and the house slowly emptied its human contents, I found a quiet corner close to Sherburn and watched him in the forty-watt half-light. Every few seconds his head would loll, he would snore quietly, mutter something to himself and then snap silent. No one had spoken to him all night. He reminded me very strongly of someone back in the early days of university, someone else who had made me feel curiously better about myself.

It was the first small-group seminar I'd attended at university, in the second week at Lancaster. I'd emerged one windy September morning from the shelter of my residence and slouched through the campus lanes to see what the next episode of life might hold. We were to be taught by a certain Professor Sherry, a name which suggested someone old and formal, perhaps a bit pompous. I knocked on his office door, even though it was slightly ajar. 'Come in!' came the hearty shout, with an accent somewhere between Quentin Crisp and Prince Charles. Pushing open the door, I made my first wary entrance into the world of academia. A number of students were already sitting in a cramped semi-circle facing the desk behind which sat the voice. Such a loud and confident greeting had in fact come from a tiny immaculate man, sporting a Chaplin moustache and a grey tailored suit. 'Please – take any seat you want,' he gestured, smiling with what looked like genuine warmth.

The other students, some dozen of them, were talking quietly among themselves in a low chatter that seemed to further exclude me. Then he began. 'My name is Norman Sherry, and since I am the titled leader of this department I wish to welcome you with a drink,' he announced, pointing behind our heads to the back of his office where a large bottle of sherry stood, surrounded by a collection of glasses. 'Please – do the honours,' he asked of the girl to my right, upon which she rose up rather cautiously and went to the back to pour the drinks. The coincidence of his surname with the tipple he was offering us didn't appear to be part of some elaborate joke, so we all accepted his hospitality with a kind of nervous grace. As we sipped at the dry sherry, he sprang daintily from behind his table and began to hand out what looked like a long poem, consisting of two separate stanzas.

As the seminar progressed, I dared to take my eyes from the poem that he seemed so excited about, to examine my fellow students. Most looked older than me, and they all seemed to be nodding in the right places. When Sherry asked a question, one of the girls had answered straight off, with a confident delivery that I could only dream about. When he put a further question to the floor five minutes later, I decided to stay silent – a sensible decision as it turned out, since the untitled poem turned out to be two entirely separate ones. Another horrifyingly self-assured girl had responded to the question by stating, 'Well – the second poem is obviously Yeats, although not one of his better known ones.' I nearly died. It was time to go home, to sign on the dole and to think of something else.

'Ah, Yeats!' squeaked Sherry, as if he were about to ejaculate. 'Well done. Exactly!' The girl who had identified the poem sat back, a smug look on her chops. 'And how might we best contrast the Yeats with the Auden?' he continued, as if the author of the other poem were also common knowledge to us. As another fearless student launched into a detailed response to the latest question, it occurred to me that Professor Sherry was as intimidating a man as I'd come across. His sophistry terrified the life out of me. And yet to the rest he was just another teacher, just an ordinary guy. Cleethorpes, the culture-free zone in which I'd grown up, just hadn't prepared me for this. But there was no way out, not for now. I was too far from the door, and was afraid that if I tried to make a dramatic exit, I would trip over someone's legs.

But salvation was at hand. Just when you think it can't get much worse, it turns out that there's usually someone at least as dumb as you are. Over at one end of the semi-circle closest to Sherry's desk sat a small blinking waif whose bent posture suggested that he was seriously short-sighted. He was small and thin, with a chin-strap beard and a pointy nose. In fact I thought I recognised him, although I couldn't be sure. Just as my eyes had wandered to this chap, Sherry had begun to pontificate about the second poem, which he told us was an allegory. I knew what an allegory was, more or less, but when Sherry threw out the question 'And how exactly would you define an allegory?' I decided once again to stay out of the firing line. I didn't know it at the time, but Professor Norman Sherry was a celebrated academic, and was already on the road to being one of the most famous and respected biographers of all time. He'd already completed a ground-breaking opus on Joseph Conrad, and was about to launch into a multi-volume biog of Graham Greene which would take him to Haiti, Panama, Liberia and the Congo – setting new standards for the genre of 'In the Footsteps of' and almost dying in the process. He was to contract typhus, tropical diabetes, suffer from intestinal gangrene and be robbed and left for dead on the roadside in Liberia. He was not the effete, pompous little academic he appeared to be that day, but I was not to know. Neither was the waif over to my right, who on hearing Sherry's question about allegory had suddenly perked up.

'It's a creature that lives on the Nile,' the waif offered,

chortling slightly in the process. Then silence. No one moved. It was difficult to believe that it had happened, and yet he had definitely said 'It's a creature that lives on the Nile'. It was the most imbecilic thing that I had heard in eighteen years of existence, but I was far more dumbstruck by the sheer balls of the person who had just pronounced the sentence than to dwell on its content for too long. All eyes were on Sherry, who had begun to twitch. For once he was lost for words. He tried to speak, but nothing came out. His gills opened and closed like a fish dying on deck. He looked desperately to left and right, as if to assure himself that he was actually in his own office, and not in bed dreaming. He turned over the palms of his hands as if he were measuring the first drops of rain from above and began to giggle, at first quietly but then uncontrollably, until he was laughing into the office air with gusto. His little body shook as he finally recovered the power of speech – 'A creature that lives on the Nile! Ha. That's bloody good. That's bloody good! Oh my dear Lord!' and he turned to face the myopic little jester who was smiling inanely to the rest of the class. Then I remembered where I'd seen him before.

His name was Mark Lammiman, the mysterious dweller of Room 1C, first spotted by my new friend John in the residence kitchen early on in that first week. He had been heard playing a flute and had also been spotted in the kitchen shaking a can of marrowfat peas as if it had been a tin of cream. According to John, the short-sighted flute player had sunk an opener into the can, upon which a jet-stream of peas had sprayed up into the kitchen air and peppered the ceiling, like wet green bullets. This had sounded promising, and I'd been keen on making his acquaintance.

He had not been back to the kitchen since, but I had seen him hanging around the residence once or twice during that first week. He was majoring in music (and doing his minor in English, much to poor Sherry's consternation) and he turned out to be something of a godsend, partly because he was a real musician who was prepared to tolerate my strumming and howling and play along with me, but also because in every other aspect of life he was so useless that he made you feel like some kind of virile god. Lammiman, as he came to be dismissively known among the kitchen crowd, was so spectacularly inept that it was a wonder how he got out of bed in the morning – or how he'd made it into double figures and got to university. I'd seen victims at school, of course, but Lammiman was on an entirely different level. I tried to be kind to him, and I did become a friend of his, of sorts – but by and large it was impossible. If you were with him for any longer than a few hours you couldn't help but be drawn magnetically into his charmed circle of bad luck. Lammiman couldn't see a thing, which didn't help, but he seemed magically destined to step in the dog turds of life. I stumbled through university, but Lammiman blundered through it. There's a difference. And so I remember him with affection because he saved me, in the most unfortunate of ways, from myself – at least in those early days when I thought I couldn't hack it, when I thought that I was unprepared for life outside of the protection of school and family. *A creature that lives on the Nile.* Perhaps somewhere, in Prof Sherry's voluminous works, Lammiman's famous answer is recorded, along with the gangrene and the tropical diseases.

A couple of nights after the allegory incident, there came a timid knock on my bedroom door. It was Lammiman, and he'd heard me strumming my guitar. 'Hi,' he began, craning his head around the door. 'Thought I'd make your acquaintance. I'm a musician too,' he continued, in a thick north-eastern accent. This seemed a generous compliment, so I replied: 'Ah – you must be the guy with the flute. You play really well. I've heard you playing. You're a *real* musician.' But my new guest had already moved past me as I sat on the bed with my guitar, and was standing over my work desk squinting at the photos of my girlfriend Helen that I'd pinned to the noticeboard.

'That your girlfriend then?' he asked, in a slightly downbeat way, as if girlfriends were a closed door to him. Before I could answer he added, 'She's a cracker!' Then, bizarrely, he began a series of strange movements, like someone trying to do t'ai chi after six pints of beer. He punched the air and kicked out with his feet in a staccato mime, each movement of any chosen limb accompanied by the chant 'Girls, girls, girls!' until he stopped, looked down at the floor and pronounced solemnly, 'Can't do with 'em. Can't do without 'em,' like some tired old rake bemoaning the downside of polygamy. It was a compelling performance, almost as good as the one he'd carried off in Sherry's study.

I decided to ask him about that one. 'Sit down, man,' I suggested, and motioned to the chair by the desk. He blinked and did as I bid. 'Brilliant that joke the other day,' I lied. 'I was thinking, how does this bloke have the balls to say that? I reckon you did a good job, shutting him up.'

Lammiman frowned. 'What joke, man?'

'The thing about the creature on the Nile.'

He looked at the floor, seeking to jog his memory. As in Sherry's study, Lammiman's natural sitting style made him look as if he were expecting a large impact at any moment. His head was permanently fixed down in the brace position that flight attendants suggest you adopt, in the unlikely event of your landing on water. From this posture my guest wafted his hand meekly in the air, adding: 'Ah, it was just a jape, man. Reckon he took it quite well. Anyway, play us a song, will you? Maybe one night we can have a jam session.'

As I obliged with some weary dirge, Lammiman suddenly jerked into a standing position and shot back across to the pictures of Helen. Pointing at a profile shot pinned up above the rest he declared, 'I'd love to do your girlfriend!' Unsurprisingly, this put paid to my warbling. 'I can easily do her for you,' he insisted. 'You just have to give me this photograph.' Playing for time, I shrugged. It seemed the safest option. 'I can do portraits, man!' he added, as though it were obvious.

I breathed a sigh of relief. Lammiman was also an artist, apparently, as well as a comedian and musician. He told me that it would take him about a week, but that it would only cost me a pint. 'Sure – take it,' I said, not really expecting him to deliver any particularly interesting goods. Anything to get him out of the room at that particular juncture. He seemed like the kind of person who might stay for ever, once you'd made the mistake of encouraging him.

And of course I did encourage him, at least as much as my public image at the university would allow me to. Despite their tank tops, the younger things of the mid-Seventies still saw themselves as cool, and Lammiman was the antithesis of hip. Just like everyone else, I wanted to be seen as a bit of a dude, and that was clearly impossible if Lammiman was in your company. People avoided him, and we were also unspeakably cruel to him that first year, once the pecking order had been settled. A group of more than five males, thrown together at random and forced to live with each other at close quarters for an entire academic year will always seek out a victim, and the status of each of the predators will largely depend upon the depths of imagination and nastiness to which they are prepared to stoop in the practical joker stakes. It's a sad but universal truth about males, and it cuts right across class boundaries. I knew about it from school, but I'd been expecting to grow out of it. No such luck. The only way to survive – to not become the victim yourself – was to hound Lammiman, and to do ever more vile things to him, publicly at least. And so we always shook up his cans of peas before he came into the kitchen, so that they would explode in his face. We would wait until he was asleep, creep into his room and set his alarm clock for early morning, placing it inside a frying pan to pump up the volume. We ordered a rotting pig's head from the campus butcher, placed a cigarette in its mouth and a pirate's patch over one dead eye and wrapped it in a box for his birthday, and so on. We made his life hell, but of course he always came back for more. Instead of telling us to shove it where we could no longer find it, he accepted the role of the victim all too easily. I suppose he'd been expecting it.

In private, I liked him. For starters, he'd brought back the portrait of Helen (and the photo in one piece) and he'd done it wonderfully. I was stunned by the quality of what he'd produced, equipped with nothing but a messy piece of charcoal, a pencil and a serious case of myopia. 'Glad you like it,' he said, blinking, 'and I was only joking about the pint, man.' I bought him one anyway. The portrait not only captured Helen's likeness to perfection, he'd blown up the tiny photo to about ten times its original size, and twisted the image in an uncanny way, as if he knew her. I treasured it, as indeed did the girl portrayed, once she eventually set eyes upon it. When John came to my room the following night to introduce me to the delights of illegal substances, his eyes fell upon the pinned-up portrait, dominating the room. Too cool to express unreserved admiration, he had simply said, 'Didn't know you could draw, boy. You should stick to that and give the guitar a rest.' I told him that Lammiman had done it. 'You facking what? Are you trying to tell me that that wanker drew that? No way!' But I insisted that the artist was indeed our pea-shaking neighbour, whereupon John allowed a single 'fack' to escape from his lips. He went up to the drawing and looked at it for several seconds before nodding approvingly. 'It's good,' he said, sitting down and opening his tin to reveal what looked like a small cake of yellowish dung. 'Facking good. Just goes to show. Mind you – he's still a wanker.'

Lammiman taught me the dangers of making assumptions about people, even though I continued to do so. He also made me feel better about myself, at a crucial time. He was Omega male, the last in the line. I felt bad about my inability to lay off the bullying, but like all young men I confined this guilt to the nether regions of my conscience. In the end, you were just relieved that you were not the target.

'Come on, Bally. Are you going to stay and shag the hostess or are you coming back with us?' slurred Blacktoft, Dirty Corner colleague and Butler's older accomplice. I was still at the party, and Sherburn was still asleep. 'How about Paul?' I asked, standing up carefully. 'Oh, he'll be just fine,' said Blacktoft. 'He always comes to these parties, and ends up snoring in a corner. He can't find his way home at night anyway. Someone'll put a blanket over him. He usually wakes up just after he pisses himself. Now are you coming?' I walked into the chill and fresher air of the night, swaying slightly. Butler, Blacktoft and myself tottered off down the dark and quiet streets, educators of the young, pilgrims through a barren land. Gibb was next, but he didn't worry me now. Neither did the kids for that matter. Perhaps it was the beer talking, but it was my colleagues in general that I found far more frightening. I didn't want to end up under a blanket, dismissed by all and sundry.

Soon after Julie's party, we had a staff meeting to organise the traditional staff show for the kids, to be performed on the Friday before the Easter holidays began. The more experienced teachers knew the ropes, and joked among themselves about previous years, but it was clear from the beginning that nothing much could be done without Paul. He would play piano during the pantomime, he would accompany the *Folies Bergère* spoof that Howell had offered to choreograph, he would play the music when the prompts came up for the kids to sing etc. As the possible running order was rattled off, he simply nodded obediently. 'So what are you going to do, Bally?' asked Julie, unusually enthused by this artistic project. Someone piped up that I could play piano and guitar, and sing.

'No way,' I retorted. 'Strictly amateur I'm afraid. You wouldn't want to hear.' Paul, silent up to that point, began to work up to a sentence.

'Oh n-n-n-not at all! He's very g-g-good. I've heard him,' he managed, kindly.

'Thanks, Paul,' I answered, wryly. Set up thus by Paul, I was nevertheless flattered by his over-generous comments. I resolved to work on something musical for the show, panicked into action by the sudden enthusiasm of the staff for the undertaking. This was obviously their muse.

At the first rehearsal, Julie, the mistress of ceremonies, ticked me off for not having decided on my contribution as yet. 'Get your arse into gear, Bally,' she complained. 'Just sing any old crap. As long as you *do* something!' I was beginning to regret not taking up her hip-wiggled offer that night – if an offer it had indeed been – since to have accepted it might have subsequently discouraged her from all this public chivvying. But hope was at hand. Trying to look busy backstage, I noticed a large music system, with a small mixing-desk and several outlets linked to a set of speakers, hung behind the top of the stage curtain. 'What's this?' I asked Baz, the woodwork teacher who was beginning to work on the *Folies* props. 'It's a beauty, man!' he replied. 'And it works. No sod ever uses it.' I asked him if he could work it, mixing table and all. 'Sure can,' he said, beaming.

For the big day, I assembled the band, Shattered Teeth. I volunteered to sing, Butler agreed to play bass, Julie was to be on rhythm guitar whilst the star, I hoped, would be Paul Sherburn, on lead guitar. Of course, none of us would play any of these things. So thunderous were the decibels that the system could pump out that we would simply pretend to perform, to the backing of Free's *Mr Big*, a historic piece of cock-rock that I was almost sure the kids wouldn't recognise. Baz could reduce the vocals from the mixing desk so that I could make a passable attempt at really singing, just to convince the audience further. As for the absence of the drummer, I resolved to inform the audience that Baz was off-stage, minding an electronic drum machine.

Julie enjoyed the rehearsals so much that for the big day she decided to put us on last, to close the show in a frenzy of music, dry ice and strobe lighting. After the pantomime and the various skits and sketches had run their course, as Julie had planned I walked out to face the school, clad in leather jacket and dark glasses. The curtain stood closed behind me. 'I'd like to introduce my band,' I hollered out across the darkened hall. As the curtain opened to reveal the members of Shattered Teeth, the packed assembly hall began to fall about laughing. Julie and Butler's presence on guitar seemed absurd enough, but there stood the tiny Sherburn, king of the ivories, victim of the music hut. 'And on lead guitar – Paul Sherburn!' I bawled out, as the tiny man bowed his Sixties hippy wig in acknowledgement of the cheers and whistles. He wore black leather trousers and an oversized biker's jacket. For an awkward moment, as the chaos below threatened to get out of hand, I thought I might have miscalculated again. Gibb and smelly breath jokes loomed large. *You'd risk losing them, and with it your authority too.* Nothing for it but to press on. 'Thank you, thank you! And now Mr Johnson, backstage with his trusty drum machine, will kick us off!' At which point the introduction to the song boomed out, the lights began to wink and the dry ice rose slowly from below the stage.

After just a few bars of the song, it was clear that the children were completely stunned. They had sat down and were blinking up at the stage open-mouthed. Encouraged, we strutted ever more convincingly, until at last, Paul's guitar solo arrived. Waddling like a Spinal Tap Chaplin to the front of the stage, he stood firm and milked the moment for all it was worth. With his wig trailing over the neck of his guitar, he began to thrust his hips and swivel, climaxing to the solo with the pained expression of agony and constipation that only a lead guitarist can conjure. The children rose as one, standing on their seats and fisting the air, in a cacophony of approval.

As the song faded out, the curtain closed and the lights came on. The kids began to chant 'We want Sherburn! We want Sherburn!' with such vehemence that the non-performing teachers, drafted in for crowd control, were obviously flummoxed. I peered through the curtains. Even towards the back, where the older fifth- and sixth-formers were seated, I could see that they'd been taken in as well. Some were talking animatedly to each other, and miming some of Sherburn's movements. I stuck my head out from the curtain. The noise was immediately deafening. 'Encore! Encore!' they stamped until it was clear that at the very least, Paul should move to the front and take a bow. Scrambling his wig back into place, Baz half-opened the curtains and we bowed, Paul's wig falling off in the process.

The effect lasted the rest of the day, during which Paul was feted and back-slapped by seemingly the whole school. 'That was amazing, sir! You never told us you could play guitar too!' they cooed. He tried to hide his pleasure at this sudden about-turn in his fortunes, but an enormous grin broke out repeatedly on his face in the staffroom. It wouldn't last, of course. After Easter they would all have forgotten and he would return to his *Wicker Man* status. But he had a happy holiday, for a change.

'How does it feel, Mr Rock God?' asked Julie in the staffroom that afternoon.

'It f-f-f-feels just f-fine!' managed Paul.

13

SURRENDERING

Lund told me that Gibb would be coming to see me teach my GCE literature class. This was a relief, sparing me the rod of him witnessing me trying to deal with Phil Gray and the harem. In fact the day I received the news I'd been with my CSE crew, checking their files and talking to them individually about their progress. I'd been told to do this by Lund, after he'd been in previously to remind them of the course stipulations. By the grace of God, Gray had been absent on that day, maybe because I'd forewarned the class of my boss's visit. But lover-boy had turned up for my checking session. Everyone else, even the harem, had brought their files as requested, but Gray's hands were empty. 'Where's your file, Phil?' I asked from the front of the class, as he sat there grinning.

'Oh – I forgot it again, sir,' he replied.

'You forgot it? You mean it does actually exist then?' I tried, hands impatiently on hips. Some of the diminished male lions in the class laughed at this, waiting to see the leader's reaction.

'Course it exists, sir!' he laughed, adopting his customary chair-swinging posture. 'It's just that – you know – I was a bit rushed this morning at breakfast. Couldn't find it anywhere.' Thus disarmed, I mumbled some threat about needing to see it sooner rather than later, but gave him no ultimatum. Despite everything, he seemed a nice enough kid. I figured that he'd produce the goods in the end – but it was beginning to worry me.

I played it absolutely straight with Gibb, selecting the most boring lesson that I could think of so that he would have no further hook to catch me with. For the June exam that year the pupils were obliged to write a series of short essay-type responses to the books that we'd been reading, and before the advent of the National Curriculum's Key Stages and the tsunami of exam-technique support books that it brought in its wake, pupils were left very much to their own devices. So instead of gathering them around me and talking about the characters in a painting, I selected a variety of different texts to illustrate the tricky art of the whys and wherefores of paragraph writing. The class oozed with the rich scent of Hull's middle class, a juicy prime-cut of seriously motivated adolescents. In truth I was an irrelevance, since they could have easily passed the exam without me. They knew this, and tolerated me in the sort of stuffy silence that was perfect for Gibb-fooling purposes.

No friendlier than he had been on the first visit, he'd at least changed his ridiculous glasses for a pair of contact lenses. As he took his place at the back of the classroom with the plan of the lesson that I had handed to Lund some days previously, I proceeded to teach the most tedious sixty minutes I have ever delivered. Never before had so little been taught to so many in so short a time, for no discernible reason. Never once did I rise from my desk to relieve the tedium, never once did I smile or betray the slightest emotion, never once did I make a joke about halitosis. As the class quietly dispersed, with not a Tracey-type in sight, Gibb appeared glued to his seat, with a thunderous expression struggling to fight past the mask of neutrality that he was professionally obliged to don. I stayed at my desk, preserving the distance between us. Looking down at the floor, he gathered himself together and fired out a bullet sentence across no-man's-land. 'You didn't exactly take any risks, did you?' he asked, half sarcastically. The bullet pinged off my helmet. I crouched low to the top edge of the trench and fired back.

'Well, no – I suppose I didn't. They have to pass an exam in June. Maybe gathering them around to talk about dancing couples might not help them very much.' At this he appeared to flinch slightly.

'Well, it's interesting that you should say that,' he simmered, his eyes beginning to blink behind his new contact lenses, 'because it might have been a better idea. I can think of a hundred more interesting ways to get the pupils to think about paragraphs, which are, after all, merely concrete representations of an author's decision-making process, don't you think?' Yes, I did think that. Good shot, Fritz!

'OK,' I admitted. 'I'll try to liven it up a little next lesson.'

Gibb proceeded to list various other things I could have done to break up the tedium, but in truth I knew some of them anyway. The techniques he described and the sort of facilitator-cum-teacher role he seemed to want me to adopt were precisely the things I felt I could do best – but I decided not to tell him. I'd surrendered and walked across the bomb-shell landscape, hands on my head. I'd take the criticism. I didn't want to fight any more. And magically, as I nodded and agreed with him over in the enemy trenches, I sensed him softening. I sensed his desire to kill me ebb slowly away.

Now it would only need an inspection from Lund and a meeting at the end of the year with Beacroft and Gibb to convert my status from probationer to fully qualified teacher, whereupon I could spend the rest of the Thursday nights of my life getting pissed, take out a humble mortgage, perhaps persuade Eileen that she should sleep with me out of kindness's sake and then rise to the giddy heights of deputy head of department within the coming twenty years. It looked like a fairly uninteresting horizon, but you never knew. You never knew what might come along. Such as Leeds RLC, for example.

This was the incident that finally turned it for me, not that Gibb or Lund were there to witness it. The occasion was one Thursday night, which just happened to coincide with one of the five-a-side crowd's birthday. The bloke whose big day John Butler decided we would celebrate in Hull city centre was one Dickie Cowlam, a social science teacher and something of a character. He was a lovely chap, big, strong and funny, but utterly incapable of taking his drink. In his mid-thirties, he lived alone in the village, tolerated by the school authorities despite a catalogue of misdemeanours that made my own behaviour look extremely sane. Then again, he was reportedly an inspired teacher, a fact attested to by ex-pupils and colleagues alike. He was one of those lucky people who never experienced a hangover, and tales of his Thursday night antics were legendary.

The best one, told incessantly since it occurred, was when Dickie had staggered home to his lodgings after a particularly heavy session. His equally renowned reluctance to wash, combined with his lack of acquaintance with cleaning imple-ments, meant that landlords had moved him on, never tolerating him for long in one place. Consequently, when he got drunk, he would often forget the whereabouts of his current address and default back to a former one, swaying back to these houses on autopilot. Turned away from a former residence by an angry tenant one wet winter midnight, Cowlam gave up the ghost and sat down on the kerbside, his feet in the roadside gutter. Cars swished by in the darkness, soaking him still further. Eventually, a police car pulled up and an officer loomed up to Cowlam's side.

'Had a little too much to drink, sir?' enquired the bobby, just doing his duty. Dickie muttered something through his false teeth. 'Perhaps you'd like a lift home, sir?' the policeman persisted, rather more kindly than was strictly necessary.

'Ah … that's the problem …' slurred Dickie, his face lit up by the police car's lights. The officer began to lose his patience.

'What's your name, sir?' Dickie murmured something in reply. 'And you say that you're lost?' Dickie nodded in the affirmative. 'What's your profession, sir?' asked the bobby, probing further.

'Teacher,' slurred Dickie.

The policeman apparently found this hard to believe. 'And what subject do you teach, sir?'

Dickie knew that. 'Geography.'

This was, of course, one of the tales floating in the air that night in Spiders, a pub-cum-club to which we'd retired after the football. We were gathered in a circle around a large table, close to the main bar. The Dirty Corner was out in force: Butler, Blacktoft and Burnsy. Rixy was there, as were various charismatic leaders of the science department. I was almost enjoying myself until two pretty girls walked in from the street, passed by our table and then installed themselves behind us for the night. Cowlam began to slaver. His sentences were becoming increasingly surreal. Up at the bar, a large group of equally large men had suddenly appeared from the bowels of the club, and they also seemed the worse for wear. As one of the girls picked up her handbag and made her way past the bar in the direction of the Ladies, one of the large young gentlemen began to shout 'Whooo-hoo-hoo!' in her direction. For some reason that I still find hard to explain, I shouted above the din: 'Are you real?'

A sudden silence descended on the room, broken only by the scraping of chairs as my former friends were beginning to stand, as if to make for the exit. Cowlam, suddenly sober, whispered, 'Are you mad, Bally?' Before anyone could really move, the large man walked over to our table and pointed at me.

'So what's the fucking matter wi' you, Shaky?'

This referred to Shakin' Stevens, a pop singer from back then who wore a leather jacket with the collars turned up, which is exactly what I was doing at the time.

'Nothing, mate. Just leave the girl alone,' I explained, saviour of the downtrodden, feminist new-man hero. I shot a glance at the girl. She was staring at me with a mixture of pity and astonishment. Butler, Blacktoft and Rixy were out of their seats, ready to bolt.

'You're fucking dead,' he announced, and lunged towards me. As I prepared for death, the man loomed large then suddenly shot backwards, as if on a length of elastic. Cowlam flinched, and fell backwards over his chair. All hell broke loose. The man was now being restrained at the bar by his drinking colleagues, some of whom were beginning to make their way to the exit. They were all wearing blue blazers, with a club badge emblazoned on the chest. I'd not noticed that before. Butler was standing and swearing under his breath 'Fucking hell Bally, fucking hell Bally' in a horrified trance. As the crowd pushed the man gradually towards the door, another enormous hulk emerged from the scrum and walked across. He leaned over the table and held out his hand for me to shake. 'No hard feelings, mate,' he pronounced, with the authority of a leader. 'Rugby crowd – you know,' and they were gone, leaving us in the bloodless silence.

When I walked into the staffroom the next morning, a strange sound began to rumble up from the Dirty Corner, like the All Blacks' *haka*. It spread across from the windows and was taken up seemingly by the whole room, until everyone seemed to be chanting *Bally! Bally!* for some unknown reason. Rixy leapt up from his chair and began the applause. 'This is the man!' he announced to the beaming throng. 'This is the man who took on Leeds Rugby League Club, and won!' So that's who they were! Rixy had checked it out with his rugby mates that very morning on the phone. My second-row adversary had been on a quiet night out in Hull with the team, only to have had the misfortune to come across a leather-jacketed nine-stone urban legend. I bowed ironically, milking the applause. I felt oddly happy. By rights I should have been dead, but I'd escaped yet again.

Things seemed to go much better after that. Even Peter Gabriel grinned at me one morning in the corridor, presumably because he'd also heard of the incident. I wasn't altogether sure that I'd wanted to be accepted into the magic circle on the basis that I went around challenging rugby league players to a fight, but in the absence of any greater achievements, it would have to do for now. In the meantime, there was Phil Gray to sort out.

Despite repeated efforts to get him to bring in the famous file, he always came up with some excuse. The best one was 'Sir – honest it's true. Just as I was putting on my bike-clips to go out of the door, I went over to get the file and who should have it in his mouth but the dog, sir? He's a real bugger, sir, when he's got summat in his gob. Won't let it go for nowt, he won't. I pulled and I tugged, sir, but he wouldn't let go.' This game of dog and mouse continued in similar fashion until the June date loomed and I finally lost patience. 'If you don't bring it in next week,' I threatened him, 'then it's over, Phil. There won't be any time to check it, assuming you've done any of the work, that is.' Of course he'd done it, he protested, feigning hurt. The harem soothed him. 'We have one lesson per week,' I reminded him. 'That's enough for us to do a bit of reading and discussion, but the rest is up to you. That's the whole point. You have to show that you can do the stuff on your own.'

Phil Gray, up to that point prepared to extend the game as far as it could go, decided it was time to make explicit his philosophy of life. He looked up at me. 'Ah – so what anyway, sir? You don't really care. You're only covering yourself anyway. If you don't give in all those files it's you that gets bollocked, innit?' The truth of the assertion hit home, but as he said it, I happened to glance at Paul Baker – the kid who'd done all the work, handed it all in on time, read the books and more, and just quietly got on with it all, despite the fact that he would probably not make the sixthform and despite the fact that he'd got almost nothing from me all year, distracted as I had been by the charismatic lout at the back.

'That's not true,' I shot back. 'What are you going to do next year when they ask you to bring something to work, or when they ask you to get some building work done for a certain date? Tell them that your dog wouldn't let you? You'll see how long you last. Daddy or no daddy.'

He sat up. 'Don't you talk about my old man!' he snapped. 'I'll bring you the bloody work, I've told you. Don't have an 'eart attack!' he crackled, suddenly looking less handsome, less untouchable.

The next week, the same one in which staff were taking bets on whether the McFees would turn up to Burnsy's final lesson, I was engaged in a more private struggle. If Gray didn't bring in the work on the Wednesday, I might not see him again. He could easily avoid me, or even stay away from school. It wasn't entirely clear to me whether the mention of his dad had pushed him away from me for good, or if he'd seen some truth in what I'd said – but I didn't want things to end up soured between us. I still liked him. He was funny and frank, and since no one had ever told him to get off his arse, the fact that he hadn't couldn't be described as entirely his own fault. But the file was becoming a bit of an obsession. I never seriously thought that the success of my coming D-Day interview with Gibb, Lund and Beacroft would really hinge on whether Gray brought in that file or not, but I didn't care. If I was going to do anything that year, I was going to get him to bring it in.

The day dawned, I walked into the class, and of course he wasn't there. Mandy was sitting next to his empty chair, chewing on air.

'Where's Phil?' I asked, panicking.

'Dunno,' replied his good lady, forever faithful.

'Has he come to school?' I shouted, losing it slightly.

'Dunno,' replied Mandy, her face as straight as a drain-pipe. There were other files to check, last-minute things to correct. I couldn't spend the lesson interrogating his slags. At lunchtime I asked his tutor if he'd registered in the morn-ing, and apparently he had. In the afternoon, I stalked the corridors looking for him, even going into the metalwork class where he was supposed to be, but there was no sign of Prince Philip. One of his more thuggish mates shrugged when I tried to corner him into an answer, there in the metalwork room, as he hammered out a car door panel like a mechanic born and bred. 'Ain't seen him, sir,' he said. The teacher was over in a corner supervising another pupil with a blow-torch, and it seemed to me that there were hiding places aplenty amongst the detritus and back rooms of this particular department, but it was no good. Besides, I was beginning to look silly.

I drove home that afternoon livid. And then I remem-bered. He lived further down Hull Road, at the far end near the estate. He'd told me as much that night in the fish and chip shop. Praying that he would come home on his bike, once he'd seen that the coast was clear at school, I parked the Beetle down a side road, ran around to the main road and into the front garden of Henry's mansion. The garden was hidden from the road by a large hedge, but by crouching down on the garden side and peering through the early summer leaves, I could see down Hull Road. If Gray came down it, I'd have him.

The minutes ticked by. Several people walked past, some
of them kids from the school. I pulled back from the hedge,
especially when an old lady walked by with a nosey poodle
who appeared to have sniffed me out. 'Come on, you silly
boy!' she complained, dragging the yapping dog off behind
her. Just as I was beginning to tire of the game, I saw a bike
in the distance, on top of which I could make out the purple
blazer of the school. At its rapid approach, I saw that it was
my man. Rushing out from behind the hedge I sprang into his
path, just as Gray had unfortunately taken his eyes off the road
ahead. 'Stop!' I yelled – and he looked up from his handlebars.
His eyes bulged. 'What the fuck …!' he screamed, almost too
late, but he still managed to swerve in towards the kerb, in a
desperate attempt to get past. I launched myself at his waist,
like a rugby league player might have done. As I made contact
with the speeding bike and Gray's body, all I could hear were
cries of terror and the metal clang and scrape of the sliding
machine. In an instant, I could feel punches and blows
coming up from below, where Gray wriggled and squirmed.
The bike was crumpled to one side on the kerb, the wheels
still spinning. Some people had stopped, across on the other
side of the road, and one of them was shouting something.

Gray wriggled free and struggled on to his feet. 'You're
fucking mad! You're fucking mad!' he shrieked, hopping up
and down. 'What you fucking doing! I'll kill you! My old
man'll kill you! Fuuuuuuuck!' he hollered one last time,
looking up at the sky. Then he looked down at his bike. 'It's
ruined! Look.' We both stepped off the road.

'It's not,' I countered. 'It's just a bit scraped.' He picked the bike up and propped it against the hedge to inspect the damage. 'So where's the file?' I asked. Gray had crouched down to the back wheel and was fiddling with one of the cogs, but at this he suddenly stopped.

'You mad bastard! You *are* fucking bonkers!' he insisted, and he doubled up, collapsing into the hedge in a fit of high-pitched laughing. I shrugged.

'OK – I'm bonkers. But I asked you for the file. I've been asking for it for six months now. So what did you expect? That I'd just let it go?' He pointed at my face, laughing even harder.

'You're bleeding. Your cheek's all cut. I love it!' and he fell back further into the hedge, chuckling. 'Rugby tackled by the English teacher! Look,' he said, recovering his poise, not a hair out of place, 'I'll bring the stuff tomorrow, OK?' I asked him to promise. 'I promise,' he said, grinning.

And he brought it. It was awful, of course. Some of it had been done at the beginning of the year, and the rest of it that night, hurriedly and scruffily, probably copied from Mandy's work, which in truth hadn't been much better. Some of it even looked like her handwriting, but it didn't matter. It represented some concrete evidence that he had done the course – which he had – and evidence that I had carried out my duties, which I had, however badly.

Gibb didn't say much to me in the final interview, the week after the kids had gone. He seemed to have come to the conclusion that it would be easier to pass me, to get rid of my presence, to forget about me for ever. He made a comment about style, and that it might be useful for me to decide on what kind of teacher I wanted to be, but I wasn't really listening. I knew what he meant anyway. I knew that I would have to seek out a middle-way between the halitosis joker and the paragraph man, between the Andrew Marvell period and the final week's rugby tackle, for there lay peace, of a sort. But I would have to find it on my own. And, of course, I had to have the last word. Pointing at my bruised and swollen cheek, Beacroft grinned and asked me, 'Been tackling any rugby league players lately then?' I smiled. 'No, not this time. I just fell off my bike.'

A couple of years later I was out drinking on a Saturday night in Hull with my elder brother, who'd come over on a rare visit. The first thing I knew, as I stood at the bar, was a full pint suddenly thrust under my nose.

'There you go, sir. Pint's on me. How you doing?' It was Phil Gray. Taller by several inches and wider than I remembered, his jeans wore the faded imprint of brick dust. Despite the working attire, he still looked like a film star.

'Hey, thanks, Phil. I'm fine. How are you? How's the building trade?'

'Fucking great, sir. Got me own little business, like. Bit o' building, bit o' supplying. You know, the old man's contacts. What about you? Still teaching then?'

'Yeah, same old stuff.' I nodded across at my brother, sitting at a table. 'Him too. He's my brother. Runs in the family.'

'Nah!' He smiled. 'He's better looking than you. Rugby tackled any pupils lately then?'

'Don't tempt me,' I japed, and made as if to grab him.

We shook hands, and he walked off into his life, leaving me with mine. What had I taught him? Absolutely nothing. I was sure, nevertheless, that he'd remembered the lecture about closing down your options. I supposed that he hadn't wanted to hurt me. He'd just been too decent to mention it.

14
SETTLING

In the summer I flew to Turkey to visit my brother, who was teaching in a two-horse town called Kayseri, tucked up somewhere in the middle of the country. Although it was most pleasant to switch off from the stress of the year just gone, see my big brother again and travel around the lovely country for a whole month – with not a single package tourist in sight – something got the better of my bowels after we'd eaten fish in a small and isolated cliff-top village, and from then on the holiday turned into something of a nightmare. Holed up for days in a small *pension*, too ill to move, my brother finally persuaded a local fisherman to take us in a tiny open boat along the rocky coastline to Kas, the nearest big town. He took us at night, so that my dehydration wouldn't worsen. I was past caring anyway, at that point. Lying prone in the wet bottom of the boat, I felt like Shackleton, alone on a star-lit sea. Hull seemed like another planet. They could repatriate my remains and read out a memorial speech in Willerton High School's staffroom: *A dedicated and conscientious young teacher, struck down in the hour of his blossoming. It represents a tragic loss to the profession.*

Unfortunately I recovered, and was back to face the kids in September. Thin as a goalpost, with my eyes pulled back into their darkened sockets, I looked as though I hadn't slept all summer. Before I'd even reached the staffroom, two colleagues hailed me with 'Bally – you look like shit!' It was an accurate observation, but life goes on. The second year stretched ahead like some never-ending line of awkwardly high hurdles. Lund had decided to reward me for passing my probation with a sixth-form A-level literature group, which was a double-edged sword. I could see that it might be interesting to take on this new challenge, but one glance at the reading list immediately made me nervous. I'd read about half of the recommended books at most, and some of them I'd never even heard of. It was OK bluffing little first years, CSE hoodlums and super-swot GCE pupils, but I had a sneaky feeling that teaching A-level was going to require some serious graft on my part.

Away from school, Henry had put up the rent rather more than I was expecting. This news coincided with a tip-off I received that there was a spare room going for forty quid a week in a shared house much closer to the school. I rang, went round and met the other tenants, passed the interview and was accepted from the first day of September. I was sad to leave my bedsit, but I'd never really felt comfortable in the rest of the yawning house, and Henry had never extended a very warm welcome for me to use it. The prospect of sharing a house with a group of other humans seemed just fine, so I decided to pack my bags and move on.

The Thursday night binges were of course scheduled to continue, but I still felt too weak to join in the football preliminaries. I was scared, with some justification, of a relapse of the dysentery I'd suffered – the condition having been confirmed by the local doctor. But football still reared its head. Ian Bridge, the head of PE, asked if I would like to take the third-year football team for the year, beginning in October, which I agreed to, failing to realise that this would require me to take training sessions every Wednesday night and worse, oblige me to rise early from my bed every Saturday morning to attend the games. Moaning quietly to Butler in the Dirty Corner about this foolish decision, my colleague rubbed his chin and pronounced, 'Ah, don't worry about it, Bally. If you do it alright you'll get promoted to grade two by this time next year. It's the only way to do it, mate. You can be a first-class nummock in the classroom, but if you don your wellies and shout your bollocks off on the touchline every Saturday, you'll get the nod – mark my words. We've all done it. It's standard practice, mate.' This was some consolation, since the dizzy heights of a scale two and the extra salary it would bring in had looked light years away to me, but I could see that Butler was serious.

Although these were significant events, they were easily eclipsed by one that took place at the beginning of a lesson with my new GCE literature class. Despite their being as distant and as serious as the previous year's pupils had been,

I nevertheless felt sorry for them having to wade through a turgid selection of poems by William Wordsworth as an introduction to the course for that year. As we prepared to wander lonely as clouds one rainy September morn of that first term, I hauled my large green bag on to the desk at the front of the silent class and began to scrabble about in its depths for a copy of the Wordsworth. Fumbling blindly among sheets of paper, exercise books and last year's orange peel, I suddenly felt something soft and silken-like between my fingers. Surprised by this unexpected tactile tingle, I tugged on the material and lifted it up through the innards of the bag. Whatever it was, it snagged slightly on some books as it reached the surface and then shot out into the light, precariously balanced between my thumb and forefinger. To my dismay, I found the sea of thirty expectant faces suddenly obscured by a small black pair of lacy knickers. Dropping them with admirable speed back into the place from whence they had come, I found myself lost for words. The class looked up at me quizzically. Its collective expression seemed to say, 'Did we just see what we thought we saw?' whilst my own most probably announced, 'Yes but let's just pretend that we didn't, OK?' Had it been Gray and the harem – already a distant memory – such a gaffe would probably have spelled the beginning of the end. But this new group was made of more diplomatic stuff. One of its more interesting members, an unfeasibly long-haired individual who, despite his unkempt appearance, was a seriously bright student, had taken to sitting at the front. For some odd reason he seemed, to enjoy the Wordsworth, but at that particular moment he seemed to enjoy the sight of the knickers even more. As they dropped back into the safer darkness of the bag, he looked at me through his mass of heavy-metal hair and grinned, ever so slightly. I raised an eyebrow at subliminal speed, just enough to acknowledge some communion with him, then managed to divert the class back to the Lake District.

The knickers belonged to Sarah, a university student who had left in the earlier hours of that same morning. I'd met her a couple of nights previously at a party to which I'd been dragged reluctantly by Rob, an old mate from Grimsby who had just moved from Oxford to Hull to begin his PhD in psychology. It often seems to be the case that psychology students are in most need of treatment, and although I liked Rob a lot, he was a wild and dangerous character wholly incapable of imagining that any of his friends might have to actually go out to work in the morning.

He'd persuaded me one Tuesday night to gatecrash a student party in one of the hovels down the terraced streets near the campus – to which I'd reluctantly agreed. In the kitchen around midnight, as I was attempting to batter a hole in the top of a 'party four' can of Watneys Red Barrel with a screwdriver, an elegant upper-class voice enquired, 'Would this help, by any chance?' Looking up and expecting to see the Queen Mother, my eyes fell instead upon a tall, dark-haired vision, can-opener in hand. She was dressed in a fetching pair of pink dungarees, and from her right shoulder hung a short fur jacket. She smiled and handed me the utensil. 'Having problems?' she asked. It may have been the beer, or perhaps the fatigue at the end of a working day, but try as I might, no words would jump out into the stale air of that kitchen. The cat had my tongue, fearing that I might sully the moment with my Cleethorpes cadences. All I wanted was for her to stay there. Eventually regaining the powers of speech and noticing, over the girl's shoulder, the hasty back-door departure of Rob with a stolen party-can under his arm, I handed her a plastic cup of the cheapest bitter and, hoping that she had no one else to waste her time with, engaged her in tittle-tattle for the best part of the next two hours. Despite the accent, she seemed thoroughly normal, witty and charming, but probably out of my league. With a simple 'Erm – would you like to meet up for a drink on Thursday?' (Wednesday would have made it look a bit too desperate), she replied magically – 'Yes'. It was a pretty *yes*, with all sorts of interesting bits attached.

I loved her from the first minute of that happy Thursday night. I suppose it was the tension. I just kept expecting her to walk off, to tire of this temporary social experiment. I learned that Daddy had sent her to university rather against her wishes, and that she was already bored and confused by the degree in linguistics she'd been bullied into taking. But she didn't seem the archetypal spoiled brat. She'd already been in London for a year, working for her brother who had converted an old Suffolk canal barge into a floating club on St Katharine's Dock. She hadn't exactly been toiling down the pit, but had nevertheless been trying to work for a living. Her father owned some sort of estate in Scotland and belonged to the Douglas clan. She didn't sound remotely Scottish.

We'd gone back to my new house that Thursday for the inevitable coffee, and the coffee had led on to the less inevitable but thoroughly enjoyable *do-we-don't-we* dance in the hall, equidistant between the bottom of the stairs and the front door. It was a cold night, and the stairs won. However, being one of those men who is never quite sure that a woman is really about to sleep with him until the voluntary removal of that final piece of clothing is inexorably and happily effected – I refer to knickers – I'd stood gormlessly by the edge of my new single bed, wondering if she was really, truly about to jump in. I still couldn't quite believe that she was standing there. 'Perhaps you should turn the light off,' she suggested kindly. I willingly obliged. As she whipped off her knickers in double-quick time, she must have tossed them unthinkingly into the darkness of the bedroom. When I woke up she'd gone – obviously having tired of the search.

But if the GCE class had noticed that day, they'd been too polite to make a fuss. If they'd looked closer still, they might have noticed that I was happier too. Life seemed to have a purpose to it again, above and beyond dragging myself to school every morning. Adding to the sum of life's great mysteries, Sarah seemed to like me, and we were spending more and more time together. She even came to meet me from school one afternoon, causing a near sensation amongst the older pupils streaming out of the gates. This raised up my status several notches. 'Was that *your* girlfriend, sir?' came the inevitable question the next day. On confirming this, several of my interrogators seemed to look mystified, as if such a union between beauty and beast were impossible. When she turned up one Thursday night at the pub – which I'd set up as an excuse in order to get away earlier than closing time – the football crowd had gawped up from their beers in a disbelieving, pheromone-fuelled silence. In the Dirty Corner the next day the comments rained down. 'Come clean, Bally. You're not really going out with that! You paid her to turn up, you wanker.'

But it was all genuine. I even got to meet the clan. We chugged slowly to Scotland in the Beetle one Friday night. Somewhere in the hilly countryside of deepest Ayrshire we turned off on an unmarked path. It twisted and turned in the darkness until we came to an old gatehouse at a clearing in the pinewoods. From there a track led towards the lights of an enormous old house, standing tall in the moonlight. Once introduced to the laird and lady of the manor, we sat by an enormous old fireplace supping whisky into the small hours, shadows flickering like clichés on the high walls. Her mother seemed to take to me, but the old man wasn't so sure. Tall and thin, dressed in old brown corduroys and sporting a leather waistcoat, he looked like the Hammer Films version of Peter Cushing – suspicious of everyone and everything. He seemed predictably disappointed by my choice of profession, and when I told him I came from Cleethorpes he looked at me with a puzzled expression. 'And where on God's earth is Cleethorpes?' he asked, reasonably, I suppose.

'Sort of down there.' I grinned, pointing past the flaming logs in a southerly direction.

When I reciprocated and finally plucked up the courage to take her to Cleethorpes the opposite happened. Whereas my father couldn't take his eyes off her, my mum was more reserved, less suspicious of Sarah than of her son's own motives for stepping into what might prove to be tricky financial terrain – namely that she had it, and I never would. But only the first part of the equation was untrue. Sarah never seemed to have two pennies to rub together, and from what I could gather, her dad had fallen on harder times after some ill-advised investments. It made me feel better about her. It helped to fuel my fantasy that my six-grand-a-year salary would impress her sufficiently to stay with me for just another week, just another month.

Meanwhile, I had to earn the six grand, and the obvious downside of my inheritance of the third-year football team was that it obliged me to rise from the snug Saturday morning sheets at a far earlier hour than I would have wished, especially given the new motive for staying put. Nevertheless, the new role as football manager was proving to be more interesting than I'd thought. For the first Wednesday afternoon training session some fourteen urchins had turned up, most of whom had played for the school team the previous year. They came in all shapes and sizes, but they looked keen enough. On that fair autumn afternoon I applied the previously learned rule of feigning competence, asking them to run around the pitch a couple of times before we got down to 'the more serious stuff'.

As they jogged and stumbled around the perimeter, I tried to think of things to do. By the time they'd run up to me waiting for the next words of wisdom, I'd simply decided to watch them play a game, seven against seven. As they sorted themselves into their preferred positions and began to play, I was surprised by the quality I'd inherited – an unexpected stroke of good luck. This was confirmed a fortnight later when we were visited one wet Saturday morning by our first opponents, a school with a rough-house reputation from deepest Hull. Their malcontent teacher ignored me and stood over on the opposite touchline, yelling a mixture of expletives and baffling tactical advice into the indifferent air. His team, with the unfortunate look of future convicts about them, attempted to visit mass murder upon my shiny new team from beginning to end, but were simply too slow to make contact. My team, still functioning on orders from the previous year, simply took them apart.

Three of the team were in my new third-year class. This was a group that had seemed a little too bubbly for comfort. The centre-forward, a large bespectacled kid called Chris, had been looking like a potential source of trouble – a little too bright for his own good, a little bit too mouthy. Already the established leader of the class because of his football prowess, he'd seemed bent on challenging me from day one, to show me who was boss. Everything I'd done had brought on some little reproach, some little gesture of disapproval. When I'd announced that the class reader for the term was going to be *Lord of the Flies*, a book that I thought they were ready for, he'd announced to no one in particular, 'Oh, it's boring. I've read it.' And, hackneyed though the idea might have been to take them out for a walk around the school grounds one leafy sunny morning – with the aim of getting them to write a poem about the six senses – it was Chris who had been the one to point it out. 'Aw, not poetry, sir! Walk around and kick up some leaves? Listen to the *rustling* sounds! That's really original, sir.' Then, worst of all, I'd asked them to write an essay about how they saw themselves as grown-ups, and the kind of job they thought they might be suited to. Chris's essay began:

'I've really no idea of what I want to be when I get older, but I know what I don't want to be. I'm not going to be a teacher. My dad told me what George Bernard Shaw said. *Those who can, do. Those who cannot, teach.*'

I'd ticked the quotation through clenched teeth as a good example of essay construction, but his cleverness was beginning to grate. Besides, he was contaminating the class atmosphere. Just as I was beginning to think that it might get out of hand, the football began. As soon as I took charge of the team, he seemed to change overnight. After the first win, he stayed behind after class on the Monday.

'So you play football then, sir?'

'Yes, Chris – kind of. We play Thursday nights after school – you know, some of the teachers.'

'Butler took us last year, sir. He was dead funny. And I never thought he'd be any good, but he is. I mean as a player, sir. I saw him play one night for the staff. He's brilliant.'

'Yes, he is good. Some of the others are too. Mr Rix, and Mr Greendale. Just goes to show, eh?'

'Yeah I know. I was going to say that. Rixy said you're quite good too. I asked him.'

I'd not realised that there'd be other, less complicated ways of solving discipline problems. I could play football, and we'd won our first school match. From then on, when the class noise ever threatened to rise above the acceptable levels, Chris would shut them up. Like Kelly at Lynton, no one crossed him. I'd been handed a different hat. English teacher, but football trainer on Saturday mornings. There was a common purpose. Football had that simple logic to it. In the classroom, try as I might, no pupil was ever really going to thank me for the homework I'd just set him, no matter how conscientious he might have been. Out on the football pitch it was different. When the team scored, they'd look back at you for approval, look to see how happy they'd made you. In the minibus on the way home there was that dumb but satisfying feeling of togetherness. The players would try it on, peppering their excited post-match chat with swear words to test me out, asking me if they could smoke, going a little too far in their questions about my private life. But it felt fine, in a strange way. It made me feel as though I was really becoming a teacher. Butler had been right. '*It's standard practice, mate.*'

Another factor which worked in my favour was the arrival of a new teacher to the department, a young graduate by the name of Mary Pomfret. I suddenly felt more senior, and found myself talking to her as if I'd been teaching there for thirty years. The Mark Lammiman factor also came into play, since she was as nervous as a newly-wed. Thin, blonde and pale, she smoked incessantly with shaking hands, casting frightened glances around the staffroom as if someone were about to steal her handbag. 'Are you Phil?' she'd asked on the first day back. Her voice was permanently hoarse, like she had a bird's nest in her throat. 'I just wanted to ask where the library was,' she continued, her eyes bulging.

'Hasn't Lund told you?' I asked, reasonably.

'Yeah,' she replied, blowing out a stream of smoke. 'But I've forgotten. And I daren't ask that Julie,' she whispered, looking over my shoulder. 'She scares me shitless.'

Much to my chagrin, she was given a sixth-form group from the off, either because Lund thought she was a genius or because no one else fancied it. The latter reason seemed improbable to me, now that I had my own group. As with the football team, there seemed to be a purpose to teaching this class, above and beyond paying the rent and having enough left over for beer and fish and chips. My A-level group was quite small, with a dozen hardy volunteers. There was some meaty stuff to get through in the next two years, assuming I survived. There was *King Lear*, *A Passage to India*, *Waiting for Godot*, some Chaucer, Yeats and Tennyson. But heavy though it looked, as soon as I launched them into something that I vaguely knew about and liked – the Beckett – some of the old excitement came creeping back. I hoped that they might get the electric charge, the voltage that had surged through me when Johnny Roe had first begun to read *Lord of the Flies* all those years back.

'*Nothing happens, nobody comes, nobody goes – it's awful!*' moaned one of the characters in *Waiting for Godot*, standing in an empty landscape. It reminded me of Steve's picture, back on the scales at Birds Eye – the cubist businessman in the desert, going 'Nowhere in Particular'. And sure enough, little by little you could see the sixth-formers wilting, see them drooping like flowers in the sudden darkness of their day. Most of them were getting it, most of them were seeing the bleakness of the play through its superficial smile of clowning and easy dialogue. You could tell that it was getting to them, at that precise time of life when they'd rather it didn't – when they'd rather believe that everything was going to turn out rosy in the garden, now that they'd passed their GCEs and marched into the happy dawn of the sixth form, with its greater freedoms, its sexiness, and its promise of the tantalising goodies of adulthood. And bang! Along comes this play, saying that it was all a waste of time, telling them not to get their hopes up. At first I thought that they resented me for having tricked them into reading it, but after a few months I could tell that they were hooked, and that they wanted more.

Then John Lennon died that December, shot by Mark Chapman outside his New York apartment. I had one of those radios that came on in the morning with the alarm. It was tuned to Radio 1. As I lay quietly dozing, reluctant to rise from the warm sheets, song after song that I knew

Lennon had written came softly from the radio, unaccompanied by the normal DJ babble. Confused, I stumbled downstairs to find Dave, one of my new fellow residents, all swollen-eyed and emotional over his cornflakes. 'They shot him!' he moaned. 'They shot Lennon!'

I drove to school in a kind of rigid silence. The world suddenly seemed a darker place. It reminded me of when Kennedy was shot. I'd come rushing in from the garden after grazing my knee. My mother put her finger to her lips and ignored me, continuing to listen intently to the radio. Every time I tried to speak, the finger returned to her lips, as if she were oblivious to my distress. It was the only time she ever ignored me.

I had the sixth-form group first lesson. Sitting in the funereal silence in the staffroom, I scrabbled through the Tennyson we had started some weeks back, and found what I was looking for: a long miserable poem called *In Memoriam*, written to mourn the death of the poet's friend, Arthur Hallam. We were going to study it anyway, but I decided to bring it forward, just to cheer things up a little further. During the class, I found the lines I wanted them to remember, that wet December day.

> *And ghastly through the drizzling rain,*
> *On the bald street breaks the blank day*

One student, a particularly sensitive girl called Cathy, threw the book into the air. 'That's too much!' she wailed. 'I can't take any more of this!' – which was exactly the reaction I'd been hoping for. They'd remember Lennon's death, and they'd remember Tennyson.

And I knew that most days, whilst their science A-level peers returned for lunch to the sixth-form centre chatting about the latest experiments and the difficulty of manipulating their Bunsen burners, the English group would trudge back, their tortured souls on fire. I'd taken to wandering over to the centre after lunch with John Butler because the jukebox had some fairly good stuff on it, but I went mainly because I wanted to watch them sitting in clumps in their common room, talking about the set books. I even wandered over sometimes and joined in. It felt good. It felt good to know they were miserable, but for all the right reasons.

15

LEAVING (AGAIN)

We reached the semi-finals of the Raich Carter Cup that year, losing to Beverley Grammar School. Note the use of *we*. By the Easter of that year, ridiculous though it seemed, I was engaged on a personal crusade to win the double – league and cup. At one point I found myself seated Buddha-like in my bedroom surveying a floor scattered with Subbuteo players borrowed from Dave, a fellow football enthusiast from among my new housemates in Newgate Street. The plastic players represented the various third years from my school team, and their positions on the carpet represented the possible tactical approaches to be adopted for the cup semi-final. Our eventual defeat was a noble one, compensation arriving three weeks later in the shape of the league title.

Life had rarely seemed so good. A week after this achievement – one which, if I'm honest, felt far more important than getting my degree – I noticed an advertisement in a national newspaper inviting applications for the post of manager at Stoke City FC, then in the old First Division. It was one of the last times I saw this quaint little ritual acted out, where a professional football team would advertise in the national press, as though the post of manager were a public one, like the civil service. I decided to apply for the job. The letter, whose copy and reply I still have pasted into an old scrapbook, went like this:

Dear Sir,

With reference to your advertisement in The Daily Mail of Thursday June 18, 1981, I wish to apply for the post of manager of Stoke City FC for the coming season.

I have recently steered the third-year team from Willerton High School to the league title of the Hull and District under-14s championship, and to the semi-final of the local Raich Carter Cup. The fact that these successes were achieved in my debut season as a manager leads me to believe that I may be of interest to your club. I feel that I have the necessary qualities of enthusiasm and organisation required for such a post, and that my experience with such a young team will stand me in good stead for helping to develop the club's youth policy.

I look forward to your reply.

Faithfully Yours

Philip Ball

When I jokingly told Lund the next day that I'd applied for the job at Stoke City, his face fell a mile. 'Stoke?' he snapped, adopting the DH Lawrence frown. 'You're applying to a school in Stoke? You're leaving us? Why on earth do you want to go there?' Lund didn't know much about football, but I'd grown to quite like him, from a distance anyway. Nevertheless, he would have been a victim, back at my school. He took things a tad too seriously, was far too intelligent to ever be happy, and most damningly had never heard of Stoke City FC. But I'd grown to appreciate the bollocking that he'd given me the year before about not taking criticism. I still couldn't take it, but at least it had made me think. So I put him in the picture about Stoke, whereupon he smiled weakly and walked off to make himself a coffee. *You're leaving us?* he'd said, giving himself away. I rather liked the tone he'd used. Some teeny-weeny tonal shift in it had suggested that he hadn't wanted me to go – that he valued me. Or maybe it was just my little fantasy. All this success was going to my head.

Cruelly, I was turned down for the Stoke job. If my memory serves me correctly, a certain Richie Barker was awarded the post, and so I carried on as before. Nevertheless, in that wonderfully noble English way, I received a letter thanking me for the application and politely informing me that the post had been filled. It also hoped that I would continue to enjoy a fruitful career as a football manager. Well, I guess that would have been interesting, but there were other things to take care of. One of them was Sarah. I could see that she was sort of happy with me, but not so with her course at the university. She'd also become friendly with another posh student called Zoe, a waster from down south who was clearly intent on sleeping with the entire male contingent of the campus. That was absolutely fine, but Sarah was spending too much time with her and I was worried in case Zoe's behaviour became contagious. Apart from that, she was several essays behind, and try as I might to help her, I found linguistics a closed book, as it were. Sarah was muttering about going back to London. We'd been a couple of times to her brother's barge, and I'd found it all pretty amazing. Growing up in Cleethorpes, London had scared me. You could always spot the provincial peasant like me, down for a day out, gawping up at the sky and pointing at the airplanes while the rest of the population hurried by, strangely unconcerned. I'd always felt on the outside in London, a city whose impenetrable and exotic social life I'd only heard of second-hand. But now that I was in with the in-crowd, I was too easily captivated by it all.

As a bonus I got to see John Cutts again. The second time I went down we invited him to the boat, and when I popped my head out from the barge's hatch at the appointed time of meeting he was there on the quayside, smoking a roll-up. On climbing through the hatch and descending to the luxury lounge below, from his mouth leapt the inevitable 'facking 'ell'. My sentiments exactly, but I knew it couldn't last. London wasn't for me and Hull wasn't for Sarah. Something had to give.

We went to the States that summer. I'd saved enough money for the holiday, and Sarah 'borrowed' some from

Mumsy. We decided to fly to San Francisco on 29 July, via the old 'bucket-shop' system whereby you turned up on the day and took the cheapest ticket available. I'd figured that no one else would be flying on that day, featuring as it did the wedding of Charles and Diana. Unfortunately, everyone else had clearly thought the same. The only flight available was to Seattle. I knew Jimi Hendrix had been born there, but I had no idea where it was. When we landed, it turned out to be one hell of a way to San Francisco.

The subsequent holiday turned out to be an unfortunately symbolic one. The photographs I took of all the places we eventually saw – the Grand Canyon, Las Vegas, the Golden Gate Bridge – were in the end nothing but wasted energy. After we returned home and handed in the five films, the shop assistant informed us a week later that none of the shots had come out. The camera lens had been broken, probably before we'd even set off. Rightly or wrongly, I felt strangely forlorn, as if the whole experience had been wiped out.

By the time I was back at school in September, Sarah was gone, in London in search of work. In her absence, I began to revert back to old ways – failing to change my sheets for weeks on end, neglecting to wash my socks, and nipping my new hobby of cooking in the bud. I had figured she might be impressed if I could cook. My mentor John had once told me during a campus therapy session: 'Fackin 'ell. Never mind about the size of your knob. Women never look at it anyway. Nah – what they like is two things. A bloke who can cook grub and a bloke who can fix a motor. Naffin' else matters.' I couldn't do either, but it didn't seem to matter once Sarah had gone.

Once she had, it became doubly frustrating to observe mating rituals all around – even in the staffroom. One morning, sitting quietly in the Dirty Corner minding my own, I overheard Butler ask Blacktoft:

'Objective fulfilled, dear colleague?'

Blacktoft mysteriously replied, 'Objective fulfilled. Over and out.'

'And was said objective worth the bother, dear colleague?' enquired Butler.

'Said objective was very much worth the bother. So much so that it is scheduled to continue, indefinitely,' upon which his interrogator concluded with the interesting, 'You are indeed a fortunate young man.'

Keeping my head buried in *King Lear*, I was nevertheless curious as to the meaning of this lively exchange. As Blacktoft got to his feet, he let slip a cryptic message in a slightly lower voice. 'It wasn't a case of marrows in sheds. Rather a case of roses in baths,' he said, and strode off to registration with a contented smirk on his face. I was stunned. The reference to marrows could only mean one thing. Since Rixy had first used the rich metaphor to describe the deeds one might get up to in the Environmental Science room, the males on the staff had continued to stare longingly at Eileen, the voluptuous newly-wed who had begun her career at the same time as me. Was it possible? Blacktoft was himself a married man, but had always had an unfortunate habit of complaining about his wife in the Dirty Corner. Roses in the bath? No – it couldn't be. Staffrooms had proved to be rather different places from what I had imagined as a pupil, but intra-staff shagging? It seemed the last bastion.

Unhealthily obsessed with this issue over the next few days, I watched Blacktoft and Eileen closely. The truth hit home after the third day of observation. Standing behind her in the queue for the kettle at morning break, the tall figure of Blacktoft looked around furtively, checking to see if anyone was watching. Satisfied that the coast was clear (I was once again scanning the pages of *Lear*), his free hand dropped to the level of Eileen's rump, upon which it proceeded to covertly caress what looked to me like a willing right buttock. I was both jealous and appalled – and then appalled with myself for being jealous. I stared into the book. What the hell did they have in common anyway? Maybe he could cook? I was pretty sure that he didn't know how to fix cars.

Interestingly, Blacktoft left in the January of that third year, taking up a scale-three post at another school in Hull. We all congratulated him on his success, and bade him farewell. At his leaving speech, he promised to keep in touch and to carry on playing football with us on Thursday nights, but by that time I had already winkled out of Butler the fact that Thursday nights (from which he'd often been absent) were his excuse to his wife for staying out late. It seemed that Eileen's hubby was a pilot on the Hull-Rotterdam ferry, which coincidentally enough steamed out from port every Thursday afternoon.

Mercifully, he was at the wheel and unaware of our presence a month or so later when the staff football team took the
same overnight ferry, invited to play a match in Rotterdam
against a small local football club whose captain knew our
head of PE, Ian Bridge. We'd been booked to sleep on the
reclining seats, not through miserliness but rather because all
the cabins were already occupied. It was rough when we set
out from Hull, and once we hit the open sea the boat began
to lurch alarmingly. Worse, my right groin was beginning to
hurt, so much so that I began to grimace with the pain.
We were in the bar sitting in a circle, and Burnsy was the first
to notice.

'What's up, Bally? Need a crap?' I told the assembled
throng that my groin was killing me. Ex-pro Burnsy was
immediately on to it. 'You were limping on Wednesday
night in the staff match, weren't you?' I nodded. 'You had
new boots, didn't you?' I nodded again. The pain was
getting worse. 'Take your shoe off, Bally. Let me look at
your ankle.' The teachers collectively held their noses as I
obeyed, and it soon became clear what the problem was.
'There you go,' said Burnsy, pointing at a small half-formed
scab on my Achilles tendon. 'Classic stuff. Your boots
have rubbed the scab too much, and it's gone septic. Always
feel it first in the groin.' Terrified by this, I asked him what
I should do as the rest of the gathering began to laugh at
my discomfort. 'Nothing you can do, mate. Wait till the
morning and we'll get you some antibiotics in town.
Meanwhile, a double whisky should do the trick.' One of

the teachers had some aspirins, which I gulped down with what remained of my pint.

Miserable, I traipsed over to the reclining seats, pulled out my sleeping bag and lay on the floor between the hard plastic rows. The movement of the boat's pitch and toss seemed even more pronounced as I lay there, feeling thoroughly sorry for myself. We were barely an hour into the crossing, and I was to miss out on the bar session. I'd been looking forward to letting my hair down a little. Slowly the aspirins took effect, and I began to drift off.

Suddenly, someone was shaking me awake. 'Bally! Bally!' It was Burnsy. I blinked up at the lights and focused on the drunken face floating above me. I wasn't even sure where I was. 'Bally – I know you're knackered, but you just have to come and look at this,' and he pulled at my arms and hauled me out of my sleeping bag. As I limped after him, hit by the sudden chill of the saloon, we emerged into a large disco area. Burnsy stopped me on the edge of the heaving mass of bodies, all dancing to a cheesy organ player, up on stage to our left. 'That one's mine!' hollered Burnsy, pointing across to the right where a middle-aged woman sat patiently to the side of the dance floor. She spotted us and waved across. 'It's fucking paradise, Bally! They're all from the fish finger line at the Findus factory. On their annual night out. They save all year and then do the overnight on the boat, leaving their old men at home!' I smiled wanly. 'Come on, Bally! You're not that knackered. They're all up for a shag. That's what they're here for. There's hundreds of 'em! And best of all – they've all got their own cabins!' And with that, Burnsy could wait no more. As he bounded off to his evening's valentine, I made my way gingerly to an empty table on the margins of the throng.

It was true. From what I could make out above the din of whoops and whirls, the entire gathering of the substantial fish finger section from Findus was there, fighting like forty-something Amazons to claim their scalps for the night. The air of desperation was entirely due to the fact that they outnumbered the males four-to-one. Rixy was already being tugged from the dance floor by at least three women, and Butler and Blacktoft – the latter invited for the trip – had already disappeared, presumably to separate cabins. Burnsy then scampered off with his lady, and as I watched in an aspirin daze from the sidelines, the entire team began to gradually slip away, one by one to their new and comfortable cabin beds. Some of the women must have noticed me sitting there forlorn, but had obviously decided that I wasn't worth it. I limped back to the bone-hard reclining seats and my sleeping bag, half suicidal.

In the bleary dawn, we were met off the boat by a minibus from the football club, for the drive to Rotterdam. For the mercifully short journey, I was obliged to listen to lurid tales of cabin sex and over-eager housewives keen on making the most of their annual fantasy night out. 'How old was yours, Greeny?' cackled some wag. 'Which one?' roared the German teacher, brought along for his linguistic skills rather than his footballing accomplishments. 'Not sure about mine either,' added Butler. 'But she looked much better after she'd put her false teeth in,' and so on and so forth. 'How did you get on, Bally? Did you ask anyone to take a look at your groin?'

'Just take me to the chemists,' was all I could manage.

On the Monday after the fateful trip, Lund announced at the departmental meeting that as a result of Blacktoft's departure, a scale-two post had become available. He then added that they intended to advertise for a scale-one teacher to replace Blacktoft, but that they would interview internally for the scale two. In the awkward silence, even I knew that this could mean only one thing. I shot a quick glance around the table. The only members of the department still on the bottom rung were myself and Mary Pomfret, the hoarse and jittery young woman who had arrived the year before and who was still giving the impression of being on the verge of a nervous breakdown. Our eyes met for a second, but she was clearly thinking the same thing. It was me versus her.

For once in my life, I felt like the front-runner. I'd been there a year longer than her, and even though I might not have been too popular with the headmaster – who still contrived to avoid me as much as possible – it seemed to me that Pomfret's neurotically nervy persona made my own relative lack of confidence look like it came from the self-doubt school of John Wayne. 'If everything ain't black and white, I say, why the hell not?' For Mary everything was grey, even the blue skies of a summer morning. Not only had she sat on so many fences she probably had piles, but she was possessed of a serious pessimism. It didn't inspire too much confidence. Her sixth-form group had already nicknamed her 'Possibly Pomfret' due to her tendency to answer any question with the former part of the phrase. Would you like a coffee, Mary? Possibly. Would you like a scale two and a hike in salary, Mary? Possibly.

Then again, I tended to like people who made me feel better about myself. She was also very funny, behind the jazz singer's croak and the shaky hands. Once in the staffroom she'd told me that Tessa had taken her aside and advised her that she might get on a little better if she could try to be 'a little less self-deprecating'. Lighting up yet another cigarette, Mary croaked out to me, 'Self-deprecating? That's nothing. I'm so far gone I'm self-defecating.' But the fact that we got on quite well could hardly hide the fact that we were now competing against each other for promotion. I needed the money and so did she. I needed a new Beetle, and she needed a mortgage.

The interviews were scheduled for the Monday, and the only thing that I'd prepared, with the covert help of John Butler, was some concrete 'responsibility' I could offer them in exchange for this potential gear-shift in my salary. John had told me to offer 'resources'. This was a suitably vague concept that covered everything from ordering chalk to building up a library of videos, some of which might even be deemed to be of educational value. Back then, actually knowing how to load a video and press 'play' was considered an esoteric skill akin to alchemy, and Butler assured me that at the very mention of *video library* I would get the job.

Meanwhile, on being asked if she had anything similar to offer the department, Pomfret would simply answer 'possibly'. The cards appeared to be stacked in my favour.

On the Saturday before the big interview, I talked on the phone to Sarah, who was weepy because there were no real work prospects in London. 'Maybe I'll come back to Hull,' she said, with the slightly annoying implication that such a move would only be out of desperation. When we'd finally hung up, Dave from the house invited me out for a drink. At the second pub we got to, who should sidle up to the bar as I was ordering but my opponent for the Monday, Miss Pomfret herself.

'Mary!' I exclaimed, pretending to be pleased to see her. 'Would you like a drink?' at which Mary grinned inanely – obviously half-cooked. 'Make it two. I'm with a mate,' she finally replied, nodding in the direction of a table at which another young woman was sitting. I introduced Dave, after which there was no choice but to go and sit with them. We joined them at their table. Loosened by the drink, Mary began to slobber and croak.

'You know, what's your name – Dave? You know … erm … that's Phil. He's all right, he is. No, he's not. He's a bastard. He's going for the same job as me, you know? Same job as me! What chance do I stand? He's already got it. That Tessa loves him. It's cos he's a bloke. Blah, blah … fucking knitting. She loves him, Dave!'

Her more sober friend jumped in. They'd obviously been talking about it before we came in. 'Oh, don't talk yourself down so, Mary,' she scolded. 'You're as good as the next man,' she huffed, scowling slightly in my direction.

'That's true.' I nodded. 'All's fair in love and war, eh? You'd better buy me a drink now, Mary, so that all debts are paid before the big day.' Unfortunately, she took me at my word, and the double vodka she plopped down for herself onto the table eventually took her beyond the slurring stage. Her friend, increasingly irritated by the whole scene, suddenly looked at her watch.

'I've got to go now, Mary, I'm sorry. I said I'd meet Jane in town. Can you get back all right?' Mary nodded, her enormous eyes beginning to bulge from their sockets. She was somewhere else. When her friend had escaped, Dave looked at his watch too.

'Reckon I'll split for *Match of the Day*,' he explained, more sincerely. Mary's lights were slowly turning off, one by one.

'OK, Dave – see you later.' I nodded, casting an awkward glance at my colleague. I offered to walk her home.

'I'm on me bike,' she whimpered, her head beginning to sag and her eyes beginning to close. 'No lights on the bike. Not here ... not here either,' and she pointed slowly at her head. 'What we going to do?'

'I'll walk it for you,' I offered, appalled by this piece of bad luck.

But it got worse. As she hit the cold air outside the pub, swaying and tottering, she announced to the street in general, 'I live in Hull. It's too far to walk the bike. Can I sleep at your place?' As I began to wheel her bike in the vague direction of Hull and she lurched after me, the quandary hit me between the eyes. She was clearly in no state to return, and yet even if I put her in a taxi, I would still have the problem of her bike. Either way, avoiding her the next day was looking increasingly unlikely. I decided to take her back for a real coffee, in the hope that it might sober her up. She agreed, but to my further dismay – as she hobbled on behind me – she started to laugh. 'Coffee, eh? I know you! You dirty bastard!' Despite my ignoring these half-volleys of slurred phrases from behind, they seemed to grow increasingly lewd as we made painstaking process down the empty streets. 'Dirty bugger ... aaaah ... fucking blokes all the same ... just want a leg-over ...' I was terrified in case some sixth-formers were out on the town, or even worse, some of their parents.

Finally we got back to my place. As she practically fell into the porch, the grim truth dawned. She was too pissed even for coffee. Worse than that, my fellow tenants were all staring through from the lounge, *Match of the Day* still playing on the TV. All the sofas were taken up. I grinned pathetically and began to haul her upstairs. I could sleep on the floor. Why did these things always happen to me? Why couldn't life just be a little bit more ordinary? About five hours later, in the pitch dark, a small voice spoke from the bed above. 'Aren't you coming in then?' it asked, the drunken slur entirely absent. 'Isn't it cold down there?' It was bloody freezing.

'Possibly,' I muttered into the dark, hoping she might get the joke. 'But no funny business, OK?'

I got the job. For the entire week afterwards, I tried to avoid her, but it was hopeless. Trying to hide in the library on the Tuesday, she came in after me and sat quietly beside me.

'You got me pissed,' she whispered. '*You* got me pissed,' she repeated, since I'd continued to stare into space. 'You took me home and you *took advantage of me*!' she breathed in my ear.

'No, I fucking didn't,' I whispered back, still not looking at her. 'Quite the opposite.' Her face went red.

'You *planned* it all!' she wheezed. 'You planned it so that I'd be emotionally unstable at the interview!' and on that note she stormed out.

'What's the matter with her?' asked Delia, sorting out library cards by the door.

'Oh, nothing,' I managed. 'We were just talking about Shakespeare.'

Where I had talked about Shakespeare had been in my sixth-form class. At the end of the year, my A-level group took their exams and ten out of the twelve passed. Before the results, I'd been even more nervous than when I'd been waiting for my own, seven years before. There were some good pupils in that class, and I'd enjoyed the emotional ride with them. Mary's group did OK, too. A-levels were powerful things. They were difficult, they demanded a maturity that some didn't have, and best of all, they set you thinking.

So powerful had the experience been for me as a pupil that I still have the dream, every late August when the term is coming round again, that I am sitting at a desk in a large examination hall. The questions are usually about history, I'm not sure why. I'm staring at the questions, but I know that I haven't revised. There's nothing I can write. The feeling of helplessness, as the rest of the hall scribbles away furiously, is stressful beyond description. And all the time I'm saying to myself, 'What am I *doing* here? I've passed these. I've got a degree. I'm a teacher, for God's sake …'

I'm a teacher. The thought occurred to me one morning in the December of my fourth year at Willerton, as I opened the classified pages of the *Guardian* and saw an advertisement asking for several English teachers for a British Council School in Lima, Peru. Darkest Peru, where Paddington Bear came from. I was a teacher, but then what? The future was rather vague. Sarah was still in London, and we were drifting apart. It was inevitable. I thought maybe she'd fancy a change, and that she'd pack her bags and come out to Lima with me. I wasn't ready for a mortgage, not just yet, so Peru suddenly sounded like a good idea. It was a three-year contract, and the money sounded fine. There was no other reason behind my application. I didn't even tell Sarah. I just fancied seeing what it might bring. And whatever it brought, I'd react to it, somehow or other.

When I was called to London for interview, it was incumbent upon me to come clean to Lund. He seemed less surprised than on the Stoke City occasion. 'OK. Thanks for telling me,' he said. 'And good luck.' He'd taught in Zambia in his early days, and seemed to understand. He also said some nice things in the reference letter, which only went to prove that he must still have thought I liked DH Lawrence and that he'd never got to hear about the Pomfret incident. It was also incumbent upon me to come clean to Sarah – not about Mary, of course, but about Peru. I told her a week before the interview. I met her for lunch on the day, but she seemed distant. 'So you don't fancy a bit of exotica?' I asked her, over pasta and salad in Bloomsbury. She looked down at her plate. 'No – not really, Phil,' she admitted, and then burst into tears. As usual, I'd got it wrong. 'Don't be upset,' I wailed across the table. 'I'll blow the interview. It's OK.'

But I didn't blow it. I got the job, and the southern hemisphere term was due to start in March. It was a school for boys, modelled on British educational values, whatever those were, and I was to teach English in secondary. After Christmas my air tickets arrived – British Airways to Paris then Air France to Lima, via Cayenne. It all sounded mysterious and far away, but tempted as I was to rip up the tickets and stay in the comfort zone, something told me to go through with it. I still loved Sarah, but there was no point in staying. Daddy was never going to take to me, and I was never going to move to London. The place still scared me far more than Peru.

For my leaving party at Willerton, gypsy overlord Stan Burns was the man delegated to write and deliver the farewell speech. I'd seen so many leave already that I never thought my day would come. Stan stood up and delivered a moving speech, making mention of my deft abilities on the football pitch, my promising career as a manager, and my endearing tendency to challenge entire rugby league teams to a fight. Just as I was thinking that he might end the speech without referring to my shining abilities as an English teacher, he delivered the following lines:

'And finally, it's a little-known fact, but Bally only got the job in Peru because of one thing. He told them at the interview that he'd had experience with *tinkers*, but they thought he'd said *Incas*.'

All that remained was to find the airport, and to see what the next three years might bring.

EPILOGUE

She was called Miss Havercroft, and she taught me when I was eight. Because junior school teachers take you for all subjects, they become important to you. You float in their orbit. You sink or swim in their pool. And I can see her now – blondish hair stacked up in a Sixties bouffant, a tight pink sweater and a pointy bra. Probably in her early thirties, she had a thin, slightly beaky nose, and was attractive in a sharp-edged sort of way. Unlike the women teachers from infant school, you knew there was no hug forthcoming from this one, no bosom of maternal warmth. She kept her distance, as if she wanted us to know that life was like that – that in the future we would have to look out for ourselves. But she was all right, Miss Havercroft. Although I was wary of her, I had no particular reason to dislike her. Kids accept what they get, and adjust to the tone the teacher sets. It's the survival instinct, and if a teacher is a predator, a prowler, you huddle into the group for protection. You keep your distance.

It must have been after a couple of months, but I re-member the day as clearly as an accident. We were doing arithmetic, and were sitting silently in groups of four on low circular tables. The room was dark, with high banana-coloured walls topped with small steamed-up windows. You could never really see outside – school and life were separate matters. We were doing long multiplication, and I simply didn't get it. The boy to my right had sensed that I was trying to copy and had curled his arm defensively around his exercise book, leaving me to face my demons. Miss Hovercraft, as we nicknamed her, of course, was hovering, checking on the progress of each group. I was still stuck on the first sum when she turned up, paralysed by my inability to write out the magical second line of numbers, the line that you have to shift to the left. I'd not internalised the trick as yet, whereas the others had. Miss Havercroft loomed above us. I can smell her now – a mixture of perfume and sour breath. She bent down and inserted her nose between the boy to the right and myself, and whispered the deathly phrase: 'Come on, Philip. You can't be that thick.' And from that point on, life was never the same again. She cannot know it, wherever she is now, but that casual little phrase changed my days and painted my horizons, for good or for bad.

If I met her now, in her dotage, I suppose I would have to forgive. She was right, of course. I was never going to be a great mathematician, and the bucket of cold water she threw over me that day at least woke me up to the fact, in a brutal sort of way. Maybe it would have been easier on the soul to have woken up to the truth in a gentler, more grad-ual manner, but it was not to be. Miss Havercroft was a bit of a cynic, looking back – a woman who spoke her mind, who was prepared to knock you down and leave you to pick up the pieces. She never taught me arithmetic, but she did teach me that life was not as sweet as it once might have appeared to be, in the rosier gardens of infancy. In that sense, she was merely the first. There were plenty more of these types lined up waiting for us, sleeves rolled up, in the dark corridors of childhood and adolescence. What I find more difficult to forgive is the language she used. *'You can't be that thick.'* The final word stuck with me throughout my childhood, like a pimple on the forehead. At least she'd had the heart to whisper it, so that the class couldn't hear. But why twist the knife? Why choose such a phrase in the first place?

And so I ask myself, forty years down the line, how many others have experienced this? It can work in happier ways too. Someone can whisper a word in your ear that sets you up for life, something that gives you the confidence to go out and stride the world like a Colossus, even if you end up flat on your face among the debris of your own making. But at least you were given the chance, probably by a person who was equally unaware that they were doing you the favour. It works both ways. There's casual cruelty and casual kindness, and everyone has their story to tell. Everyone can tell you about the teacher that made them or broke them, and they can tell you what the weather was like that day, and the colour of the socks that they were wearing.

A few years later, at secondary school, I took home my end-of-year report, written by my form master, the Latin teacher Alf Manning. I don't know why we called him 'Alf'. It certainly wasn't his real name, but it mirrored the fact that we quite liked him. It was a neutral sort of nickname, no harm intended. Alf was a hip sort of chap, young and skinny with an Afro perm. He seemed unlike the stodgier gown-wearing community of teachers who floated around the corridors of that old grammar school. He seemed vaguely to be on our side, his hairstyle a little nod in our direction. But he kept his act fairly straight, and he was smart enough not to come over to the other side.

As form master, Alf's job was to read the report, glance at the accumulated marks and write a concluding remark at the end. Nowadays you have to write a mini-thesis, but back in those distant days a phrase or a sentence was enough. Anyway, my parents opened the sealed letter, read the report in silence before tea, and then left it on the table for my perusal. They said nothing, which meant it was OK. I was always in the middle somewhere, half decent, nothing special. Already knowing most of my marks, I looked down to see what sort of comment Alf Manning had conjured up. I was fourteen and, having to choose my O-level subjects for the next year, I was hoping that maybe Alf might have some ideas for me. The concluding remark was a half-sentence, as if he'd written it in a tired slump, bored at the end of a long evening of teacher tedium:

Has the makings of a moderately good linguist.

At first it seemed innocent enough, but then I looked more closely. The word 'moderately' jumped off the page. You won't be good at anything, it really said. You can only be *moderately* good at things, even the things for which you get the decent results. Call me neurotic if you will, but at that tricky point in my life, the comment came down on me like a hammer blow. Alf didn't mean it. Unlike the junior school teacher before him, he had no darker purpose. I knew that back then. But because he seemed like a good guy to me, it made the comment all the worse because it came over as truthful. Why insert that little word *moderately*, unless it had meant something to him? 'Don't get your hopes up,' he appeared to be saying to me, and so I took his advice.

Back in my home town twenty-five years later, I arrange to meet an old friend in a pub. We sit down at the back of the lounge and proceed to natter about how life is treating us, who's in and who's out, who's up and who's down. When it's my turn to get the drinks I walk over to the bar with the empty glasses, only to stop dead in my tracks. It's unmistakably him. The Afro cut has been toned down, the brown cord jacket has been replaced, but Alf Manning still has the same rounded John Lennon specs, the skinny frame and the long swan neck. He looks good. He's talking animatedly to another man at the bar, and his voice is the same, oddly deep for the small body and quite fruity, like a radio presenter. Even if Alf had undergone plastic surgery I would still have known the voice. Standing a yard or so back from the bar, the phrase *'Has the makings of a moderately good linguist'* is resonating in my head. I'm caught between wanting to hurt him, to take him to task for his confidence killer, and just saying hello, across the years. Whatever I choose, there is an enormous compulsion to at least speak to him, to face my nemesis. It's what every pupil dreams, years down the line.

The barman is looking quizzically at me, so I shuffle up to Alf's side and order a couple more beers. Absurdly, I turn to him and utter, '*Salve, magister!*' (Greetings, teacher!), using the Latin phrase which he taught us to holler out when he came into the classroom at the beginning of Latin lessons. Momentarily taken aback, as if he is about to be assaulted, he frowns then replies, '*Salve discipulus!*', relaxing his stance. It's a Tuesday night and the pub is fairly empty.

'Hello, Alf,' I open, suddenly remembering that he is not called Alf at all. His neck is slightly scrawny now, the skin sagging. He fixes his eyes on me, looking for clues. It won't be the first time some daft ex-pupil has accosted him in a pub.

'Hi,' he tries, obviously flummoxed. I step in.

'You taught me Latin years ago, back in the grammar school.'

'Oh yeah,' he replies, suddenly looking as if he wants to get back to his pint and his friend. 'Don't do that any more now. Retrained as an English teacher. Not much call for the classics now.' Out of politeness, since my beers have not yet appeared, he asks me if I live locally. I tell him I live in Spain, and have done so for some time – at which point I am bursting to use his famous phrase, written in a tired moment twenty-five years ago. I don't know how I am going to follow it up, but I feel powerfully compelled to tell him that the moderate linguist speaks Spanish, and a bit of Basque – and that I've done OK, if nothing special. But I know that it will be impossible to explain exactly why I want to tell him that. In the blinking of an eye, the urge to hurt him back – to hold him responsible for the messy sort of person I feel I've become, standing there in the carpeted lounge of The Nottingham Arms – suddenly fades.

'Oh! I'm learning Spanish,' he offers, breaking through the sudden silence. 'The wife and I are going to night classes. Sort of helps a bit when we go to Spain every year. Thinking of getting a place down there.' I suggest that the Latin background must help, and he nods vigorously.

We went back to our drinks and to our respective friends and lives, and I knew that I would probably never see him again. It didn't matter. But as I sat at the back of the lounge watching him that night, aware that he could have no idea of what I was thinking, something clicked back into place – the feeling that despite the fatigue, the frayed edges, the fumbling and the fooling around, something in my teacher journey had been worthwhile. The incident reminded me that the kids might remember me too, for better or for worse. They would remember me for what I was wearing, and for the things that I'd said, right down to the tone of my voice and the cut of my poorly pressed trousers. I owed them something for that. I sensed an obligation in there – an obligation to try to get it right.

I was trying, but it was turning out to be rather more complicated than I'd imagined. The road to oneself is paved with the fuzziest of intentions.